OTIS

OTIS

*Giving
Rise
to the
Modern
City*

Jason Goodwin

Ivan R. Dee
Chicago 2001

Library of Congress Cataloging-in-Publication Data:
Goodwin, Jason, 1964–
   Otis : giving rise to the modern city / Jason Goodwin.
    p. cm.
   Includes bibliographical references and index.
   ISBN 1-56663-385-0 (alk. paper)
   1. Otis Elevator Company–History. 2. Elevator industry–
United States–History. 3. International business enterprises–
United States–History.   I. Title.
  HD9715.9.E434 O854 2001
  338.7'621877'0973–dc21

2001028195

To all Otis employees
past, present and future

Contents

	Acknowledgments	ix
	Prologue	xi
Part One	Elisha Otis	5
	Competition	21
	Hydraulics	37
	Swansong	52
	Abroad	63
	The Hidden Hand	72
	Otis Elevator Incorporated	88
	The Otis Elevator Industry	101
	Abroad Again	109
	The Indicator Years	117
	The Search for Control	126
	The Great Depression	134
	Service	140
Part Two	International	153
	World War II	165
	Postwar America	168
	Postwar Europe	189
	Percy Douglas Tours the World	195
	The American Dream	204
	Breaking the Mold	213
	Breakaway	235
	The Management Revolution	247
	Takeover	259
	Epilogue	264
	Appendix	273
	Index	280

Acknowledgments

Y OU ENTER AN ELEVATOR AND IN SECONDS you're at the top of the
Eiffel Tower, the Petronas Towers or any of thousands of skyscrapers
around the world. That quick trip actually took about 150 years. In 1853
a restless tinkerer named Elisha Graves Otis created the first "safety hoist"
and gave rise to city skylines—and spectacular views—around the world.

Like the elevator itself, *Otis: Giving Rise to the Modern City* is the product of countless details that have created the history of the company and
the industry Mr. Otis founded. It's a story of technological achievement
and the evolution of the industrial world as we know it. But more than
that, it's the story of the relentless dedication of the people who transformed one man's brilliant idea into a company operating in virtually
every country of the world, a company synonymous with its product.

A few of those people were as essential to this book as hoisting ropes
are to an elevator. Former Otis President and current United
Technologies Chairman George David was the inventor of the idea for
this book, giving it the momentum and resources it needed. Although an
"elevator man," as they say in the industry, for just 15 years, he was cap-
tivated by the company's products, its engineering, its geographical
dispersion and, above all, its history. Hubert Faure, a former Otis chairman himself and an important part of the company's history, supported
this project with enthusiasm and encouragement, as well as incredibly

detailed recollections and astute observations. The style of leadership at Otis is historically "hands-on," and that was demonstrated as well by former Otis Presidents Karl Krapek and J. P. van Rooy and current President Stephen F. Page, who provided both guidance and support for the project.

This book has been a decade in the making and, in its earliest stages, was guided by a small committee of historians and experts from the world of publishing, as well as by George David and Hubert Faure. My thanks to Larry Hughes, publishing consultant with Harper Collins Publishers, who chaired the committee and identified a publisher, and to committee members John W. Field, former president and CEO of Warnaco; Dennis Flanagan, former editor-in-chief of *Scientific American;* John A. Gable, executive director of the Theodore Roosevelt Association; Glenn Porter, director of the Hagley Museum and Library; and George Smith, president of the Winthrop Group. Thanks are due particularly to Judy Bremer Olson, who coordinated committee activities and provided notes that later helped me in guiding the project.

I owe a debt also to Erik Warners, retired manager of Otis' Netherlands company, and to other Otis employees in Japan, France and around the world who shared their stories with me. Several retired Otis executives not only offered their insights on company history but also read the manuscript scrupulously for accuracy and technical precision. They are Mike DiZio, Gary Faltin, Al Saxer, Jim Siegel, Roland Tillison and Mert Meeker. Mert, who sadly passed away during the project, loved the elevator business, and this book is dedicated to him and the thousands of Otis employees responsible for the company's legendary greatness.

Otis archivists Michele Aldrich and Dennis Barrow provided invaluable research and ensured that the manuscript was accurate. Thanks also go to John S. Cox, who edited the manuscript, and Peter Good and Kirsten Livingston of Cummings & Good, who provided the book's inspired design.

If this book advances understanding of the achievements of this remarkable company, it is because of the contributions of all these people.

Jason Goodwin

February 2001

Prologue

A SKYSCRAPER IS THE FIRST THING a visitor to Otis' factory in Japan sees as he approaches Shibayama across the flat fields of the district. In any city in the world it would not merit a second glance, but, standing here alone in windswept lowlands close to Tokyo, it draws the eye irresistibly, and its oddity is not dispelled when the visitor, coming closer, sees that the tower is practically windowless. Five hundred feet tall, sheathed head to foot in gunboat grey, the tower seems as sheer and mysterious as something out of science fiction.

Even to those who understand the tower, it remains marvelous. Architects talk of its being built by a new method which shaved as much as a quarter off the time normally taken to construct a building 39 stories high, a method known as inversed lining. For the Shibayama tower a huge concrete pad was first floated at upper basement level, from which work could proceed in both directions, up and down, overturning a century-old approach to skyscraper erection which involved digging foundations down to deep basement level and then building upward floor by floor.

Yet the structure's integrity had not been compromised for the sake of speed—on the contrary, sensitive to Japan's extremes of climate and geology, the architects had incorporated further new technologies which made the building unusually secure against wind damage and earthquakes. Resonance-suppression panels, for example, looking like nibs which projected from the upper stories, helped to break the force of high winds eddying around the building, and gave it the strength to withstand winds of up to 75 miles per second—an event reckoned to occur once in 500 years. Engineers had also installed a revolutionary system to control vibration, essentially an enormous weight in the attic that would shift automatically to counteract tremors.

All this effort, all this research, had gone into the construction of a building nobody would ever rent, for it concealed no penthouse boardrooms, no condominiums. Returns on the $28 million project would be measured in terms of scientific progress and competitive advantage, not cash. For in formal terms, the Shibayama Test Tower was nothing more than an enclosure of space. It contained 11 separate elevator shafts, fitted with a battery of instruments and machines, to allow Otis engineers to try out new technologies, components and ideas in a controlled environment. It would ultimately enable the world's biggest producer of elevators and escalators to create elevators capable of handling more traffic, at higher speeds, over shorter periods, more safely than ever before.

By 1990, in line with a renaissance of research and development within the company, Otis had built test towers in America, China and Europe to coordinate and perform research all over the world.* Each tower, to some extent, reflected a regional bias in the elevator market. The tower in Bristol, Connecticut, for instance, was designed principally to test the behemoths of American elevatoring—the hotel and office elevators. The European tower was correspondingly smaller, reflecting the European taste for apartment elevators. The Chinese tower was chiefly for instructing workers in quality-control approaches.

At 39 stories, not including six underground floors, the Shibayama Test Tower was the biggest that Otis or any of its rivals had ever built. It was designed from the outset to cope with anything Otis' engineers could throw at it—double-deck elevators moving at a breathtaking 42 feet per second (the Bristol tower, by contrast, was restricted to 32 feet per second), even elevators still on the drawing board which would reach speeds of 49 feet per second. It was designed, too, as part of the globalization of Otis

---

* So perfectly did they express function in their form, that at the behest of the architectural historians the British government actually listed one test tower as a national monument.

engineering capabilities, with backup from Otis' research-rich parent company, United Technologies. Otis' premier projects were to become children of the superhighway—the product of intense collaboration via e-mail, video conferencing and, of course, plain old-fashioned face-to-face meetings between engineers from all over the world.

In the speech to mark the tower's official opening on February 19, 1998, many of these points were addressed by George David, chairman and CEO of United Technologies, the parent company of Otis, Carrier, Sikorsky Aircraft, Pratt & Whitney and Hamilton Sundstrand. Everyone present knew—and not only because George David liked to repeat it—that behind the tower lay more than Japanese construction savvy, or even the company's determination to increase its penetration of the Japanese market for elevators. It stood, in some part, as a symbol of faith in the kind of company that Otis was, blazing a trail American companies would have to follow.

The future, David was certain, belonged to those companies that could straddle the globe, as the barriers to world trade continued to fall one after another and a global economic order for the 21st century began to emerge. At the time of the tower dedication, some 15 percent of the world's population enjoyed three quarters of its wealth. But others were clamoring to join in, and the great closed societies of the postwar world had flung down their barriers. As the 20th century drew to a close, perhaps half the world's population was poised to make the leap Japan had made in four decades, from a subsistence economy into a full-fledged, integrated component of the developed world.

While some traditionalists viewed the prospect with alarm, David saw it as an opportunity, and Otis as a model. The test tower in Shibayama was conceived as a world-class facility for a global enterprise. True, its ultimate ownership remained in the United States, but Otis still maintained more employees in more cities of the world than any of the other UTC companies. Otis' 66,000 employees, of whom fewer than one in 10 was an American, operated in 1,900 cities worldwide—not just in the capital cities of the 222 countries where Otis had a presence,* but in regional capitals and business and industrial cities of the hinterland.

---

* Every country in the world, except six.

Working on customers' premises, speaking the local language, adapting its products and methods to match local needs and expectations, Otis had worldwide experience perhaps unrivaled by any American company. Its name and influence were woven into the industrial fabric of dozens of countries. Otis in Japanese meant "good elevator," while the company's links with Japan went back to the 1890s. Most French would have said that Otis—which was manufacturing in France before World War I—was a French company. In the United Kingdom or Australia, Mexico or Brazil, China or Canada, Otis had been a familiar name for well over a century.

By the late 1990s the company had seized the invitation to participate in the great economic awakening. To survive in the global economic market as the playing fields were gradually being leveled, a company had not only to offer the best it had but also to prove its willingness to help host countries achieve their ambitions. So the most widely spoken native language within the company was Russian. In India, Otis had in two years made investments totaling $12 million. In Kuala Lumpur, Malaysia, the world's tallest buildings, the Petronas Towers, symbolized the region's determination to succeed, with the help of Otis elevators. In China, Otis employed more than 4,000, making it the largest elevator enterprise in that country, itself the largest construction site in history. In every part of the world save one, Otis outstripped its rivals, the sole exception being Japan, where its market share nevertheless had tripled in 20 years.

Backing this unique achievement was an unremitting focus on quality. If standards worldwide were converging rapidly, at Otis they were being made to converge. In 15 years Otis in China had achieved the remarkable goal of producing escalators to a standard acceptable in Japan, home of the sternest critics of reliability. In Japan itself, with the new test tower, Otis had gone further than any of its rivals in establishing benchmarks of research and design.

More than just a stupendous engineering achievement, more than a challenge to Japanese manufacturers to match a new benchmark in elevator technology, the tower encapsulated Otis' way of thinking about the world, and how it sought to operate within it. It stood for Otis' position as a global company. The alternative to building it was to retreat from one defensive position to the next, as much of the rest of the world followed in Japan's wake and into the ranks of developed nations. Survival demanded that the processes that would likely shape the 21st century should be co-opted, not resisted, that Otis should learn to embrace and benefit from the palpable desire and ability of other nations to cross the threshold into the developed world.

Japan was doubly significant to Otis. Nowhere else could Otis' ambition to set the world's standards be more concretely, more visibly, achieved than in the country which exported not only its goods, but also its expectations, to the entire Asian region. In spite of the looming financial firestorm, Asia's cities, sleeping tigers, could be expected to grow rapidly from third-world, low-rise, low-value megalopolises to vertical, well-heeled, high-productivity urban giants. A revolution that had taken America a century to achieve, and Europe 30 years, was expected to be complete in Asia within a decade. Even after the Asian economies went into recession in 1997, Otis would forcibly associate itself with the standards the rest of Asia had come to expect from Japanese manufacturers. Otis, as ever, knew it had to be there.

OTIS

Part One

Chapter 1

Elisha Otis

On a late May day in 1854 a man in a black overcoat and stovepipe hat stepped off the *Thomas E. Hulse,* a small paddlewheeler with a single upright stack, onto the wooden town dock at Yonkers, New York. Down by the water's edge, a railroad gang was laying the new Hudson River Railroad, soon to link Yonkers to New York City. Downstream on the other side of the tracks, the parish cemetery ran off into the distance, with the steep escarpment of Yonkers Heights rising to the eastern horizon. Remnants of the old Dutch farm town were still to be seen—old gabled farmhouses nestled among clumps of trees—but paved streets had come to replace dirt lanes and cart tracks, and clapboard houses were filling in the pastures cleared by the early Dutch settlers. The waterfront had changed too, the river bank now crenellated with landings and wharves, where red brick and rusty tin announced the presence of low factory buildings and their cluttered yards. Wherries and sailbarges hunkered on the water. In the distance to the south lay Manhattan's wooded hills.

Alfred Wilde sniffed the air appreciatively. He liked the bitter sea-coal stench he knew so well. He tipped a penny to one of the boys perching on the dockside railings, and followed him along the waterfront. The boy pointed out the bedstead factory that Wilde had come here to visit, took his penny and ran off.

The factory was a plain three-story brick building with a tin roof already turning to rust, standing on a jetty ringed by old oak pilings. A drawing made a few years later shows it jammed between the river and the railroad—an unrivaled position for the time. On one side of the building stands a boiler house with a 40-foot chimney; in front runs a gap-toothed picket fence that divides the factory yard from the railroad lines. The artist's impression, though, is one of life and bustle: the factory chimney belches soot, in the background a paddle-wheel steamer is forging upriver, a masted schooner is loading from the jetty, a two-horse dray is crossing the yard, and a sawyer has his bench set up in the doorway. The weather is fine, and a man is lounging on the outside staircase, smoking a cigar.

But no smoke was pouring from the chimney on the day Wilde called, and at first glance the building appeared to be empty. A mechanic himself, Wilde knew only too well the false starts and phantom opportunities that threatened anyone entering industry in those days. America was still a young country, after all. New York, with half a million inhabitants, was the biggest city in a country of a mere 12 million people—4 million of them black slaves in the South. Boston was already a half-Irish city, but while Native Americans had not yet disappeared, the huddled masses of Europe had not yet come, and the United States was still essentially a white, Protestant preserve. The vast majority of Americans in the 1850s lived on the land, slaughtered their own livestock, made most of their own clothes and traded their surplus crops for a colorful array of privately issued banknotes.

But in this quiet, rural world men like Alfred Wilde were stirring up a second revolution. Their cotton mills—like those that Wilde ran at Cohoes upstate—were the first big industrial ventures to establish a beachhead in the country, along lines initially laid down in England, where the Industrial Revolution had begun. Where cotton manufacture led, other enterprises were trying to follow. America was full of inventive men trying uncharted markets.

Wilde made his way up the riverbank and crossed a yard to the shop door. He saw a small three-horsepower engine and heard the hiss of steam from its boiler. A young machinist stooped over an old lathe. A couple of oil cans stood on a work bench to one side, a desk on the other. Plates of iron and iron rods were stacked against the walls. A heap of coal lay in its bin. The ground was strewn with wood shavings and slag that had spilled from the ashcan as it was carried outside. Everything, in fact, was just as Wilde had supposed it would be, apart from a small cannon lying in its wooden cradle near the door, like a relic from another revolution altogether.

The man who rented the shop was one Elisha Otis, and if Wilde was initially disappointed to learn that Otis senior was away, he soon found the young man minding the machinery perfectly capable of discussing his needs. Some 67 years later, that young man could still recall the visit, at the end of which Wilde left for Cohoes with some rough-sketched diagrams of an elevator suitable for hoisting freight, and Charles Otis kissed the Union Elevator and General Machine Works Co.'s first unsolicited order for a No 2 Hoist Machine, value $300.

The power of advertising had lured Wilde to Yonkers. Earlier that month he had witnessed an interesting exhibition at the New York World's Fair. This had been a splendid occasion, as everyone agreed—managed by P. T. Barnum, the impresario, funded by the New York Chamber of Commerce and modeled on the first World's Fair held in London two years earlier. On a site now occupied by Bryant Park, west of the city reservoir on 42nd Street, the committee had erected a huge pavilion of wrought iron and glass to display and market some of the new wonders of American invention.

When the Fair first opened, in 1853, some 50,000 people streamed through the gate at 20 cents a head and made their way slowly along the enormous aisles to the equestrian statue of George Washington that formed the Fair's centerpiece. But attendance dropped gradually, and in 1854 Barnum had revamped the displays, boldly replacing Washington and his horse with Elisha Otis and his hoist.

The ironic significance of replacing horse with hoist was largely lost on contemporaries, of course. Six feet tall without his top hat, Elisha Otis hourly stepped into the shaft and onto the open platform of his machine. Put into gear, the platform lurched skyward; a drum squealed, a rope squeaked, wheels rattled, and in the midst of this din, at a rate of about 12 feet a minute, Otis was winched to the top of the shaft.

The *New York Recorder's* official artist, who had been idling all morning beneath the palms, set busily to work with his block and pencil, on a drawing which would be reproduced thousands of times and come to decorate Otis offices around the world, illustrating an event that has long since eclipsed the bigger show it was a part of. It wasn't Otis going up that dazzled the crowd—it was Otis not coming down with a crash after he slashed the hoisting rope with a saber. "All safe, gentlemen," he announced, as the brakes kicked in. "All safe."

Barnum paid Otis $100 for this stunt and apparatus. Elisha was not too proud to take the money from the man who had given the world the Bearded Lady, the Feejee Mermaid and the man who dived into a teacup from a circus roof. And wisely so. Mr. Wilde of the Cohoes Cotton Mills was in the audience, together with representatives of Johnson, Cox and Fuller, of Spuyten Duyvil; a visiting businessman from Charleston, South Carolina; a Boston manufacturer of linseed oil; even a contractor for the U.S. Assay Office building on Wall Street—one of the very first buildings to be erected using wrought-iron floor beams, and so a precursor of the skyscraper. All of these men watched Otis' exhibition with interest, and were sufficiently impressed to have placed orders with Otis' Union Works by the end of the year.

For when Otis had severed the hoisting rope with his saber, the lift had fallen only a few inches, then stopped with a jolt. The mechanism was simple, it was automatic, and it promised to make the hoist safe for the first time in 2,000 years. By executing this stunt, before a gasping crowd, Otis had heralded the birth of the elevator industry.

Hoists and lifts and pulleys were not a new idea. From early times men had sought ways to raise and lower heavy loads. Massive stones had been maneuvered to raise the largest structure of the ancient world, the monumental pyramid of Cheops at Giza, Egypt, to a height of 512 feet. Archimedes, the father of mechanics, who flourished around 236 B.C., reportedly employed ropes and pulleys, and devised a machine in which the hoisting ropes were coiled on a winding drum by a capstan and levers. In one version of the machine, the capstan was turned by men walking inside it—just as little dogs, in the medieval world, turned spits over a fire, and donkeys, in our own time, were used to raise and lower buckets in a well. In the turbulent centuries that followed the collapse of the Roman Empire in Europe, the so-called Dark Ages, Christian monasteries shone as beacons of light and learning amid the gloom; but for protection they often retreated to inaccessible mountain tops, and well into the 20th century both goods and visitors approached monasteries in Greece and Syria by means of a roped hoist, drawn up by a capstan.

Already in Roman times, engineers seem to have hit on the idea of enclosing the hoisting platform within a shaft to prevent its swinging wildly from side to side. Hoistways "have been found in the ruins of the palaces of Roman Emperors" (Encyclopedia Britannica 1939). The Roman Coliseum was completed in 80 A.D., and to this day the visitor may inspect the elevator alcoves—something short of an enclosed shaft—which could raise groups of gladiators, or packs of wild animals, straight into the arena overhead.

There is no evidence of the use of counterweights, however, before 1670, when an anonymous reporter recorded a machine installed in Turin, Italy, that could raise and lower a single person enclosed in a cage by means of a crank and a counterweight. A similar contraption, which traveled in a three-foot niche in the wall, was installed in the home of one Edward Weigal of Jena in Germany two years later. Nobody knows why these early passenger elevators were installed, but certainly the Austrian Empress Maria Theresa had three put into various places in the year of her death, when she had grown very fat and too weak to handle stairs. In one, which she had installed in the Capuchin Church in Vienna in order to visit the coffin of her late husband, she was reportedly stuck on November 2, 1780, an early—perhaps the very first—incident of what elevator people nowadays call an *STK in elv*. Among the great, the desire for secrecy was as much a spur to elevator development as obesity: Andreas Gaertner, a mechanic of Breslau in Germany, is supposed to have invented the device by which tables groaning with food could be winched through the floor of a private room, thereby dispensing with servants and their eavesdropping. A similar contraption was at work in Moscow in 1814, more for show than secrecy. Presumably only the central portion of the dining table descended, like a sort of vertical lazy susan; otherwise the dinner guests would have had to untuck their legs from under the table, and risk sliding off their seats through the well into the kitchen below.

Not until 1830 was a fixed hoist put to industrial use, when an English cotton mill, possibly steam-powered, was equipped with a pulley and an endless rope for raising bales of cotton. The Industrial Revolution, which had begun in England at least as early as the early 1800s, spurred further applications, and by 1835 a machine known as the teagle was installed, driven off the central steam engine by a belt, controlled by a hand rope, and operating in an enclosed hoistway. In the same year a more sophisticated version of the twin-bucket well was inaugurated, the so-called rising cupboard, described as an arrangement of "two cupboards which balance each other and are attached by cords, fastened to staples in the exterior surfaces of the tops and bottoms of the cupboards; while the cords run on two cast-iron wheels."

All these advances were convenient, but from ancient Egypt to modern Europe the mechanical hoist was scarcely an essential. Labor had always been abundant and cheap. After the pyramids, the tallest buildings in the world were the great medieval cathedrals; their spires were not in daily use, and no one had ever suggested the need for hoists and hoistways in them.* Nor did it seem that the pattern would change in the New World either. In 1841, New York City raised its own gothic spire to 284 feet, and Trinity Church remained the highest structure in New York for 52 years.

The growth of industry in America seemed, at first glance, like a rerun of the Industrial Revolution that had swept Britain 40 years earlier. It produced the same red brick factories, the nondescript workers' housing spreading across the fields, the soot and grime, and the same poetic disaffection. To many contemporaries, the blossoming of American industry seemed spurred by the same Anglo-Saxon genius for invention. But the pattern of American industrialization was different in one crucial respect, as we shall see.

Elisha Otis was born in 1811 in the hamlet of Halifax, Vermont. Like most Americans of his generation, he grew up on a farm—set in a lush hill country whose towns were the size of villages and whose villages have sometime since vanished from the map. Vermont's entire population could have found elbow room in a modern city block.

---

* Though in the fullness of time Stigler-Otis put an elevator in St. Peter's in Rome. It was mentioned in Otis' in-house publication, the *Indicator,* for April 1910.

Elisha was a reluctant farmboy. Planting and reaping meant work by rote, and he found the cycle of the seasons monotonous. Machinery, by contrast, was unpredictable and lively, and lent itself to improvement. He hung about the village blacksmith's shop, tinkered with whatever farm machinery he could lay hands on, and in 1829, at 19 years old, set out with his father's blessing to take up a job in Troy, New York.

All along the web of waterways between Albany and New York City, hundreds of general mechanics were driving the American Industrial Revolution. They kept close to running water, which provided the power to turn machines and the means to float their products off to market—down the Hudson, up the Erie Canal—and their machine shops were the laboratories of the new age. As they spread, so they began to alter the colonial pattern of sturdy independent yeomen and their farms. The fur traders' outposts had been gobbled up by brisk little commercial communities turning out iron, cloth, flour and a few other simple necessities. Most "manufactories" were still small-scale affairs, run as wet-weather alternatives on family farms; but it was only another 20 years or so before America came to grips with steam and mass-production, before American weapons, mechanical harvesters and specialized machine tools were to provide a spectacle at the World's Fair.

Elisha, in heading for Troy, moved as the United States was moving, from country to town, from agriculture to industry, from cash to credit, and from tradition to invention. He dreamed up new ways to harness the power of a turning wheel. He fitted out—for richer men—entire factories two, even three stories high, in which articles descended from floor to floor in an ever increasing state of finish and perfection, "never known," as his son recalled, "to have to alter, remodel or rebuild the machine after it was once constructed and put to use."

When one business folded, he started another. If a machine was too slow, he knew it right away, and he was not by nature a patient man. He was no sooner thinking of a thing than he was clambering over it, half-built, up to his elbows in axle grease. He was, to be sure, a stern and righteous churchman, and his Puritan God gave him a furious sense of imperfection. Almost everything he saw could be done better—faster, cheaper, more accurately—and he went at it with the energy of a man possessed.

It was a survivor's instinct that drove him from task to task and place to place. Industry presented a long and rolling frontier, ranged by men like Otis. Like the other American frontier, this one had to be strictly watched; and it needed a wakeful man, self-reliant and determined, to maintain any sort of position on it for long. For every shallow settler's grave, every smoking farmstead in the West, the East could show you a bankrupt who had failed to keep up with the progress of industrial development. One of Elisha's most ruinous ventures was the machine shop he built and equipped on the banks of Patroon's Creek, shortly before the city of Albany diverted all the creek's water to its drinking supply. But a man of Elisha Otis' skill and inventiveness was unlikely to be idle very long.

Next he started to manufacture carts, entered haulage. Finally he was rescued by the offer of a job in a bedstead factory. To his employers' delight, he devised an automated lathe that turned out bedstead rails four times faster than a man could make them. The factory failed for all that, but when one of the partners, Mr. Maize, moved the concern to a better location, close to the markets in Bergen, New Jersey, he brought Otis with him to install the turning machines, and kept him on as master mechanic. In the winter of 1851–52, Maize entered into a partnership with Barnes and Newhouse in order to shift his operations once again, to Yonkers, where Newhouse had a sawmill on the Hudson he was anxious to improve. With Maize's experience, Barnes' capital and Newhouse's property, the sawmill was replaced with the bedstead factory that Alfred Wilde saw standing idle by the Hudson a few years later. Elisha Otis moved to Yonkers with his family to superintend the organization of the factory and to install the necessary machinery, as he had done before.

The difference between industrial development in America and Europe was partly a matter of attitude. Americans, as Alexis de Tocqueville had observed, were not like Europeans, and above all they had no peasantry. The crudest American log cabin, he recorded, sheltered men of independent habits, who read the newspapers, discussed public and foreign affairs and intended to do well for themselves. Labor in America possessed a kind of dignity which the slum dwellers of the Old World could scarcely dream of.

The roots of this distinction were historical and economic. Population was abundant in the Old World, where millions of agricultural workers were drafted into the industrial cities, and their labor was cheap. For hundreds of years, European notions of value had been grounded in property. Land was relatively scarce, and as a form of wealth it passed down generally unchanged from one generation to the next. In the New World, conversely, land was abundant. It was workers who were scarce—especially in the North—and their wages were correspondingly high. The relative shortage of working men had a stimulating effect on the progress of U.S. industries,* and influenced its direction.

The labor squeeze certainly fed into Elisha Otis' thinking about factory organization. Partly for the sake of speed, and partly to remove a burden from the shoulders of a well-paid workforce whose time could be better spent elsewhere, Otis turned his attention to making a hoist to move heavy lumber. Power-driven hoists were already being used elsewhere—indeed, Newhouse, Otis' employer, had a furniture factory on Hudson Street in New York City with a hoist that Otis must have examined. Hecker's Mill on Cherry Street had one made by Henry Waterman, a New York mechanic ("a very crude affair operating between two floors...");[1] and the Boston firm of George H. Fox and Co. was already shipping freight elevators to various parts of the country. By 1852, Fox's elevators used wire rope, which was less liable to break than hemp. In the event of a disaster the operator of the lift was expected to throw a lever to brake the car, via a rotating pinion under the platform that connected to the rack on the guide beams. As a safety measure it was not very effective, since it depended entirely on the quick wits of the man in the car.

The lift that Otis constructed in his machine shop on site and installed in the bedstead factory followed existing patterns—a platform set between vertical guide rails and raised and lowered on a rope wound around an overhead drum, the drum turned by belting that looped across the factory floor to the central, continuously turning steam engine.

---

* In 1846, Sir William Armstrong built a hydraulic crane at Newcastle Docks in England, based on principles discovered in 1796 by Joseph Bramah. But this did not lead to a boom in hydraulic elevators. The development of hydraulics had to wait for conditions to be right in America, in the 1870s.

The difference was the automatic safety device that Otis devised and coupled to his machine, which was to take him to the World's Fair two years later.

Like most great inventions, it was simple. Hoists were intrinsically dangerous in a world where all machinery was dangerous, but the most serious cause of accidents was a fraying rope, an overloaded platform or the failure of the belt that connected the drum to the factory's central steam engine, which could send the car or platform into free fall. What Otis first did was to notch the hardwood guide-rails which prevented the car from swinging out of line. Wooden guide-rails were surprisingly strong, often made of oak that set like iron, and they were not abandoned in the industry until the beginning of the 20th century. Otis then took a flat-leaf spring—a cart spring, in fact—and fixed it to the roof of the car, connecting it to the hoisting rope so that tension on the rope would draw the spring up, and draw its two ends in. Only if the rope broke, or slipped, was the tension released, and with that the spring would automatically flatten itself against the roof of the cab. Shoes on either end of the spring would then be rammed home into the notches carved on the guide rails, and the cab brought to an abrupt halt.

At first sight it seems incredible that Otis did not seek a patent on his safety right away. Patents were a mechanic's lifeblood—so many were registered in the second half of the 19th century that one patent officer is said to have resigned in the belief that he had registered everything that could possibly be invented. The strict patent laws of the United States gave inventors proper protection, and this was an enormous spur to human ingenuity. Patents could draw an industrial bottleneck into a man's pocket, a process Elisha well understood.

But it was not until seven years later that he registered his patent in an automatic elevator safety. Nothing in his apparatus was really new of itself, like a species of valve, or the shape of a blade; in a sense, he had merely bunched together some existing ideas in a new way. Perhaps he never fully appreciated the significance of what he had achieved, never quite believed in elevators as a discrete branch of industry, in the way he believed in railroad brakes, ingenious automatic bread-baking ovens or his own turning machine. In the industrial world that Otis understood, invention implied producing a direct effect on manufacture; the safety hoist was a minor convenience, at best. The surest proof that Elisha thought about his invention in this way comes from the fact that nobody stole his idea: safety elevators in the 1850s were no more obvious to potential rivals than to Elisha himself.

Yet by coincidence his own employer, Benjamin Newhouse, very soon learned the advantages of the automatic safety. In 1852 an accident occurred at his Hudson Street factory. One of the hoists—possibly a Waterman machine—fell several stories, and two men were either killed or seriously injured. The lever-operated safety proved predictably inadequate in the emergency. Newhouse immediately gave Otis orders for two safety hoists, while his neighbors, the picture-frame manufacturers Searls and Williams, were sufficiently impressed to come in with an order for their new factory, too. All three machines were built and installed within the year 1853, for $300 apiece.

Elisha was still working for Newhouse, but his future seemed uncertain once the hoists were built. The bedstead factory was not succeeding, and when he learned that the works were to close, Elisha considered going west to join the California gold rush.

Perhaps beneath his impulse to go west we can make out some explanation for his relative indifference to "vertical transport." Elisha Otis, despite the direction his own career had taken, belonged by birth to an America of farms and fields, linked by rivers and great trails. Spurred by the arrival of the railroad, early industry expressed itself in horizontal terms—cattle and crops moving across the face of the vast continent. America was very broad, not very high, and it was still growing, too, but sideways, state fitted onto state like a gigantic jigsaw puzzle. The greatest city on the continent faced the great plain of the sea; it was spreading north across Manhattan, with the financial district forever threatening to burst its bounds and move northward into the Midtown area. Chicago boomed as a huge low sprawl of wooden shacks, wooden theaters, wooden pens, all to be swept away by Mrs. O'Leary's fire in 1871, but for now staring out across the lakes and plains.

With stone docks, railroads, fences and the frontier, of course, America was spreading west, erecting the towns and then the railheads that would pull it all together. The landscape was still being drawn and plotted. Whole cities existed in the heads of their hopeful founders, in dusty lines scratched in the soil. "Unimproved" farms were being offered—tracts of virgin forest waiting to be felled, buffalo ranges waiting to be settled, plowed and fenced. Industry, such as it was, belonged to the rivers, as the wagon trails lumbered forward into the Plains, then to the railroads.

Elisha Otis, above all, worked to contribute to this horizontal world. His thoughts ran on turbines, wheels and lathes, on better railroad brakes and stronger railroad bridges. Even after he had set up as an elevator manufacturer, he turned dreamily back to a project for manufacturing rotary bread ovens, which threatened persistently to ruin him, and in 1852 the most vertical considerations in Elisha Otis' life were his upright morals and his stovepipe hat.

Whatever his dreams of California gold, he soon abandoned plans to leave Yonkers and head for the West. In Yonkers, after all, he had a works plant that Newhouse had provided for him at the foot of Vark Street, which could continue to house him and his family, while Newhouse was happy for him to remain in the factory machine shop at a small rent—keeping an eye on the building, no doubt, and hammering away at his new invention. Accounts show that he invested part of his savings in a second-hand lathe and a small steam engine to run it, now that the factory's big engine lay idle. His eldest son, Charles, was also old enough to help out, and Elisha may have reckoned that the boy needed an apprenticeship. All the same, times were hard. After shipping the picture-frame makers' hoist in November 1853 there were no further orders until Elisha accepted $100—perhaps with some relief—to make and install the small safety hoist that he delivered to the World's Fair in May 1854.

Business was steady in the next couple of years. After the fair Otis sold an elevator every month, for a grand total of $2,975. In 1855 the value of orders almost doubled to $5,605 from only 15 elevators, and more than doubled again in 1856 to $13,488. Some 53 Otis safety hoists had been installed, mainly in New York City, when an advertisement in the *Yonkers Examiner* calling for "three steady American BOYS, 15 to 17 years of age, who will not abscond in the first year...if well treated" and "given a chance to learn," pointed to the growing prosperity and confidence of Otis' enterprise. It also foreshadowed the crucial reason behind the elevator's success in America, a shortage of ready and steady labor.

On March 23, 1857, Otis installed the first-ever commercial passenger elevator, in a department store owned by E. V. Haughwout and Co., "importers and decorators of French China and manufacturers of Silver Plated Ware, cut glass and table cutlery," on Broadway and Broome Street, New York City. The idea of a department store then was new, a marriage between the street-level shop and the multi-story warehouse, but Otis' contribution to it was not a great success: the machinery was too noisy, the concept too novel, and the public preferred to trust the stairs to reach the fifth and highest floor before the lift was actually abandoned in 1860.

Change was coming, however. The age of immigration was dawning with the first steamers crossing the Atlantic, and if most newcomers meant to go West, many joined the swelling populations of the East Coast cities. Land rents in New York City doubled in the decade to 1856. Architectural styles were changing. Jeffersonian classicism belonged now to the rustic past. It expressed a belief in republican government derived from ancient Greece and Rome; it offered columns in place of trees, capitals for leaves, its buildings sprawling wide and low like figures on a country picnic. All this was giving way to a Venetian gothic more suited to the commercial activity that was remolding the country. Gothic was spikes and spires and the pointed energy of a new form of wealth.

The American urge to height and monumentalism surfacing in the 1850s was struck by the business downturn of 1858, a cyclical depression that showed how far along the industrial and commercial road the United States had already traveled. Its roots were agrarian but also international: the end of the Crimean War had damped down the demand in Europe for American grain, and European credit had pulled in its horns. A run followed on the U.S. banks; railroad securities plunged; factories closed, and "from the month of May last," Charles Otis wrote in his journal for 1858, "business matters in this vicinity and even in the whole country have become less and less active. During the months of July and August, there was scarcely any business done competitively, and the general complaint among all classes was of the almost unparalleled dullness in business."

It was Charles, Elisha's older son, who had accepted the Cohoes Mills order from Mr. Wilde back in 1854, and it would be Charles and his brother Norton, rather than Elisha himself, who would found the fortunes of the Otis Elevator Company. All through the year 1858, Charles kept an informative and entertaining journal; and signed a peculiar contract with his own father that speaks volumes about the differences between the two men.

Elisha had roved the frontiers of technology, like a cattleman watching his fences, stepping in here, improvising there, adjusting and maintaining and inventing all along the broad boundaries of mechanical and industrial technology. Charles gave him his due in a memoir he delivered to the public in 1911 on the centenary of his father's birth:

> *He could invent, design and construct a perfect working machine or improve anything to which he gave his mind, without recourse to any of the modern drafting room methods. He needed no assistance, asked no advice, consulted with no one and never made much use of pen or pencil in designing the various machines...of which he was the inventor.*
>
> *The trend of his inventive genius was mainly in the direction of machinery, and when, either in his ordinary pursuits, or in reading or conversation, his mind was led to a needed advance in almost any form of mechanism for the attainment of improved methods or ends, the desired result was reached by him more as an inspiration than by a process of slow, laborious reasoning and experiment.*

Charles in his youth plainly considered Elisha as part tyrant, part idiot, for Charles' approach to business, as to life, was rather different.

By 1858, Charles was working in the shop as his father's foreman, at a salary of $900 a year. In the contract he drew up with Elisha in February of that year he undertook to work 10 hours a day, and "to attend to the business beyond those hours on extraordinary and pressing occasions without extra charge. It is not understood," the contract continued, "that I am never to be absent from the business in working time, but that I am to be allowed opportunities of visiting or other recreation as is usual among men to a reasonable extent..." Charles wrote *men,* not *gentlemen,* but he wished his father to know that he was not a mere factory hand—as his father had been at his own age. He had pretensions to a sort of urban gentility that his father had never entertained.

On Wednesday, January 27, we find him heading into the city from Yonkers in a new pair of doeskin trousers. He spent the morning with his father and younger brother Norton looking at hoists, discussing the terms of a lease for a sales office, and meeting Newhouse and another man before Elisha returned to Yonkers on the 11:30 train–a steam locomotive that flew Old Glory and pulled four wooden cars from 31st Street to Peekskill. Thereafter, Charles had lunch with his friend Alvord at Crooks Saloon, after which they strolled about town and Charles had the bumps on his head read by a phrenologist for $4.50. He seemed to be in no hurry to return to the shop; instead he picked up an accordion in for repair, and after some sharp bargaining bought a watch and chain for $75.

Charles and his brother Norton seemed to know what they wanted in life. On the face of it, Charles' journal reflects a young man of his age and time–confused in love, muddled by minor vanities, beset by a mixture of self-pity and conceit. One day he is preening in his doeskin trousers and paying court to Loretta Chambers. The next he is complaining of the fickleness of women and burying his head in his hands. But every day reveals his determination to be better than his father–more reasonable, more businesslike, more successful. Elisha, at the same age and with a similar impulse, had quit the family farm. Charles stayed with the business, and his concentrated energy would build it up.

Elisha was "a very conservative and conscientious manufacturer," one report had it, who "for a considerable time made a practice of not entering into one contract until the last one taken was completed to everyone's satisfaction." His sons were not craftsmen in this sense; they were instinctive industrialists. The phrenologist Charles had seen in New York City told him that he was a "perfect driver, inclined to be boss [with] great determination and strong Will," and he and his brother wanted to pile on production; they wanted to be rich. Norton eventually pursued a political career. Charles, more than either his father or his brother, drove the elevator business.

In March 1858, for example, he was as hopeful as his father that Elisha's new rotary oven patent would prove a success–the elevator business was in the doldrums. By May, though, Charles was referring distantly to "these hundred thousand dollar Air Castles." "For the last three months," he wrote, "there has been great calculations made on the oven patent; so much has been expected from that, as to throw a sensible pursuit of business entirely in the shade as a matter of comparatively slight importance... I can feel like taking hold of our regular business and by giving it strict attention, endeavour to make it thrive. I feel like going to work with the intention uppermost to pay the debts first, and get clear of these annoying creditors which might be accomplished if the effort was made."

Charles' pompous resolutions must have irritated Elisha. A further clause in the contract he drew up with his son contained a gag order: "It is understood that I am not to volunteer advice or opinions concerning that part of the business not placed in my charge," to which Charles disingenuously agreed. Over the next few months it was Charles who grew irritable. His father was still plugging away at the oven patent, and interrupting the management of affairs that Charles was forever trying to establish in a period of business depression. "No sooner will daylight appear than father will break loose again and kick me heels over head if he can, forgetting all the past, go crazy over some wild fancy for the future and get into debt again worse than ever...."

Much of Charles' journal is inspired by normal juvenile grumbling; but Elisha Otis did find it hard to change the pattern of his career as a general mechanic and inventor, which in his son's view would fatally taint the name they were making for themselves as manufacturers and installers of safe elevators. And if the view of the son—and the evidence of his later career—are to be believed, it must be said that the business world at large trusted Charles rather more than his father. Elisha worked on easy credit all his life, and Charles found himself endorsing his father's bills and loans. In January 1858 Elisha managed to quarrel so badly with Newhouse that he faced eviction. By July, Charles described a business "settled right down on to a rock bottom," with creditors bringing suit over $7,000 worth of debt, on top of a $5,000 mortgage, and five out of 15 hands laid off. In the circumstances, Elisha seemed determined, as ever, to widen the directions of his enterprise, but Charles could bear it no longer. Sometime in 1859 he left to work for a competitor.

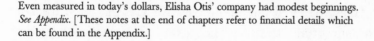
Even measured in today's dollars, Elisha Otis' company had modest beginnings.
See Appendix. [These notes at the end of chapters refer to financial details which can be found in the Appendix.]

Chapter 2

Competition

ALTHOUGH OTIS' 1857 HAUGHWOUT BUILDING elevator was the world's first commercial passenger elevator, technically speaking the fact of carrying passengers was of little significance. The principles involved were the same as for freight. Yet the fertile genius of Elisha Otis had nonetheless established a second milestone in the development of the modern elevator by demonstrating that elevators could be run in store or office buildings, which, unlike factories, had no central steam engine.

He had devised an elevator with its own independent source of power—the small steam engine drive he developed in 1855. All previous hoists had depended on continuous factory-line shafting, belts run from the factory's main power source. These belts traveled in one direction only. Altering the direction of the elevator itself required a relatively elaborate "shipper" mechanism to engage a straight or crossed belt that operated the winding drum. The independent engine, though, could be configured to turn in either direction at the tug of a rope running through the cab, and with it the way was clear for the installation of lifts in hotels, offices and apartment buildings without central engines. Charles Otis was not blind to the significance of its development, and the quarrel between father and son had been patched up by 1860, when they filed a joint patent on the improved oscillating engine. Charles had come back to engineer significant improvements to the machine Elisha had designed a few months earlier.

Charles returned not a moment too soon. The outbreak of the Civil War one year later coincided to the month with the unexpected death of his father, caught in a diphtheria outbreak. Elisha himself had taken an enthusiastic part in the lead-up to the war, and between John Brown's raid and the actual opening of hostilities he helped raise a militia, the Zouave Wide Awake Artillery Corps, which drilled and stamped about on the green at Yonkers. The artillery in question was the very cannon that Mr. Wilde had passed on entering the machine shop a decade before,* which the Yonkers authorities guardedly permitted the troop to fire "at some safe and suitable place...between the hours of 7 and 8 o'clock PM, and with as little annoyance as possible."†
A splendid photograph shows the Zouave Corps standing in front of the Union Elevator Works, looking fierce and bellicose with their beards and brass buttons; Otis himself, so people said at the time, was a ringer for John Brown.

Had Charles, with his younger brother Norton, not been sharing responsibilities with their father at the time of his death, the business would likely have gone under. As it was, Elisha had left the business "in a very embarrassed state," and creditors moved in swiftly. One M. S. Driggs, a warehouser, wrote Charles that "we think it very remarkable...from the manner it appears you are much displeased because we do not consider the death of your Father payment in full." Shortly before he died, Elisha had made over all the factory tools and fixtures to his son, as security for a chattel mortgage; and after his death it was left to Charles and Norton to keep Otis abreast of the rash of technological advances and applications that broke out in the 1860s, wedding the industry to a process of continuous improvement that lasted into the 20th century with the invention of the electric gearless. For despite the double crisis of 1861, orders could be found among the bills and demands. The brothers themselves had saved $2,000 to invest, and they held a string of decent patents in the business.

---

* and which represented part-payment for the very first safety elevator Otis ever made.
† Oct. 2, 1860. Donald Shannon, *The Annals of Vertical Transportation,* 1953

In spite—perhaps because—of the war, the 1860s were crucial to industrial development. Thanks in some measure to wartime demand, the U.S. economy became self-generating. Already by 1860 the United States was the world's fourth-largest manufacturing nation in terms of output. As the decade advanced, the number of manufacturing enterprises rose almost 80 percent, and the numbers they employed grew by half as many again.

Labor shortages brought relentless advances in machine production; machines lent themselves to mass production, and mass production to standardization. Thanks to the prolific output of American agriculture—flour and meal production was the biggest single U.S. industry in the 1860s, slaughtering and meat packing from then until 1914—all industry was boosted. And America never had deficiencies of power: water and coal and, later, electricity were to be found or produced in greater abundance there than anywhere else on earth. Finally, the whole of the United States represented the largest free-trading zone in the world—trading facilitated, as the 19th century wore on, by the explosion of the railroads.

The rising volume of business fostered demand for fast and efficient ways of moving materials through a building. Not only materials—Americans, too, seemed to be in a flurry of activity, chasing markets around the country on the backs of the railroads, staying in bigger and bigger hotels and processing their paperwork in larger and larger offices. Elevator manufacture became an increasingly specialized craft, feeding on developments across the field of industry, as success brought the need for an ever more intricate understanding of the market and the machinery that supplied it.

For unknown reasons, the firm was called N. P. Otis & Brother. Charles concentrated on office work while Norton drummed up sales and supervised at the factory. Their product was uniformly sturdy, neat and reliable—an important consideration in those days, when customers expected to carry out their own repairs.

Their reputation grew—not without promotion. They frequently faced customers who still found any elevator a marvel, people who had to be taught first what an elevator did, and only then why Otis' did it best. Charles worked hard on his elevators and engines, but both brothers watched their sales in a fiercely competitive market, and passed up no opportunity to advertise their wares, scattering flyers as they traveled to far-flung installations. The flyers aimed to both set and satisfy expectations, and drew on testimonials like this one of January 1868, from the owner of the St. James Hotel in New York City, which might almost have been dictated by the brothers themselves:

> *Gents*

> *As it is now just one year since your "Passenger Elevator" was put in operation in this Hotel, I desire to express to you my entire satisfaction of its operation.*

> *Its principal feature is its noiseless operation, combined with steadiness of motion, and most perfect safety.*

> *Our guests who have been in other Hotels where Elevators are in operation, are universal in their comments over it.*

> *The superiority of its motion is so noticeable that it commands their admiration and scarcely a day passes but I am commended, and congratulations extended to me, for my good fortune in obtaining so perfect a machine.*

When it came to discussing noiseless operation and steadiness of motion with distant clients, Norton, the younger brother, was the better salesman. He retained all his life an easy and affable manner, which is perhaps the birthright of the second son, no doubt polished in these years of commercial traveling. He was in Troy in September 1862, putting in an elevator for a coffee merchant, when he wrote Charles for 50 circulars to distribute around town or leave with the buyer to give out to the visitors who were sure to come and look. Already, he reported, "there has been quite a number of the heaviest dealers in to see the machines and [they] seem to think them a first-class arrangement and look and act about them as though they were some new discovery that had just come out." By 1868–prefiguring the later rivalry between two cities–Chicago businessmen were being advised that Otis Patent Safety Hoisting Machines "are used by most of the leading houses in New York, and about one thousand of them are now running in the United States, Canada and Cuba."

In 1870, Otis put out a 70-page catalog which assured hoteliers, among others, that travelers would be "delighted with the novel luxury of the elevator, [and would] naturally dilate upon it among their most noteworthy experiences of travel." It was true, too. Five years later a hotel guest wandered into an empty elevator and sat down on the bench, supposing he had found himself a snug and quiet little sitting room to read the paper. The elevator boy returned, slammed the doors, pulled the cord, and "up went the car with a whizz!" The poor guest leaped roaring to his feet—"Heavens and earth! An explosion, I'll be bound!"— then fell to his knees in prayer. The elevator boy told a story well, and "Heavens and earth! An explosion, I'll be bound" became that hotel staff's favorite catchphrase.

Much of the Otises' energy went into countering competition, which had sprung up from the outset. Elisha's automatic safety had not (perhaps rather surprisingly) wiped the field of competition. There was much business outside New York that Otis could not possibly have reached, and advertising was still at such a primitive stage that plenty of people who needed a hoist had never heard of Otis. Safety was not the only issue, either. People considered costs, the efficiency of the working parts, the speed of travel, the advantages and disadvantages of wire ropes and steam engines. Nor were the Otises alone in trying to get elevators out of the factory ghetto. In 1859 a rival, coincidentally called Otis Tufts, invented his steam-driven Vertical Screw Railway, an extraordinary device, wildly overengineered, heavy and expensive, by which the elevator cab rose like a nut on an enormous screw thread—20 inches in diameter—turned by a steam engine. It became a principal sight of the city when one was installed in the Fifth Avenue Hotel, and the Prince of Wales was taken to admire it when he paid a goodwill visit to America in October 1859. But at $25,000, Tufts' elevator could hardly compete with $3,000–$7,000 drum-winding machines. As the royal entourage steamed up the Hudson, it had been Elisha's little cannon that bravely greeted it from Yonkers, from the door of the Union Elevator Works.

Events moved rapidly. Comparing rival systems would grow yet more complex with the arrival of hydraulics in the 1870s and then, in the

1890s, electricity. By the turn of the century, when passenger elevators were standard for new hotels, apartment buildings and offices, the appearance of the cab, the quality of the ride, the noise level and steadiness of operation had all to be taken into account. New elevator enterprises could be established on the back of a single improvement in any part of the whole design. Indeed, they could be established, in the right location, without any improvement at all, given the costs of transport across the Hudson.

Tufts' screw elevator was not merely radical in design: it offered an alternative approach to elevator safety—there could be no free fall if the car was clamped onto the screw. Tufts in 1861 secured a patent on the use of multiple lifting ropes and argued for the benefit of this as a passive safety measure. Otis, alongside other manufacturers, took up wire roping, invented in Germany in about 1831, and Otis maintained a barrage of facetious propaganda against the whole concept of a passive safety system, boldly welcoming the scrutiny that Otis Tufts had attracted to the dangers of the lifting rope itself.

"Any lifting rope or other labouring member that can be made," warned the Otis catalog for 1869, "MUST fail at some time, and MAY fail at any time. The fallacy under consideration may be set in a striking light by asking the question: why, if six ropes are safer than one, are not twelve ropes twice as safe as six, and sixty ropes ten times as safe?... We would better untwist all our cables, and simply string the wires straight and distinct, in groups like a harp."

The 1870 catalog deals with safety and danger in lurid terms, suggesting that the need for elevators was proved less than 20 years after their introduction to New York.

"Hoisting Machinery," the catalog confided, "presents one of the most peculiar and difficult problems ever solved in Mechanics. It is subjected to a duty and responsibility, so to speak, such as belongs to no other kind of apparatus. Its work is to lift great loads to great heights, where gravitation, the firm friend and support of all other machines, becomes a tremendous foe, and if one iron sinew fails for a moment—a merciless victor, hurling lives and property to a terrible destruction."

The catalog reveled in providing details of grisly accidents, all suffered in rivals' machines. Pointing to a newspaper headline that read

"Lamentable Accident," the catalog piously suggested that "CRIMINAL RECKLESSNESS AND WHOLESALE MANSLAUGHTER" would be more appropriate, the crime being a failure to buy Otis. Horror stories were followed by gripping accounts of how the Otis positive safety feature had prevented disaster. Otis' reputation was apparently so solid, and its safety apparatus so reliable, that the engineer of a New York tobacco firm had airily spliced and respliced a hoisting cable which was "repeatedly broken," secure in the knowledge that in every case, "the safety ratchet and pawls have arrested and locked the car in its position aloft, without the slightest damage resulting."

People were certainly beginning to worry about elevator safety, because elevators were making their way into the mainstream of daily life. Newspapers tackled the issue. They entertained their readers with lurid accounts of deaths and injuries on the one hand and demands for reform on the other. Otis' first passenger elevator, after the Haughwout, was not in production until 1866, having to overcome ingrained prejudice against vertical transport.

Another rival safety system—and one that, like Tufts' multiple roping, found favor with the public—was invented by Albert Betteley of Boston around 1860. By operating in an almost airtight shaft, a falling elevator would be made to glide downward on a cushion of compressed air. It was actually an accident that attracted Betteley to the idea. A platform hoist carrying seven boxes of sugar crashed to earth and came to rest in the cellar of a Boston store. Surprised to see the boxes perfectly undamaged, Betteley examined the shaft and the cellar and discovered that the cellar was airtight. Having proved his conclusion by experiment, he took out a patent on the air-cushion safety device, which Tufts ridiculed as patenting a hole in the ground. Over the years the reliability of the device was improved, most notably by a concern called Ellithorpe, which was eventually to sell out to Otis. In 1879 the Air Cushion Company performed a test drop in Boston, with eight people riding in the cab when the ropes were cut. Unfortunately no provision had been made for the release of air as the elevator car dropped, so the doors blew out and all the passengers were injured. But the following year, rather incredibly, a number of visitors were induced to step into a trial machine displayed at the Chicago Exposition. "The car fell 109 feet," *Harper's* recalled, and "the passengers walked out smiling, and the crowd cheered with wild enthusiasm."

However confidently Otis spoke to the world through catalogs and flyers, the brothers were never complacent about safety. There was, for instance, one weakness in the original Otis safety device that became more apparent as buildings rose in height and the cables were lengthened: while a cable break near the car would activate the spring and pawls, a break on the other side of the pulley block overhead might occur in such a way that the weight and resistance of the cable as it flailed up to the block maintained the pressure on the spring. By the time the severed cable whipped over the block the car was traveling so fast that the brakes couldn't grip the ratchets. The introduction of hydraulics rendered the mechanism dangerously obsolete, because cars now traveled too fast altogether. Charles meanwhile had taken out a total of 31 patents relating to safety devices, nine of them in collaboration with Norton, who himself had 15 patents in his own name, seven with R. C. Smith, and six with others; and it was customary to offer a real smorgasbord of safety features, many of which were redundant.

But safety was by no means the only arena in which Otis found itself in competition with other makers. On the one hand, the barriers to entry into the business were low, and would remain so for decades: any competent mechanic might cobble together a hoist, and in days when transport was slow, a local outfit could offer a fast, relatively cheap service to neighboring concerns. On the other hand, the elevator was a relatively complex machine involving a number of working parts, each of which was open to improvement. While introducing all the time a bewildering array of additional safety devices, the Otis brothers concentrated their energies on improving the engine that controlled the car.

Otis' product in the 1860s was dominated by successors to the oscillating steam engine that Charles had patented with his father in 1860. A belt was still needed to transmit power from the engine to the elevator winding drum, but a belt-shifting device could be done away with, for a dedicated engine could be fitted with a three-way steam valve to close or open steam inlet parts at will, allowing the engine pistons to go into reverse motion or, by closing both inlets, to bring the engine, elevator machine and cab to a halt. The engine was operated from within the cab by a running rope, sometimes coupled to lever-and-wheel operating devices for ease and safety. By the standards of the day, there was nothing much wrong with these machines: they were accepted as reliable and found to be easy to operate and maintain, although their maximum speed was about 200 feet a minute, which limited their use to five- or six-story buildings. Moreover, the oscillations of the engine transmitted themselves to the cab. All the same, steam engines continued in use into the early 20th century, long after the introduction of hydraulics, and even after electricity.

Competition was stimulated by demand, of course, which inspired invention, although it is very hard to say which was chicken and which was egg as buildings began to rise higher and higher. In 1853 work had begun on the Cooper Union Building in Cooper Square in New York City: it would have been the first to use wrought-iron floor beams had the beams not been diverted twice to other destinations while construction was in progress. Cooper Union was the first to include an elevator hoistway in the original plans. Curiously, the building seems to have waited almost 70 years before an elevator was actually installed, in October 1914—an Otis electric gearless machine, still functioning in the 1950s.*

The elevator put into the Haughwout three years later was not a great success, but the store itself—five-storied, built in the palazzo mode—survived, flourished and pointed the way for others to follow. In 1862, *Harper's* magazine wrote of Broadway: "Twenty years ago it was a street of 3-storey red-brick houses. Now it is a highway of stone, and iron, and marble buildings." The article complacently concluded that "of course in all this the city has lost much of its old town character, and becomes every year more and more a metropolis." American business boomed in new directions as the Civil War ended. Production rose, and there was more demand for warehousing, transport and distribution. A tide of contracts and administration and paperwork raised the demand for space—the first private office buildings in the world, the first great hotels,

---

* The delay was not a record, though: St. Peter's in Rome was completed in 1626 with an elevator shaft not filled until 1900.

insurance company buildings and apartment blocks, all breaking away from old models that were really no more than converted private homes. Most of the new constructions required elevators—"veritable chain reaction bombs, destined to overturn the real estate market…[elevators] equalized rents on every floor of commercial buildings, instantly annulled safe economic investments and, conversely, created new and extraordinary ground rents."*

The first office building with an elevator was the Equitable Life Assurance Society Building, which went up in New York City in 1870. Its architect was George Post, who clinched the case for an elevator with the building committee by saying that "if they would build the building six or more stories high and put elevators in, he would be personally responsible for renting the upper floors if there was any difficulty in doing so." On January 4, 1869, Charles Otis wrote his brother: "We have lost the Equitable. Tufts has got it."† Post's prognosis, meanwhile, was correct: thousands flocked to the Equitable Building just to appreciate the views, and the building owners enjoyed a very good return on rentals. A little farther along Broadway the New York Life Building and the Park Bank Building—neither originally designed with elevators in mind—had been rising at the same time, standing together, so the magazine *Real Estate, Building, and Architecture in New York* assured its readers, as "the three most imposing and artistic office buildings in the country." If they missed their neighbor's distinction in elevator firsts, Park Bank and New York Life were quick to catch up, and Otis secured orders from both. New York Life took two five-foot steam freight elevators at $1,500 apiece in March 1870 and one eight-foot passenger elevator, costing $12,500, a year later, and in August 1871 Otis Brothers moved in themselves, neatly announcing that "Our Passenger Elevator, illustrating its advantages over all other machines, can be seen at our office."

By 1870, Charles Otis' longstanding determination to get a grip on the business had borne fruit. In 1867 the company was able to post an impressive account of assets and liabilities, which both in ratio and sum total had been transformed from their position only a decade earlier,

---

* "La Dialectique de l'absurde," in *L'Architecture d'Aujourd'hui,* No 178, Paris 1975.
† Otis, of course, later won it back, with hydraulics.

when the shop was saddled with debt and the value of assets barely reached three figures. Stock, tools, fixtures and uncompleted engines were now valued at $52,499.61 alone. In addition, $27,623.69 was due for collection, there was $2,030.93 in cash on hand, and the company's real estate was worth $4,890.43. Against these assets of $87,044.66 the company owed $21,517.32. An earlier effort to boost the capitalization of the business by bringing in Charles' old friend J. M. Alvord ended, as it had begun, in disappointment: Alvord's expected inheritance had not materialized, and in April 1867 a check-up on his handling of the company's financial operations revealed that he had been embezzling funds. Now, barely five years after Elisha's death, the brothers faced a level of demand that strained their resources. In November 1867, Otis Bros. and Co. incorporated as a trust, to the tune of $225,000, with Charles as president on a salary of $3,600, and Norton as secretary and treasurer on $3,000 a year.

The money was enough to purchase the assets of the old partnership and provide a solid base of working capital. In 1868, Charles secured a loan to mastermind the move to a new location built for the purpose down the road in Yonkers on Wells Avenue and Atherton Street, where Otis would stay–and grow–for 100 years. As ever, Charles' personal probity proved an asset to the company, just as it had done when he endorsed Elisha's notes in the 1850s: "I have applied to the Continental Insurance Co. for a loan of $10,000–ordinarily they would not loan that amount on a factory property," Charles contentedly wrote his brother, "but will let us have it as a personal favor."

In 1869, perhaps as a consequence of the move, which had allowed work to go on faster than in the old shop, attempts were made to cut costs and examine practices. In February, Charles wrote Norton: "Dear Brother, When we came to make up our annual statement on the 1st of January I found that on $80,000 worth of Engines made by us during the past year, we have made less than $5,000 profit. This state of things has powerfully suggested to my mind the necessity of taking some measures at once for reducing the cost of our machinery to the fullest extent as it must be apparent to you as well as myself that we cannot raise prices under present circumstances, but on the contrary, the tendency must be towards a reduction." The trouble was no longer a lack of space or machinery, Charles thought; it was managerial. "We have never had an excitable man to direct and organize in the shop. What we want is a man with large practical experience to superintend in machine work, but who will make an investigation into the manner in which things are being done and institute reforms whereby the same labor will produce nearly or quite double the amount of work. Such a man as will not fear to make it known when a workman is doing but 1/2 a days work and receiving a whole days pay and who is capable of discovering it when such is the case."[2]

As the letter goes on to note, Charles had not only found the man– William Lockwood, "a very civil quiet gentlemanly man"–but had already appointed him, at $30 a week, on a par with the existing foreman, Wilson, whose position had been growing dangerously unassailable. "We have been altogether too much in the hands of Wilson," Charles warned his brother, "so much so in fact that he could dictate constantly to us at any time and put us to great inconvenience by simply absenting himself from the shop." It is hardly surprising to find Charles writing two months later to complain of Wilson's behavior, "blocking the wheels to some extent so that we shall arrive at the desired result much slower than if he took hold and helped along." It was still good management that the enterprise required, and Charles spelled out his philosophy of excellence: "We must aim to manufacture at the minimum cost if we expect to thrive," he repeated, "and this I would achieve without having a single man who works for us underpaid but rather paid more than he can get otherwheres, but I would see that every man and boy in our employ was made to execute the fullest amount of work possible in the time for which he is paid. I would have no idlers around the shop waiting for their machine to run off its work at the slowest possible rate of speed at which the machine can be made to run. And it is my firm conviction that our ultimate success or failure depends very much on the manner in which this question of production is managed."

How far the atmosphere had changed since the 1850s, when Charles had expected time off at work and when, to judge from his journal, whole wet, dull days passed without "much doing in the shop"! Even then Charles had kept a keen eye out for slackers, though. "I returned to the Shop," he had written in his journal for February 19, 1858, "and found Billy in the engine room intent on doing nothing, or as near it as possible, having his lathe belted on a slower motion than I had directed, which he quickly changed when he saw me." Charles remained all his life a machine-shop man, driving operations there at full speed, quick to spot a bottleneck amid all the whirr and apparent industry of the place, a stickler for excellence, too—for safety in his elevators, for efficiency in his engines, for keeping abreast of orders, "to do justice to our customers by giving them their machines at the time they want them instead of 4 to 6 weeks after," as he reminded Norton. By 1870 much progress had been made in standardizing components: "*Each piece of every machine is as nearly as possible a perfect duplicate of the corresponding piece in every other machine,* hence we can always supply any parts which may become worn or injured by use, without any delay or trouble."

Visitors to the new Yonkers Works were invariably impressed; shortly after the move a book called *Great Industries of the US* chose to examine Otis' operations in admiring detail. It described a three-story building for machine shops, finishing shops and pattern offices on the Wells Street side. On Atherton Street lay the cabinet and wood-finishing shops, with workshops for varnishing and painting. Timber could be seasoned in heating chambers at the building's rear, beside the carpenters' shop and lumber yard. Underground cisterns supplied the buildings and fire-fighting equipment. A basement housed the boiler, a blacksmith shop and stores. The author spoke of "the exquisite judgment and skill with which means are adapted to ends," and went so far as to describe the engine as "quiet as the action of a pair of human lungs in perfect repose."

Otis' 1870 catalog must have exerted a positive influence over the author of *Great Industries of the US,* because he paraphrased large chunks of it and was so unctuous and enthusiastic about the Yonkers Works that his text might have been composed, like the St. James Hotel's testimonial, by Charles himself. By then Otis was expanding the factory built four years earlier yet again, "working day and night, with a double set of hands," in order to meet demand.

The rise of business by the end of the 1860s was reflected in the growing rivalry and competition that characterized the construction world. The field of industry widened with every passing year, and communications swelled—newspapers, the telegraph, cheap printing. The

Boston-based Otis Tufts, as we have seen, posed a continuous threat to Otis' business even in New York, where Tufts had scooped the Equitable contract in 1869. Therefore, Otis evidently responded to a wager made by L. A. Bigelow of the Tufts Manufacturing Co., to the tune of $10,000, that a Tufts machine would prove, "on a fair competitive working test," more economical than the Otis product. "We beg you to say to Mr. Bigelow that we wish this working test made with the least practicable delay," Charles had signed on, but was the trial ever performed? The records are sadly silent.

What this curious episode did suggest, however, was that at bottom Otis and Tufts recognized each other as good competitors. The rivals started to negotiate a merger as "the Union Elevator and Machine Co." in March 1873. The overture seems to have come from Bigelow, then treasurer and general manager of the Tufts Elevator Works, who laid out the nub of the business with naive candor in a letter of March 12, 1873: "The union of our two manufactories gives us the opportunity to very materially raise our prices to somewhere near the point our competition has gradually driven us from." This was a novel, and perhaps easier, way of dealing with Charles' complaint five years earlier of an inadequate profit on turnover, and it was a road Otis was to take to its end over the next 30 years.

In this case, though, the final deal was never cut: the prospectus was printed, the financial arrangements worked out, and dividends of 15 to 20 percent were predicted on the capital investment, yet the proposal simply withered away. On inspection, Tufts' patent for multiple hoist ropes proved invalid, and the Otis brothers may well have revised their own view of their competitive position after peering into Tufts' inventories and analyzing its prospects. "We will say now that we are experimenting with a new Rotary Engine, having one of 50 horsepower operating our shops with great success and we believe the problem of a good Economical Rotary Engine is about to be solved," Bigelow had written; but it wasn't, and the Otises were perhaps rightly unimpressed.

In any event the 1873 depression seems to have killed the union proposal off. Building construction was cut by half its 1872 rate by the September Panic of 1873, and America slumped into its worst depression before the 1930s. Markets remained stagnant until 1879. Tufts Elevator Works itself did not survive: all its patents were bought by a Boston manufacturing firm that actually made Tufts' equipment, and as a postscript the famous Vertical Screw Railway, installed with such fanfare and expense in the Fifth Avenue Hotel in 1859, was quietly retired in 1875.

With Otis suffering from the depression, Charles himself seems to have wavered in his impressive determination to stick to the elevator business and make it go: by 1875 he was reporting to the board of trustees on a plan to manufacture a new mowing machine invented by Rudolf Eickemeyer, pointing out that "the Elevator business for the last eighteen months has not been very thriving, and if we can safely add to our business...it may be advisable to do so." He was sufficiently cautious to pull back from a project to run a foundry on the site, preferring to rent it to more experienced operators who "have since furnished our castings at lower rates and of a more satisfactory quality than we have ever had before."

Only the depression refused to go away, and by 1877 the president's report made for desperate reading.

> *The past four years cover a period of business depression unprecedented in the history of this country.... There is absolutely no fixed value to any kind of real or personal property except stocks and bonds, whose apparent value is determined by the number of people and amount of capital available for gambling in them. Real Estate is absolutely dead, the only transactions in it being through the Sheriff and the Auctioneer, and sales are almost invariably for the amount of the mortgage—or less.... Our own business has felt, in the loss of business, the prevailing condition of things. By careful and conservative management, we have been measurably free from losses in the way of bad debts.*

In the same report he was able to say, with some relief, that Otis had sold out its interest in the haymaker for $30,000, enough to make up for the losses incurred in a field already dominated by large corporations engaged in cutthroat competition.

Even more satisfactory, and of longer-lasting benefit, was Otis' timely shift into hydraulics, inaugurated in March 1878 with the delivery of a hydraulic passenger elevator to a Broadway establishment. Hydraulics and economic recovery came to Otis hand in hand, so that they were in an excellent position to capitalize on the rising market—a circumstance Otis sealed in May 1878 by buying deeply into William Hale's Hydraulic Elevator Company of Chicago.

Chapter 3

Hydraulics

THE RELATIVELY SHORT DEPRESSION OF 1857–58 had stimulated Elisha
Otis' work on the oscillating steam engine; and it was rather as if the
depression of 1873–78, too, had been sent to give elevator manufacturers
a jolt, forcing the Otises to concentrate all their technological efforts on
improving and inventing their machines. The depression of the 1870s
saw the elevator industry establish the technology that would be required
by the next building boom—a boom heralded by the erection of the
Boreel Building on Broadway in 1879.

Steam elevators worked by driving drums onto which the hoisting
rope was coiled; but only so much rope could be wound onto a drum,
a practical limit to greater height. The first hydraulic elevator had been
invented in Paris in the mid-1860s. Léon Edoux had a watertight cylinder sunk vertically into the ground beneath the elevator shaft,
containing a plunger connected directly to the bottom of the elevator
car. Pressurized water was pumped into the cylinder to raise the plunger
and car; it was pumped out again to descend. The earliest hydraulic elevators did not use counterweights, so that the whole weight of the
machine rested on the plunger. But the absence of counterweights meant
smaller shafts, a useful means of saving space in the days of thick-wall
construction. At least in the public mind, safety seemed guaranteed by
the "lollipop on a stick": the elevator could not fall because it stood on

a column of water that could find its way out of the cylinder only through controlled openings.

In Europe especially, such machines proved popular. Europeans had a curious fear of ropes, and the plunger elevator was well suited to the three- or four-story building that Europeans preferred. In the United States the demand for tall buildings led elevator manufacturers away from the plunger type, which involved drilling a hole in the ground as deep as the shaft was tall, toward a roped hydraulic, using ropes and pulleys to increase the height and speed of travel. For every traveling/fixed pair the speed and rise of the elevator equaled twice that of the hydraulic piston. The practical limit was roping over six such pulley pairs, giving a 12:1 ratio such that the cab traveled 12 times as far, and 12 times as fast, as the piston itself. With the roped hydraulic machine the cylinders could be laid vertically or horizontally, often one on top of another in the basement.

Ordinary water-main pressure was used at first, later giving way to pumping devices that raised the pressure to 100, 200 and even 800 pounds per square inch—the higher pressure allowing for smaller pipes and more efficient transmission. Like steam-operated lifts, hydraulics used a running rope inside the car to control the water flow, and the travel was, as one might imagine, remarkably smooth. Otis was not in advance of the technology: the first roped hydraulics were installed in Boston as early as 1868, and the vertical hydraulic was patented by the Whittier Machine Co. in 1871. Otis got into the act by roundabout means—through the relationship the brothers forged with William Hale.

Hale, born in 1836, had gone from Wisconsin to Chicago in the 1860s to work for a paper manufacturer. As early as 1837 the new town of Chicago, with 4,718 inhabitants, was the biggest in Illinois; the railroad and the canal arrived in 1848, and by 1870 the railroad, in particular, had bolstered Chicago's claims to be the most important city in the Midwest. Hale soon began to dabble in real estate, as Chicago began its meteoric rise from a small settlement to the leading metropolis of the interior. A year before the Great Fire, more than 330,000 people lived and worked around the busiest railway hub in America, and State Street was a mile of hotels and shops, with the eight-story, 225-room Palmer House as centerpiece. St. Louis and Cincinnati were left behind.

The city, however, was built almost entirely of wood. The summer drought of 1871 dried the buildings out, and when fire broke out on October 8, 1871, the prevailing wind sent it ripping north and east across the heart of the city, leaping across the Chicago River before exhausting itself the following day in Lincoln Park. In 24 hours, 17,000 buildings were destroyed, 300 persons killed and 100,000 left homeless. Damage was estimated at $88 million.

This proved to be the beginning, not the end, of Chicago's story. Overnight, it seemed, the phrase "Chicago Shall Rise Again!" was coined. Some businesses were up and running within 48 hours, and a host of promoters spread out across the country, touting the investment potential of the city.

The Great Fire wiped out Hale's buildings, too, but he promptly built one of the first new Chicago office buildings and became fascinated by the elevator that went into it. Construction was going on all around him. A flock of eager young architects, attracted by the opportunities reconstruction offered, poured into the city, many to work for William LeBaron Jenney, who pioneered steel-frame construction: Louis Sullivan, who was to be known as the "father of the skyscraper," Daniel Burnham and John Root, among others. Starting from scratch, with space, cash, steel, elevators and, notably, a new, uniform building code and fire regulations, these architects were able to design buildings bigger and more efficient than anything built before.

Hale realized that the elevator industry was a sound investment, and he bought up patents belonging to a Boston mechanic named Cyrus W. Baldwin, who had invented the water balance elevator in the early 1870s, a sort of hybrid hydraulic in which the car was raised and lowered by emptying or filling a bucket-like counterweight which ran up and down the shaft, linked to the car by a cable passing over an overhead drum. It was a very simple device, capable of great speed and rise—speeds of 1,800 feet a minute, rather astonishingly, which would have required a building several hundred feet tall—and ludicrously dangerous, in retrospect. The car was pulled to a stop by a brake which gripped onto the side rails. Baldwin, then Hale, contracted out the actual manufacture, to Otis, among others; but the device was rapidly superseded by hydraulic-pressure systems. Baldwin soon mastered these and invented a vertical-cylinder machine that would become the Otis standard model.

With remarkable speed Hale established himself as a major player, with Cyrus Baldwin as his genie of the lamp. Hale's own gift was for promotion rather than manufacture, and his elevator interests soon eclipsed his construction work: contracting out the actual manufacture, he rapidly built up a business that spread from Chicago to New York, and via agents to Paris and London. After several months of fierce competition in New York, Otis and Hale came to an agreement that stemmed the costly competition between the two companies. Hale would assign Otis the rights to sell his elevators on the East Coast if Otis would stay out of Hale's Midwest market. Meanwhile Otis would manufacture for both markets. In 1875, Otis Brothers took over Hale's patents, and Baldwin, the inventor, came to work for Otis in Yonkers. Obviously it made sense for both Hale and Otis to have Baldwin working close to the factory.

By early 1878, Otis was manufacturing hydraulic passenger elevators to Baldwin's specifications, and Charles Otis invented the speed governor that made them safe that year. The board moved on May 10, 1878, to buy deeply into Hale's concern, the Hydraulic Elevator Company of Chicago. From then on, Otis would have exclusive manufacturing rights over Hale's hydraulic elevators, delivering them to Hale to sell in the Midwest, while Otis took the East and Pacific Coasts. Otis' speed in responding to the hydraulic challenge, and Hale's swift compliance, established the Otis Co.'s preeminence in the market for the next 20 years.

A visitor to Yonkers in the 1870s would have been hard-pressed to recognize the semirural collection of fields, barns, bowers and factories that had characterized the town in the early 1850s. By 1875 both Charles and Norton had moved into capacious new houses built for them "at regular shop rates" by company craftsmen, along the serendipitously named Buena Vista Avenue, Yonkers, on the banks of the Hudson, overlooking the Palisades.* Elsewhere the view was less restful. There were

---

* Not the first move the brothers had made: a letter from Charles to Norton in 1866 speaks
  of a house which "will be just about done by the time you get back and then we will have
  superb accommodations."

railway lines to New York City and a sheaf of local enterprises making rubber, morocco, hats and illuminating gas: an altogether more gritty industrial scene. The huge cemetery where Elisha had been buried—along with other victims of the diphtheria outbreak—remained as the sole patch of green. Along the riverfront, land was being busily recycled.

Otis' enterprise too had changed. In addition to the laborers, there were now proper engineers, with classroom training in an increasingly specialized field. Colleges and universities were offering engineering curricula that built on the major advances achieved since mid-century: the discovery of laws governing the behavior of fluids, thermodynamics, heat engine cycles; the measurement of horsepower; the principles of mechanical advantage; and the kinematics of machine elements, including gears. The laws of electricity, too, were being laid out as the century advanced: Gauss' Law, Oersted's Law, Faraday's Law and the theorems put together in James Clerk Maxwell's *A Treatise on Electricity and Magnetism* of 1873, all of which underpinned the subsequent development of electric motors and generators.

Gone were the days when an inspired inventor could knock off a working machine without drawings and juggle different lines of business. Instead of self-taught mechanics whose rudimentary workshops were the test beds of invention and whose work in factories was the wellspring of progress, degreed engineers were gathering formally in professional societies and at technical meetings to exchange ideas and generate further advances—men who, by an old definition, could do for a dollar what any fool could do for two. At Otis the precision tooling and manufacture which hydraulic systems required and encouraged involved far more detailed specification than the old steam engines, so a line of draftsmen had to be employed. Systems of financial control and forecasting had grown more sophisticated. There is a reference in the Otis books to an order "sent by telephone" in 1880. In 1882, Otis presented its first typewritten letter to the finance man being recruited as treasurer, tapped out faultlessly by an early trained stenographer.

Increasing professionalism raised the stakes, but the Otis brothers always believed in producing the best, demanding the best, and paying the most. Careful thought was given to the procedures of the factory and the office, as the contract signed by Rudolf Schmidt as engineer and draftsman in 1878 suggests: "He shall see personally that all measurements, surveys, sketches, and particulars of work for fulfilling orders required at either an office or factory or in making estimates for work are procured and put into proper shape and kept in such systematic order as to be always available for reference and use," the contract said, and more to the same effect. Although he was expected to travel about–"from place to place in every direction whenever and wherever the proper performance of his duties so require"–he was kept on a short leash. There was to be no absenting himself from the shop, in the leisurely pursuit of pocket watches and a city lunch: his expenses were to be such "as are absolutely necessary and entirely reasonable." The expansion of business from an intimate family concern to an impersonal system required not only formal controls but a formal statement of trust as well.

Like stenography and telephony, the spread of elevators was beginning to spawn its own new language. Otis' first machines were bluntly known as hoists; in passenger use they were sometimes described as lifts. But both lift and hoist were hard Anglo-Saxon words, bearing implications of effort and struggle. Only in England, where the lift was relatively slow to catch on, was the word retained with all its industrial force–and logic. You could *lift* a body *down*, the English pointed out, but the only direction you could *elevate* people was up.

Neither hoist nor lift quite survived the American genius for advertisement. Polite, attractive, faintly euphemistic, the word *elevator* began to appear in the Otis catalogs in the 1860s; there is no evidence of its prior use. "The King [of Naples] has had a machine made," wrote Greville in his memoirs for 1830, "like a car which is drawn up by a chain from the bottom to the top of the house. It holds about six people who can be at pleasure elevated to any story and at each landing-place there is a contrivance to let them out." This charmingly ingenuous description of what was then a noteworthy spectacle exposes the word *elevate* for what it was, a word almost magical, thoroughly kingly, implying an almost fairy-tale expression of will, like a satisfied wish. To most people the word *elevated* whispered of high social standing. In Australia, the depression of the early 1890s forced companies to advertise for the first time, and they promptly dropped the word *lift* in favor of the suave word *elevator*. The French language imbued *ascenseur* with an almost religious quality. The cars went *down* as often as they went up, but somewhere in the mind, *down* was the yawning pit, the mangled car. It was the *up,* not surprisingly, that caught the imagination.*

Until then, people used all variety of euphemisms. In 1835 the English talked of "rising cupboards"; 10 years later of an "ascending room," referring to a contraption that raised 10 or 12 people to the upper viewing gallery of the Coliseum in Regent's Park, London; and the idea of the elevator car as a room in its own right did linger for a surprisingly long time. Tufts called his screw-mounted elevator a "vertical railway" in 1859; the *New York Times* preferred the "movable room." It was not until the early 20th century that passenger elevators became recognizably themselves, designed to look like elevators in their own right, rather than like lobbies or antechambers connected to the design of the whole building. Perhaps the late Victorian taste for drapes and upholstery, for potted plants and heavy blinds, helped to obscure the fact that the elevator, having no windows, was unlike any other room in the house.

A large part of the cost of a passenger elevator system could be apportioned to the car itself. Otis' determination to go after the quality market soon brought cabinetmakers onto its payroll, so that its products might be not only the best but perceived to be the best. "The car is a sumptuous apartment, about seven feet square and eleven feet high," boasted the catalog for 1870, in describing an installation at the Congress Hotel in Saratoga, "domed overhead with skylights, ventilators, and chandeliers, supplied with gas through a flexible tube; below richly carpeted, with a large mirror and luxurious sofas around three sides. The sides and domes overhead are finished throughout with panels, pilasters, brackets, carvings and mouldings in richly variegated colors of bird's-eye maple, French walnut, tulip-wood and ebony, lighted up with chaste and appropriate touches of gilding. As a piece of rich cabinet work, (manufactured wholly in our own works in Yonkers) this car has been pronounced second to nothing produced by the most celebrated New York makers." Earlier Charles had put it more succinctly in a letter to his brother, "VanDerbilt (*sic*) and all the big guns of New York are there and

---

* As late as 1951 thrifty Indian operators were refusing to take passengers down in an attempt to save power.

have made some pretty thorough examinations of it and pronounce it the best thing in the world."

To travel in an Otis passenger elevator of the period was, no doubt, a sumptuous experience. With the car doing little more than 100 feet a minute, there was ample time to settle on the sofas. With a smart uniformed bellboy in attendance, variegated colors to admire, a marvelous chandelier and chaste gilding, the passenger must have felt that the journey was something worth talking about back home. Charles, with his engineer's aesthetic, would have preferred something "making the car look lighter and a little more cheerful inside," and he suggested replicating the Congress Hotel design at less cost, with white wood pumiced and painted, to save "all that expensive veneering"; but if a customer wanted veneering and pilasters, gas light and French walnut—why Otis would give him the rankest luxury without a murmur.

Through rope gearing, the hydraulic elevator offered the potential for much higher and faster elevator ascents. Flamboyantly signaling an end to the long depression in the country, the Boreel Building in New York was the first of the really large commercial buildings that rose as high from the sidewalk as brick bearing walls could take them. In New York it was followed by the Morse Building of 1878, the original Temple Court (1879), the U.S. Bank Building (1880), the Mills and Potter Buildings (1881–82), the Produce Exchange (1881–84), the Welles Building (1881), Western Union (1883) and the Washington Building (1884). As the pent-up demand for new construction finally found its outlet, business was brisk.

America's cities were burgeoning. Immigration swelled to a flood after the Civil War—by 1890, famously, there were more Italians in New York City than in Naples, more Irish than in Dublin, more Germans than in Hamburg. Almost a fifth of the nation's population was foreign-born, and in a city like Chicago that proportion reached almost 90 percent by 1880. Between 1870 and 1890 the number of cities with more than 100,000 population doubled, though not only foreign immigrants swelled the tide. Many Americans were being pushed off the land by a gradual decline in agricultural prices, and they were drawn to the steady wages and material comforts of town. The business of supplying a new urban population became easier and cheaper. Transcontinental railroads brought country produce to the city, while everywhere improvements in machinery, distribution and organization, especially in centrally important industries like iron and steel processing, oil refining, meat packing and heavy machinery production satisfied rising demand at prices that just about halved across the board between 1865 and 1890. Visiting foreigners sometimes mocked what they saw as an American tendency to gigantism and boastfulness; yet few could deny the verve and energy of the country.

Some observed that America was evolving a new kind of city—the Vertical City. It is often said that the elevator created the tall buildings of America. The truth is, of course, that many factors conspired to make them possible—including boastfulness. Iron-frame construction was increasingly widespread from the 1860s and developed into fireproof buildings within a decade. Wind bracing came in the 1880s. Central heating, which was available by 1861, was standardized in 1885. Plumbing in America was already well advanced by the mid-19th century, and the existence of pathogenic organisms was understood by 1870, when the office of sanitary engineer was recognized. By the 1880s the problem of lighting was being solved by electric filament bulbs. Construction equipment was increasingly power-operated, and the resulting speed with which a building could be erected had a positive impact on its economic viability. These were all technological prerequisites of monumentally large buildings, but with them had to come systems of organization on site, and access to finance on a colossal scale. In the absence of regulations, or when regulations were weak, tall buildings led to more tall buildings.

Iron-frame construction and the elevator advanced hand in hand to make the skyscraper a possibility. The impetus to height was there all along, and some very tall buildings were constructed from masonry alone, but the sheer volume of the necessary masonry foundations set economic limits to height. Buildings of eight, even 10, stories could be built of masonry; but for every story the piers and walls had to be thickened by around a foot at the base, eating into valuable rental space until the whole process became self-defeating.

Elevators, though, could make higher floors as valuable as the lower—often even more valuable, once people realized that they could escape the grubby, rowdy street without risk and get a good view in the bargain—or as an Otis catalog put it, "enjoy a purity and coolness of atmosphere, an extended prospect, and an exemption from noise, dust, and exhalations of every kind." If this drove all real estate prices up in a neighborhood—if higher and higher was the only logical economic response—it is worth recalling that skyscrapers were still more than the fulfillment of utilitarian economics. Victorian city streets were dirty: badly drained, littered with dung and flies, polluted by the coal smoke of industry and of private homes. Traffic was often chaotic and unpredictable. The new skyscrapers were clean and gave tenants electric light, central heating and ventilation, hot and cold running water, big windows and amazing views, which was more than could be said of run-of-the-mill low-rise constructions. They were well protected—there was an army of attendants to see to that: doormen, elevator attendants, cleaners, messenger boys; and many could service the needs of tenants right there in the building, with restaurants and coffee shops, barbershops and newspaper stands.

The very American penchant for tearing down old buildings to put up new has tended to obscure the fact that the tall office buildings were invariably so well built that many of them are still functioning a hundred years later, and have proved themselves not only adaptable but also architecturally and aesthetically delightful.

For the skyscrapers were about more than money and hubris. There were other, more human reasons for business districts to huddle together: people needed to meet, send messages, move paperwork from department to department and office to office. The arrival of the telephone in 1876, which might have been expected to transform the situation—to make it possible for people far apart to talk together—ironically had the opposite effect. Telephones generated more links, more business, more demand for paperwork and postage, and any enterprise worth mentioning joined the cluster of businesses that settled around the downtown exchange. The telephone was also a direct prerequisite for super-tall office buildings. Without the telephone, the new offices would have been impossibly remote.

But to concentrate on tall buildings themselves is to miss the point about American urban development. The elevator, steel construction, telephones and all the other paraphernalia of the high-rise belonged, like high-rise buildings themselves, to a larger process of change. The first tall buildings were office blocks. Their appearance raised the real estate values of neighboring plots, paving the way for more office blocks to be built. Homes, factories, workshops and rooming houses, which had previously been shuffled together with offices in city centers, were squeezed out. The reach of a city matched the rise of its downtown, as people began to commute from residential suburbs using new and reliable forms of public transport.

Ultimately the transformation of the American skyline came down to a desire for change. Americans were eager to experiment. When New Yorkers looked at Broadway and saw only a line of three-story brick houses, they clamored for the trappings of a metropolis. And they recognized few constraints over what a metropolis might be. In Europe the same conditions might be said to have existed—more business, telephones, elevators and money, just as in the United States—yet the process never took off there, and buildings remained five stories high, however massively they approached the street, until after the Second World War. Americans wanted to see their cities soar; Europeans, on the whole, preferred to improve and embellish their inheritance.

The book *Great Industries of the US* had rhapsodized on the Yonkers Works in 1872. In 1881 the April issue of *Scientific American* devoted its entire front cover to the elevator revolution, with a lavishly illustrated article on Otis' manufacturing methods. One illustration showed the Yonkers Works, an enormous palace of a building with 34 windows on its three-story façade, and a vast central chimney belching smoke. Beneath it were shown Otis technicians testing a hydraulic piston-case for the approval of a bowler-hatted spectator whose gaze is directed toward the pressure gauge and whose ample mustache suggests he may have been Norton Otis himself.

The article, under the heading "American Industries," was unstinting in its praise of "the pioneer house in the business." Otis had overcome the difficulty of establishing uniform standards across a wide range of specialties by combining "in this one establishment all the facilities which their long experience has suggested necessary.... Their workmen have been especially drilled...they use no low-priced, poor quality materials, and all their productions have that thorough adaptation of parts, careful adjustment and uniform strength which have obtained for the Otis elevators so large a share of popular favor through so many years." After extolling the organization and perfection of the machine works, the article described Otis' rigorous testing procedures, the principle of hydraulic lifts, their safety, and Otis' work on steam elevators. Steam, it appears, was no longer recommended for passenger use, hydraulics being cheaper in an unpowered building. "Hydraulics are to be found in most of the recently erected prominent buildings devoted to public use, or for business offices, hotels, apartments, or private residences, as well as in factories and warehouses, and their simplicity, economy and efficiency, united with the growing public conviction of their entire safety, render it extremely probable that the field of their future use will be rapidly and greatly enlarged."

In 1883, Otis clinched the largest elevator contract that had ever been awarded, with a $69,800 bid for the Produce Exchange. A New York newspaper covered the announcement with an article that reflected on changing priorities. Ten years earlier, it said, such a sum would have been considered a wasteful extravagance. Now elevators were as necessary to a building as a roof.

Almost all passenger elevators were now hydraulic. Of 1,250 Otis passenger elevators in service in New York, only 136 were still steam-powered in 1884. Freight elevators were changed more slowly: the majority were still belted, and independent steam-operated lifts still outnumbered hydraulics. Quantity was not necessarily synonymous with quality, however, and not only Otis benefited from the burst of elevatored buildings. "The demand for elevators in lofty buildings has produced a spawn of rickety rattletraps which ignorant and penurious owners catch at because they are cheap and which ought to be forbidden to hazard human life under severe penalties," a critic observed in 1884, repeating an argument Otis itself had been using for years: "The Otis patents cannot run forever and it would be no oppression to compel all elevators to have these only perfect guarantees of safety." Otis was already advertising with the slogan "The Standard of the World," and in New York City alone, as the company boasted in 1882, with Otis elevators carrying 50 million people a year, there had never been a single passenger injury in one of them.

J. L. Hubbard, an importer, had been the company's financial backer since entering into partnership with the Otis brothers in 1867, when they formed a trust; he sold out all his stock in 1880—alleging later that he had been defrauded by Charles and Norton's artificially lowering the stock's value before the sale. Two years later, at the beginning of 1882, Charles and Norton decided to follow him out of the company, offering all their stock and patents to Hale for $350,000.

One can safely guess at the reasons for this decision, which ended Otis' days as a family firm. Charles and Norton were born relatively poor; Charles, in particular, had experienced hard times, both as a child and as a young apprentice in the fledgling elevator company. Together they had driven the business into the big leagues, feeling their way into the stratosphere of business systems, accounts and bond issues, and learning to respond to the needs of an ever-widening market. They trained on the job and learned by their mistakes, but it had been all hard, remorseless work, and Charles himself was in poor health. William Hale was prepared to take the business over, leaving Charles and Norton to enjoy their wealth, bolstered by the rent the company would pay them for the land they retained in Yonkers. Norton saw himself in politics, on the public stage. He was already involved in local affairs, where his talents for salesmanship and mediation were appreciated. Charles, more prickly and socially self-conscious, a man who stood stiffly on his dignity, perhaps already had visions of gentlemanly living. Within two years of his retirement he was touring Europe.

In May 1882 the transition to a new management team led by Hale was complete. Charles and Norton were retained as consultants, at $300 a month. "One of the main objects of this offer...is to secure the hearty cooperation, influence and support of the brothers," the board minutes declared. William D. Baldwin—no relation of Cyrus Baldwin, the inventor[*3]—was offered the job of treasurer in October, and the next month the incumbent resigned. W. D. Baldwin took his place, with a $1,000 raise in pay. Hale had head-hunted him from France, where he was working as the representative of an American firm, and by March 1883, Baldwin had

---

* Cyrus Baldwin's position in the company was gradually to erode as he tied himself to the development of gas engines.

a place on the board of trustees. The business was rationalized, in view of its continuing expansion, into four departments: sales, manufacture, construction and finance, each under one of the trustees, and accountable to the president.

From his office in Chicago, Hale had been giving the Otis brothers advice in business matters before they retired, helping them move the company from a relatively informal family concern toward a more structured operation; as president he sped up the process, taking direct charge of all the company's activities, and introducing the best new business practices used in Chicago. Otis elevators were now at work in 272 cities in the United States, and Hale's reorganization began to create some sort of order from an ad hoc variety of agencies, direct installations, market share agreements and the like.

The bulk of his efforts was directed to legal and bureaucratic reforms. Both in the factory and the office, processes were rationalized, and the causes of common errors were analyzed. Work was no longer to begin without written confirmation. All materials relating to an installation were to be assembled at the factory and delivered in one go, as far as possible—a directive all the more logical now that contract terms specified half-payment when the machinery was delivered to the building, and payment in full on completion. As for the installation contracts themselves, they were to be more carefully worked out, and no longer routinely to "include anything other than the elevators themselves." Hale had no compunction about protecting his investments: poor old William Lockwood, Charles' "very civil quiet gentlemanly man," was informed that his services were no longer required. Suppliers were scrutinized: Beals and Walworth, who had taken over the former Otis foundry, lost their contract. Even the old ratchet safety, on which the company's fortunes had been founded, was dismissed without tears in March 1883, its death knell briefly sounded in the minutes of a busy trustees meeting. New offices were rented in New York City. In 1883, Otis inaugurated its own elevator inspections in the city, and soon thereafter took over a service shop in New York, while the *New York World* clamored for official inspections (begun in 1885).

Feelers were put out to Norton to see if he wanted to return as vice president in 1885. Norton seemed poised to venture into business again, and had established a new company of his own, which may have rattled Hale. But the approach came to nothing, and Baldwin moved up to take the job on the understanding that he would resign if Norton changed his mind. Business continued to improve, with strong demand from the new outsize office blocks. In January 1886 it was reported that in just five new buildings in New York City, 67,000 people were lofted and lowered daily by Otis elevators, some carrying 30 people at a time. Some 114 elevators in the city—which contained 3,500 altogether—topped 100 feet. In October 1886, Hale reported that the American Elevator Co., Otis and Hale's export wing, was showing profits.

Nonetheless, Charles and Norton returned to the board on February 15, 1887. The five-year period in which the brothers had promised not to go into the elevator business independently was up, the velvet fetters broken. Charles and Norton bought up a respectable but not significant number of shares, and Hale, tendering his resignation in order to return to Chicago, moved that Charles be elected president. No doubt the works felt the need for a hands-on machinist like Charles, and he was soon authorized to spend $10,000 on improving the machine tools and reorganizing shop-floor practices. It may be that their return was connected with the trustees' desire to buy the Yonkers factory (which the Otis brothers still owned and leased to the company) to facilitate expansion: Otis paid them $80,000 in June 1887.

Chapter 4

Swansong

UNSTINTING PRAISE HAD BEEN LAVISHED on Otis before Hale took over, but in five short years, such was the speed of U.S. industrial development, the Otis plant had lost its edge. When Charles returned in 1887, he wasted no time in examining and enumerating its deficiencies. He found all the heavy machinery crammed into one end of the basement, where it could be reached only by a small hatchway, and an elevator so underpowered that the heavy castings had to be manhandled by blocks and tackle. The steam boilers were "old and presumably weak": the insurance company had actually set a limit to their pressure, while the engine itself turned over at 112 revolutions per minute instead of the prescribed 130. The foundry was dark and cramped, and so small that it was "incapable, in fact, of turning out much if any more than half the castings required."⁴ Some $20,000 worth of ground–eight lots–was scattered with coal, sand, pig-iron, hydraulic pipes and the like, all so haphazardly laid out that a gang of laborers was employed merely to fetch and carry stock, and keep the tracks in decent repair and free of snow and ice. The sheer acreage of the storage yards in itself required two watchmen–"at an expense of Nine Hundred Dollars per annum"–to keep an eye on the yards and their entrances, although as far as Charles could see, there was no real way of preventing theft, trespass and idleness anyway with the men sauntering out at will to the local bars and strangers wandering in to "engage the attention of the workmen."

Tearing through the machine-shops, Charles saw far too many men crowded onto slow machines. He recognized skilled men performing tasks that could have been easily automated: each man instead was turning out his product at different speeds, and variable quality, not only from man to man but even from one job to the next. What tools and machinery they used were old and worn, "entailing losses from slow and imperfect work, from break-downs, necessary repairs, and consequent loss of the use of the tool, and from expense in repairing. I found a 35 horse engine driven to 76 horsepower, with a consumption of fuel sufficient to give double the last-mentioned power with an improved modern engine," he recalled in near despair. But it was more than a question of equipment: the building itself, "though one of the best in its day," was too narrow and low-ceilinged for modern appliances. To Charles, always a stickler for punctuality and precision, it was a nightmare.

Poring over the books of the business only confirmed his suspicion that the company's profitability disguised a failure to keep up with the rising volume of business. Otis was scarcely garnering a third of the available business on its own doorstep, in New York City, yet the plant was overstretched and relied on expensive overtime work merely to fulfill orders. "Other concerns in this line...have sprung up...and are making great progress in acquiring the business and absorbing its growth," Charles lamented; competitors were using Otis as an object lesson in how not to run a business of this sort—they were learning from Otis' mistakes. "One concern has spent from two to three hundred thousand dollars in building a new factory and furnishing it throughout with the latest improved machinery and tools, so that they can now produce and sell at a good profit a given machine at the same price which it costs one of their neighbours to produce it," Charles warned, adding, "Another comparatively unknown concern has risen and stretched itself, built, furnished and completed a new factory at a large expenditure of money, and is now ready to enter the field at our own doors, and walk off with our business...."

The *Scientific American* had commended Otis for the sheer variety of its work, supplying not only "hotels, offices, mercantile buildings, and residences," but also "elevators and hoists for warehouses and factories, furnaces and mines, winding engines for inclined planes, screw and gear combination lifting powers, with many special modifications of engines and appliances to meet the demands for all kinds of service." By covering every possible contingency and need, Otis had raised and enlarged its reputation across the board. But now, it appeared, there were gaping holes in the product line, injuring Otis not only in head-on competition but also by repute, for "many customers are deterred from coming to us by the statements of our competitors that they cannot obtain what they have been persuaded they want, of us." Otis' dominion of the factory elevator, for example, which had once brought the company a regular $10,000–$12,000 profit every year, had apparently collapsed, and while still convinced that the Otis vertical hydraulic possessed "greatly superior qualities as an elevator," Charles recognized a growing demand for horizontal machines—now "a standard article in elevators"—which Otis could not supply.

Hale, back at his business in Chicago, was aware of this challenge, but unlike Charles he saw it primarily as a sales and marketing problem. If competitors were managing to turn customers away from seeing Otis, "this must be stopped," he wrote to Charles in August 1887, "and the best way to do it is to go for these horizontal fellows on their own dung hill." By that he meant a policy of trashing the opposition and slashing prices. Hale was a businessman: he had, after all, approached the elevator industry as a speculation, in the aftermath of the Chicago Fire. He had first hired Cyrus Baldwin to do his inventing, then turned to Otis to carry out his manufacturing, and finally used the Otis name and assets to run an efficient business on the East Coast. As president, he had aimed to sharpen the business style of the company and to maximize profits on every deal. He had sought out, and got, the other Baldwin, a non-elevator man, to be his treasurer; and the treasurer, significantly, had risen to second-in-command. In 1886, Hale had begun "to investigate and report…upon the expediency…of combining with other elevator builders in business matters of mutual interest." He had built up an office system which was in itself irreproachable but which seemed to Charles far too expensive for the business the company was actually doing.

Charles was an elevator man. Single-minded in pursuit of his dream since youth, he had allied with Hale in order to leapfrog into hydraulics and to maintain the volume of work at his precious factory. The two men were separated by a difference in emphasis—one that would resurface throughout Otis' history, and the history of manufacture at large: Hale always looking for a way to improve sales, Charles for a way to perfect his machines.

Charles sought to redress the balance between office and factory by building up production. Hale himself had no doubt recognized the gap, and his resignation in favor of Charles seems in retrospect remarkably amiable and far-sighted. Hale had decided to hand the business back to the people who could beef up the production side. It took three years for the relationship to sour.

Aghast at the way the works had been run down, Charles ran through his $10,000 in a twinkling and almost immediately "appropriated" the sum of $50,000 for "the purchase of land, erection of new and repair of old buildings, purchase of new tools and machinery." In August 1887 he was to be found buying the rights to a liquid indicator, buying tools, installing traveling cranes in a new, long machine works, increasing foundry capacity by half. In October he was getting the engineers to work on a horizontal hydraulic machine, and in December enthusiastically pouring money into Cyrus Baldwin's gas engine technology. "I regret having to say that…other concerns in this line, formerly unknown or but comparatively little known have sprung up and…by investing large sums in buildings and in greatly improving their facilities…are making great progress in securing the business. This should not and need not be. We are, by position and reputation, age, knowledge, ability, capacity and resources and in every way the giant of the business and if we fail to use our strength and advantages…we have only ourselves to blame." Two months later a letter arrived from Otis' new rival, C. R. Crane, at the Grand Hotel, Paris, proposing a merger, and perhaps it was partly in anticipation of a negotiation that Charles got to work on plans for a horizontal hydraulic—the very machine for which Crane had become famous.

In the end it was Stokes & Parrish of Philadelphia who ducked under the Otis umbrella first, purchased for $50,000 outright in April 1888. The company was incorporated in Philadelphia, with Charles and William

Baldwin as directors. But all year a correspondence was being conducted under the dark heading "Crane Matters." Crane appeared to be launched on the same road as Hale and Otis, eager to buy out Stokes & Parrish and Whittier Machine himself; when Otis scooped Stokes, though, he seemed ready to come to terms. "I saw Charlie Crane the other day," Hale wrote Charles in February 1888. "We are to go over the whole subject again, but I thought I would do nothing more until you closed with Stokes. When that is done, I think I can present a plan of operations which will be satisfactory all round." So it would prove, although negotiations were complicated by Crane's bullishness and the separate involvement of Whittier. "I rejoice daily that you are at the head of Otis Brothers & Co., instead of me," Hale wrote in March, although he took a very steady view of all Crane's bluster and price slashings. "I do not take a great deal of stock in all they say about selling so many elevators, and doing so big a business, and making so much money. I have never seen anyone who could sell for less than anyone else and make more money than the parties who got a good price, and in all my business experience have seen lots of people try it and fail."[5]

"He will get tired before we shall," Hale wrote;[6] people would soon get fed up with Crane's erratic pricing and increasingly shoddy work, adding:

> *Having so much cheap work on their hands, and it being absolutely neces-sary...to show a profit on the business, he will soon be compelled, if not already doing it, to slight the work, and do it as cheaply as possible, for the sake of the profit. They have often done this in the past, and the result has been that the work comes back to us, at better prices.... A year ago they took a contract away from us, with a great flourish of trumpets, and now the same parties decline to have their machine under any circumstances.... I certainly do not propose to be driven into any arrangement or concession which does not meet the approval of my better judgment, and I am sure you will not be. If we can stand firm, and let the whirlwind pass by, there will be a calm one of these days, when the costs will be reckoned up, and it will be found that such methods of business are neither profitable nor desirable.*[7]

Meanwhile Otis, Hale and Crane were sidling up to an agreement to reduce competition and bring others into collaboration. Whittier, blowing hot and cold, now making overtures, now giving Otis "difficulty in bringing him to an understanding of the situation, and bringing about an arrangement which will be mutually beneficial," was to be given "the benefit of competition" by Otis and Crane, suspending a market share agreement in New England in May. Crane was meanwhile to join Otis in buying Graves Elevator, short of control. At last, in August, Otis Brothers & Co.'s capital stock was raised at a stockholder's meeting from $500,000 to $600,000, C. R. Crane buying the additional stock in four certificates of $25,000 to make Crane the largest investor in the company, though the trustees doubted his motives sufficiently to refuse him representation on the board. The money was easily spent by Charles, who in the year 1888 ran up bills of $153,000 on renovating and enlarging the Yonkers Works, and still bayed for more. None of the new allied companies advertised their links to Otis: all were to remain operationally independent while pooling their technological resources, in what has become known as a business trust.

Charles had a perfect and well-placed confidence in the growth of the elevator market. Only a global cataclysm driving "the remaining inhabitants of the earth" into huts could "seriously interfere with the elevator business, or prevent its continuous and extensive growth." The threat of a recession, which he scouted in his report of September 1887, only strengthened his determination to spend on modernization and improvement, while Hale counseled retrenchment from Chicago. "It is almost the universal rule that in trying times such concerns as are not up to the times, whose facilities are poor and behind the age, are the ones which go under," Charles insisted, and pointed to the experience of cotton kings who found that it paid to change all their machinery every eight or 10 years to keep up with technological improvements.

"The eastern part of the country is fairly well built up, but large structures are still being built in the western and northern cities," he reported in 1887. He was being, perhaps, too cautious. Two years later the *New York Times* predicted that "of all the business buildings and a considerable portion of all other buildings that were erected over 20 years ago there will not be one in a hundred remaining 10 years hence." American cities, it wrote, even East Coast ones, were engaged in a scramble for land—for "enclosed space" in which to conduct the steadily increasing volume of business. Two forms of rapid transport had been introduced, the *Times* article pointed out, which utterly revolutionized the demand. The elevated railroad drew far-flung regions into the daily orbit of the city. The elevator allowed businesses to grow where they stood, without need for territorial expansion. It was widely recognized that the arrival of hydraulic elevators had checked Wall Street's plans for a move north in 1878. More and more people could be brought rapidly into larger and larger buildings, whose development created a greater demand than the country had previously known for architectural skill and science in their construction. "It may be consistently stated," the *Times* concluded, "that American architecture as an independent school began its existence with the invention and adaptation of the elevator."

In these circumstances no expenditure that led to high volumes and high quality, Charles thought, could possibly be wasted. "Low prices increase sales; large Works require large sales; large sales, large purchases; and the manufacture of machinery on a large scale tends to reduce costs," he told the trustees on March 6, 1888. The market was there for the taking. High quality formed the basis for the company's reputation: the Otis name was already a bankable asset, and it was important to be able to say, as the catalogs did, that no accident in an Otis elevator had ever proved fatal. A contractor would have to think very carefully before he signed up with a competitor. The main thing was to be there, ready for the inevitable contract, ready on price, on technology, on quality. What young competitor could say, as Otis could, that its elevators would run five years without a hitch? What competitor could set such a premium on its product?

Charles worked furiously to remedy the deficiencies of the works. He bought land apace. He erected a new foundry. He built a new, wide, high-ceilinged machine shop. He bought new boilers and a new engine, doubling power at little extra cost of fuel. He replaced old tools wherever possible, exchanging skilled workers for unskilled, and attempting to convince the trustees that almost any new machine tool would pay for itself, if not within three months, then within a year. He reorganized the layout of the factory and brought in a new time-check system so that one watchman's services could be dispensed with and idleness found out. Visitors were made to carry passes. Stock-holding systems were reviewed as the storage space was reorganized, and it became possible for an accountant to add up a balance sheet at the close of each day's business. He had his own wells drilled, saving $400 a year to the city mains. He reinvigorated the production of "factory machines," an Otis standard. He quizzed workers and engineers on processes and improvements—doubling the strength of the cut gears, for instance, or working out ways to ensure proper lubrication of machine parts. He watched the workers closely and weeded out malingerers and undesirables—bad morale, he thought, was fatal to manufacture.

He even dreamed of an elevator machine, "into one end of which the crude materials could be placed, and out of the other end, in the shortest possible time, and with the least possible expenditure of power, and no cost for labor, completed Elevators should come, perfect in every particular, packed and boxed, and ready for shipment."[8] This hyperbole was contained in a good-humored presidential report, and yet the fancy seemed to prey on his imagination. "The machine would not be subject to the caprices of men; would not strike or rob its employer, intentionally or otherwise, nor thwart his purposes and destroy his business for sinister and selfish ends and objects." Perhaps it may be seen as a reflection of Charles' incipient paranoia; certainly it suggests, in the character of a man who always dealt better with machines than men, the flaw that drove him from office two years later.

Meanwhile, in the real world, Charles defended his program with characteristic verve: of course, retooling and expansion was expensive; of course, it was hard to implement when the work of building elevators had to continue all around it, he admitted. "A poor factory, well run, will do better than a good one, broken up and out of order," but "the transition period had to come sooner or later; and it was better that it should come at the earliest moment possible." He would not allow his listeners to concede "for a single moment, that because another establishment sowed its seed three or four years ago, and is now enjoying the fruits, that, therefore, seed-time and harvest are forever past, and the only thing left for this concern to do, is to go down to Egypt and buy its corn."[9] True to his company's reputation for high quality and fair employment practices, he would not countenance wage cuts, or wholesale firings, either: "This method of procedure means usually, only a

senseless and inconsiderate determination to wrench from the bread and
blood of the working man, what it is desired should accrue to the pocket
of his employer."

Indeed, far from seeking wage cuts or firings, Charles Otis had a tender solicitude for the factory men, as a hand-scrawled letter to Baldwin,
the treasurer, in July 1889 attests:

> *Mr. Nichols is it seems to me doing us good service and a good deal more*
> *than returning to us the value of his apprenticeship. He has just devised a*
> *means of saving as I calculate at least 60 days work of one man... by intro-*
> *ducing a bludgeon punch to punch the holes instead of lowering them down*
> *to the yard and drilling them.... It seems to me that it will be but simple*
> *justice to him, to pay him something... as I am inclined to believe that per-*
> *sonally he has not much means and possibly has not the means of obtaining*
> *much if any. He has never even hinted to me on the subject but I think we*
> *ought to do what is right by him....*[10]

Of course, there was a hard-headed reason to avoid firings wherever
possible, as long as "our factory is '...a machine...' of a fragmentary and
imperfect kind," relying for all the machinery on craft skills which were
too precious to discard lightly. America was beginning to solve its peren-
nial labor shortage, but men who knew their job were as rare as ever.

"The only reliable and substantial basis upon which a manufacturing business can be built is the uniform excellence of its products,"
Charles warned the stockholders once again in 1889. The elevator market, he explained, was inherently unstable. One year buildings would
be torn down to make way for bigger ones, and the next year everything would be still. Profit on any job was a matter of guesswork;
building went on at such a rate that "orderly and systematic methods"
were thrown to the winds. Plans changed on the job, leading to delays
and losses for contractors, "which it is generally impossible or impolitic
to collect for.... Every man and every gang is in the way of every other,
and it is a rough-and-tumble scramble over and under and through
everybody and everything," he said. The only certainty was quality.
"So long as regard is had to this fundamental principle, a business will
grow by natural accretion as everything in nature grows under favorable

and healthful conditions. To overlook these things and allow Cheap John, penny-wise-and-pound-foolish methods to creep into your Works, buying and employing the lowest priced material and labor, advising and selling machinery badly proportioned and ill-adapted to the purpose for which it is required, will inevitably lead to growing dissatisfaction of customers, declining trade, and ultimately in the decay and ruin of business...."

Charles in his excitable and impassioned way could put a case with verve and confidence, but he did not know any longer how to wring more investment from his stockholders. The three years of his tenure as president were years of pleas and arguments, marked by furious tussles with the sales department over optimistic promises, laying of blame, and mental anguish. Charles worked harder than anyone else and was consequently always difficult and demanding: as early as 1867 his accountant had resigned in exasperation when he was asked to file a fifth and perfectly superfluous copy of accounts. "What would you have more?" he cried, "[A] facsimile of my petty cash? This today; what tomorrow? A copy of my Journals? Or perchance a facsimile of the facsimile I rendered yesterday?... What then?... An extra twist to the 'red tape' of Suspicion—an extra eye-hole in the office door!" Giving a passable imitation of a man driven genuinely half-mad by the Otis brothers, he had stalked off to find a situation where he would not be treated, as he grandly said, as a mere "Chevalier d'industrie...not worthy of business confidence...."[11]

Charles could never feel that his work was done; he could never rest easy that the company was dominating the market as it might. "The boring mills have been run till 10 o'clock during 48 evenings in 1889," he told the stockholders, "while in 1888 the mills were run all night during 230 nights, and the entire shop was run until 10 o'clock during 234 nights." These were statistics he gathered himself, poring over the records and the schedules, pencil in hand. In January 1890 his superintendent, A. G. Mills, who had suffered all kinds of epistolary combat with his chief, wrote Charles that "we are in the 400 in the elevator line," having sold 400 elevators in 1889. It was the kind of benchmark Mills knew would please him. When the figure was more accurately marked down to 399, Charles was no longer around to know of it.

His address to stockholders for February 1890 was valedictory. The warning on "Cheap John" methods was Charles' parting shot, fired on the day he retired "on account of ill-health," at the age of 51. Perhaps he recalled the phrenologist's verdict that he would "live to be an old man" if he took care of himself. He would live another 37 years after retiring in 1890, surviving both his younger brother and his first wife, and dying shortly after marrying his nurse, at the age of 88.

Chapter 5

Abroad

Elevators had quickly established themselves as a widespread form of mass transport in the United States, but the rest of the world changed far more slowly. In the 1860s, Americans were observing how European workers performed mulish and degrading tasks for want of proper machinery; the fact was that European labor was comparatively cheap, and work patterns long established. Nor did Europe evolve the kind of giant office block, let alone the skyscraper, that characterized downtown areas of the major American cities. In part this was a conscious decision of Europeans to preserve the jewel-like quality of their cities as they had evolved over centuries. In part it was a subconscious respect for history, for religion, even for monarchical power: there was something indecent (if not illegal) about a private construction towering over the churches and palaces that ostensibly gave direction to society.

It was a class thing, too. The highly idiosyncratic owner of Gramercy Flats in New York had refused to install an elevator in his building because he did not want any of his tenants feeling inferior or superior to one another: high-level apartments already attracted premiums in elevatored buildings in America. In Europe the opposite held true, where generations of stair-climbing urbanites had established pretty precise class strata between floors. The second floor, or *piano nobile,* was always the best, with perhaps large louvered windows on the street, a view of trees and gardens at the back, and handsome, well-proportioned rooms reached from the hall below by an impressive curving staircase. Attic stories, by contrast, were crammed with tiny box-rooms for servants, or for the legion of impecunious artists who hacked consumptively in European garrets. This was as true of London, where the private house ruled supreme, as of Vienna or Paris, where apartment living was an old tradition.

Yet influences were at work, even in Europe, which stimulated demand for vertical transportation. The Grosvenor House in London was the first hotel in the world to be provided with passenger elevators for the convenience of its guests: the Grosvenor, significantly, was built at Victoria Station, one of the world's busiest, which handled Britain's railroad connections to the continent of Europe. In other situations, though, provision for the masses was largely an American requirement. When, for instance, giant department stores were built in Europe, they came with an American accent. The Magasins du Printemps opened in Paris in 1874, openly modeled on similar stores in the United States, where a huge range of goods were displayed in different departments and arranged according to quality and price. It was the first store in Europe to have elevators.

European lift manufacturers initially supplied the demand, but they could never really garner the same experience, or compete in such instructive competition, or grow as large and resourceful as their American counterparts. Otis, of course, was a giant even in America. A European contractor could approach Otis with almost any project, secure in the knowledge that his order had a precedent, that he was not providing a manufacturer with a test tower. It was for just this reason that the Parisian authorities finally buckled to the pressure of time and called in Otis to work on the Eiffel Tower, the centerpiece of a world's fair planned to celebrate the centenary of the French Revolution.

World's fairs were very much in Otis' line. One of the earliest of them had launched Elisha's career as an elevator man in 1854, and since then both Otis and the concept of an industrial fair had gone from strength to strength. In the days before mass media, these fairs offered companies like Otis wide publicity. They expressed the way industry was creating a genuinely international community of interests—they really were world's fairs, speaking a language that could be understood as read-ily in Germany as in Chicago. Every year there were more marvels to be displayed, and more people came and looked at them. Engineers, scien-tists and architects came, of course, to be stimulated and challenged by the collections and their layout, so that Paxton's glass and iron Crystal Palace of 1851 influenced the design of European shopping arcades, and the Paris Exhibition of 1889 introduced the world to electric street light-ing—while the exhibits themselves helped to inform the scientific or industrial communities of new developments in their fields, in days before easy international travel and the prolific specialized literature we currently take for granted. The display of American machine-made watches at Philadelphia in 1876 was an example of the way knowledge spread. The Swiss had examined the processes, copied them, and returned to Chicago in 1892 with machine-made watches of their own.

But lay people who felt involved in technological progress in a way their fathers might never have done visited the world's fairs, too. The Eiffel Tower is too familiar a landmark to surprise any longer, but old photographs reek of incongruity, with men and women in long skirts and bowlers, feathered hats and tail coats, surrounded by iron strutwork and hard plating, a nakedly industrial backdrop of rivets and girders.

The entire tower project aroused furious antipathy when it became clear that the organizers of the Paris Exposition of 1888 were determined to push ahead with their ambitious scheme for erecting the tallest struc-ture in the world close to the center of Paris. "A gigantic kitchen chimney," the intellectuals called it, but too late. The commission had already spent heavily in preparation for erecting what they saw as a perfect symbol of France's scientific, artistic and technological achieve-ments—and hoped, through gate sales, to make a good deal of money, too.* Because of this, elevators were essential from the start.

The European market for passenger elevators had grown in tandem with American demand, but not, as we have seen, at anything like the vol-ume. In most European countries respectable lift producers did exist, and it was the intention of the commissioners to make the tower a showcase

---

* And did so, beyond wildest expectations: scheduled to be dismantled at the end of the show, it has received about 6 million visitors annually in recent years.

of French technical prowess. The various sections of the tower—the inclined legs to the first platform, the more deeply curved section of the legs up to the second platform, and the straightforward straight run to the top—were put out to contract with domestic firms. No one, it soon appeared, wanted to bid for the middle section: nobody knew how to deal with the curvature. Ascenseur Otis Cie., the Paris office of the American Elevator Company, which was Otis Brothers' European branch, had a crack at the tender, but the commission rejected it on the basis of its rules against foreign involvement; instead it extended the bidding time.

Meanwhile Otis' first foreign sale was made in 1862, when the schooner *Mary Ellen* carried a freight hoist from Yonkers to St. John, Newfoundland—loaded right from the dock on Vark Street! In 1873, D. Tomas Urmaneta of Santiago, Chile, had the honor of ordering a small passenger elevator from Yonkers, instigating Otis' first foreign sale in this line, while two freight machines were installed in a sewing machine factory in Glasgow. Only the previous year, an observer noted, "in the business streets of London, one of the tourist's sights is the porters who carry on their backs barrels of flour and other materials...transferring cargoes to the upper floors of the huge storehouses." In 1876 a Viennese visitor to the Philadelphia World's Fair wrote a paper to explain the American love affair with the elevator—marked proof, if proof were needed, that the contraption was not widely used in Europe.

But demand was rising: Hale recognized it when in 1880 he formed the significantly named American Elevator Company to market Otis' elevators in London and Paris. Four years later, as president of Otis, he brought the company under Otis' control, and by 1885 some 25 passenger hydraulic elevators were installed or on order in London alone. Given the costs that attached to shipping, and the difficulties of managing installations at such long range when mails were still slow, it is a testament to the quality of Otis' product at that time.

"Otis Brothers & Co. still stand at the head of the elevator business of the world," Charles Otis told stockholders in early 1888. "During the last two years we have extended our name and reputation and have shipped our products to almost every civilized country of the globe. We have opened up a large acquaintance and trade with Australia.... Our London connection

is promising well, and we are acknowledged to stand at the head of the business there—even by the old well known and long established elevator concerns in that city, and, notwithstanding the well known prejudice of the English people against American products, we now have if not the largest by far the best, most satisfactory and profitable business in our line on the other side of the Atlantic. Our business along the Pacific Slope has also been satisfactory. We have during the past year shipped elevators to China and South America...."

Under the circumstances, Otis Brothers & Co. was perfectly aware of the publicity value of the Eiffel Tower. Outside the United States, Otis was in much the same position with regard to educating its potential customers as it had been in the 1860s at home, when Norton traveled across America with his flyers and testimonials. Nor was its ambition any less: it was unthinkable that the tallest building in the world should not be equipped with Otis elevators. Much heartache and expense was to follow from this line of reasoning, as it happened, but the company was delighted with its $22,500 contract in July 1887. For all the vicissitudes and bitterness that the project eventually provoked, the Eiffel Tower was to be an acknowledged showcase of technological skill.

Otis, then, was pleased but hardly surprised. The company had known all along "that, although the French authorities were very reluctant to give away this piece of work, they would be bound to come to us, and so we were preparing for them," as Hall, Otis' Paris representative, later recalled. When he was actually invited to consult with the tower commissioners, he surprised them with the admission that the project "has required a great amount of preparatory study and we have worked on it for three years." He continued by saying: "This is the first elevator of its kind. Our people for thirty eight years have been doing this work, and have constructed thousands of elevators vertically, and many on an incline, but never one to strike a radius of 160 feet for a distance of over 50 feet." The "piece of work" that Otis got in July 1887 was for the most contentious and awkward section of the entire tower: two of the curved legs.[12]

The job did not, at the outset, appear impervious to solution. Indeed, the scheme that Otis proposed and finally built was ingenious, although, in the view of one recent technical paper, it contained no single element so radical as to be beyond the capability of French engineering. The issue was possibly cultural: Europeans had a block about roped elevators. Magnificent work was done in Europe to perfect the direct plunger machine, which, by maintaining contact with the ground via a rising-plunger shaft, appeared to offer the promise of perfect safety—although the illusion might have been dispelled by the horrible fate of Baroness de Schack, in the Grand Hotel in Paris 10 years earlier, as *American Architect and Building News* breathlessly reported:

> *She took her place in the car, with a superintendent and the man who worked the apparatus. Instead of descending, the car began to mount with alarming rapidity. The casting which united the piston to the platform on which the car rested had broken... the piston darted downwards with fearful speed to the bottom, while counterweights, now much heavier than the car and its load, pulled the car up at a dizzy rate. Arriving at the top floor, the car was rammed against the top beam. The shock... broke the chains which held the counterweights, and the car went flying down to the basement. The weights fell with a report almost equal to a cannon shot.... The three occupants of the car were dead.*[13]

Nevertheless, Europeans refused to give up their love affair with the piston elevator. This being the case, European makers were less familiar with rope systems at the level of detail, and the devil was in the details.

This was reflected in the attitude of the commissioners—or rather of Eiffel, who advised them—toward Otis' winning bid. Naturally, absolute safety was a precondition of any installation of such prestige; and naturally, Otis offered a modified version of its original notch and spring safety, adapted for the rails that replaced the guides on the incline and that promised to halt the car within 10 feet. But now Eiffel, through the commissioners, demanded that Otis send its best man over to discuss the whole project: Thomas E. Brown, the chief engineer, whose presence in Yonkers during the first year of Charles Otis' reorganization of the factory was practically indispensable. Charles now blundered by consenting to the French demands. Having reluctantly lent the commissioners its top-level engineer, the company naturally found itself conducting a top-level dispute with Eiffel over safety.

Eiffel insisted that the Otis design should incorporate a rack-and-pinion safety device, like those used on inclined railways. Not only did this afford an extra measure of safety, but—and here Eiffel dished up a true surprise—the commissioners apparently were set on having a car that could be manually lowered by the operator in the event of a failure. This, of course, reset the parameters. The Otis system did not allow for this requirement; moreover, the rack would be noisy and slow. "I should favor giving up the whole matter rather than allying ourselves with any such abortion," Hale wrote to Charles Otis. The company had wanted the kudos of the Eiffel Tower, but instead they were to be made to exhibit Stone Age technology. "We would be the laughing stock of the world, for putting up such a contrivance."[14] Thomas Brown refused to approve the change and returned to New York.

It seemed likely that Otis was being made to suffer for the mutual antagonisms that had arisen between Eiffel and the commissioners. Eiffel was being excessively cautious, knowing the commissioners' mood. Otis held the trump card, though, provided the company had the nerve to play it, because time was running out. The Exposition was to open on May 1, 1888, and the contractual deadline for the work was January 1. Yet continuous modifications to the tower's framework as it was being built forced Otis to wait until the lines of the legs were properly established, and it soon became clear that January was an impossible target. Eiffel immediately threatened to stop payment. Charles wrote him a long and steady reply, pointing out how the designs had been altered, staunchly defending Otis' reputation and concluding: "...after all else we have borne and suffered and achieved in your behalf, we regard this as a trifle too much; and we do not hesitate to declare, in the strongest terms possible to the English language, that we will not put up with it.... If Mr. Eiffel shall...treat us as we believe we are entitled to be treated...well and good; but it must be done at once...otherwise we shall ship no more work from this side, and Mr. Eiffel must charge to himself the consequences of his own acts."

Otis, notably, won all its arguments in this case: its elevators were in operation on the day the Exposition opened, free of the odious rack and pinion, and notably smoother and faster than the elevators installed by local companies in other sections of the tower. Newspapers reported

Otis' lifts to be among the best American exhibits at the fair. For Charles, the entire project vindicated his efforts to restructure the production facilities at Yonkers. Had reorganization been delayed, he told the stockholders, "the heavy Eiffel Tower Elevators could never have been constructed, in the time we had, if at all; and the contract would have entailed very heavy losses and damage, resulting, in all probability, in law suits and general disaster, both to us and to Mr. Eiffel."[15] Fame and reputation had its price all the same: the cost to Otis of delays and overruns, not to mention the enormous amount of time and energy the project devoured, was prodigious.

Otis' confidence, however, remained unshaken. "It is fully decided that a Tower will be erected in London higher than the Eiffel," Baldwin was writing in 1889, "and it is of the utmost importance that the information Mr. Gilman [Otis' London representative] has written to the office for should be sent to him without delay. Will you please see that it is?"[16]

In 1884, W. F. Hall, vice president of Otis, took a vacation in Australia. Melbourne's population was growing fast, and the city possessed, like many a Midwestern town, a frontier mix of the rugged and the refined: cast iron houses, bluestone Houses of Parliament, streets of European flagstones, pubs for ranchers and clubs for lawyers and businessmen. There was a boom in construction, and Hall soon found an enterprising landlord to whom he explained the logic of the American way. Mr. Prell, by name, was building a four-story office block without elevators when Hall convinced him that the upper floors of a building served by a good elevator would yield rents equal to the ground floors; furthermore, with an elevator he could go higher. Prell did just that: he added two stories to the building and installed one of Melbourne's first passenger lifts. The speculation was a success, just as Hall had demonstrated: over the next four years Prell went on to build three nine-story buildings on the lower slopes of Queen Street.*

Prell and Hall triggered a latent boom: the population of the city was rising, export prices were high, and the government and private firms were borrowing heavily from abroad. Old buildings in the city began to fetch high prices: speculators drove up land values, and soon

---

* Two of them, 31 and 34, were still standing in the 1950s.

every section of the community, from banks to churches, was involved in the land boom, as Melbourne began to sprout with red-brick "skyscrapers" and enormous, Renaissance-style hotels. In 1887 a company was formed to supply high-pressure hydraulic power through seven miles of mains: normal mains' water pressure was too low in summer to work.

Otis moved rapidly from agency to factory. In 1887 the Austral Otis Elevator and Engineering Company was formed in the city. But perhaps the similarities with home turf were misleading: economically, the Melbourne freedom to boom and bust was very American, but the financial and social ties of the city were with Britain, and Austral Otis' business declined rapidly after the British firm Waygood opened a subsidiary factory there in 1890, allying with the local firm of Johns as boom turned to bust. By 1892 some 70 percent of all the elevators connected to the hydraulic mains were Johns machines. This outcome was not good for Waygood, either: it had spent heavily and now sold out at a loss. When Waygood re-entered the Australian market, it was as Waygood-Otis, of England.

Chapter 6

The Hidden Hand

I N THE SUMMER OF 1893 a virtual city rose on 600 acres of marshland on the shores of Lake Michigan. The White City, as it was called, was erected for the World's Columbian Exposition in Chicago, ostensibly to celebrate the 400th anniversary of Christopher Columbus' arrival in America, but in reality–given the way Chicago had snatched the honors from under the noses of New York, St. Louis, Washington and Philadelphia–to signify Chicago's remarkable recovery from the fire of 1871. As the fair's publicity journal put it, "As it was true of old, that all roads led to Rome, it is equally true that all roads lead to Chicago."

The exposition ground was called White City to distinguish it from the Black City–smoky, sprawling, industrial Chicago, a city whose population had swelled from 400,000 at the time of the fire to 1.25 million, many of them first-generation immigrants. They gave the town a rollicking, radical, criminal air, which New Yorkers thought showed that Chicago was not a city at all but an overgrown frontier town. The White City was there to demonstrate that Chicago's raw energy could be refined–though to many visitors it reeked of a uniquely Chicagoan bravado, a pageant played to Chicago's swelled-headed complacency. This was perfectly true, but it was fun, too, and ran deep in the Chicago grain: a hundred years later, one of the city's department stores had an elevator operator who called out the floor numbers down to street level, when he would fling out an arm and cry, "Chicago!"

At the Columbian Exposition the visitor was dazzled by a grand confection of canals, pavilions, museums and railway stations, sculpturally disposed to form an ideal urban complex, perhaps the first planned public space in America since Jefferson's time. In contrast to the pell mell irregularities that characterized 19th-century American cities, the White City was embellished with broad avenues and public squares, delightful parklands designed by Frederick Law Olmsted, classical buildings and classical vistas designed and arranged by such architects as Daniel Burnham and John Root. Around the water basin, deferring to Richard Morris Hunt's grand dome, the pavilions of the Court of Honor were corniced at a uniform height, abiding by formal axes, every one grandly porticoed. The White City was a classical master plan for America.

Some 21.5 million paying customers visited the Exposition—the profits were exemplary—and they left wondering how it was that everything that real cities lacked the White City seemed able to provide, and all for 50 cents a head—cleanliness, systematic planning, courteous security personnel, public drinking fountains and restrooms, a moving sidewalk and the convenient rail link to the Loop. Partly, they understood, it was the triumph of the new, clean power of electricity, the unseen, silent power behind so many of the Exposition's displays. Ten thousand Edison bulbs had been installed in a Tower of Light by the General Electric Company. The world's first Ferris Wheel, and the pavilions along the shore, were all picked out at night by incandescent bulbs. The elevated railway was electric. The 50 gondolas that cruised the canals and the lake were electrically powered. Even the lake steamers running between the fair and the Loop followed a string of electric buoys.

One can hardly overestimate the extent to which electricity revolutionized the world, or credit, retrospectively, the sheer breakneck speed of electrical development in the late 19th century. At mid-century, when Elisha Otis demonstrated his safety elevator, electricity was still a curiosity with no known applications. The first clumsy dynamos were then developed, and in 1873 a reversible dynamo was harnessed as a motor, immediately sparking efforts to apply this knowledge to the transmission of power. Between 1880 and 1884 huge advances were made by pioneers in electric traction. Thomas Edison solved the difficulties of electric light; in Paris the Siemens brothers exhibited an electric tram car and an electric elevator; in New York City, Edison established the world's first public electric supply station. J. P. Morgan supplied the funds.

In all branches of the new science there were many practical difficulties to overcome. Edison almost burned Morgan's house to the ground, while Siemens' elevator was a flimsy rattletrap, and the best electric elevators of the early 1880s were restricted to freight use—simple motors running at constant speeds that merely substituted for old steam engines and slotted into the belt-shifting and pulley mechanisms of line-shaft-driven systems. They were far too rough and jerky to compete with hydraulic passenger lifts. Then in 1883 a Viennese engineer exhibited a four-man, 75-foot-rise elevator powered by a directly connected electric motor, and a year later William Baxter, Jr., installed a patented direct-current, worm-gear machine that drove a winding drum in a building in Baltimore. At Otis Brothers, William Hale, the father of Otis' hydraulics, sensed that something was happening in his world.

Electricity, as it turned out, did not immediately transform the elevator industry; but Hale had had the foresight in 1884 to appoint Thomas Brown to the new position of chief engineer, with instructions to monitor the development of this new form of energy. Brown, as already noted in connection with the Eiffel story, was a first-class engineer, the first to work for Otis and one of the last to interest himself, in a purely amateur way, in electrical science. Within 20 years, electrical engineering was a separate discipline.

For the moment, however, electricity was young, and initial efforts to perfect electric traction concentrated not on elevators but on the development of streetcars. Tall office blocks had been encouraged to cluster downtown by the spread of hydraulic elevators capable of fast, silent ascents. Low-rise competition—from light industry to shops, but most importantly residential buildings—had been pressed further out toward the city's rim. The year 1889 was the first in which Americans heard of the *commuter,* who bought a "commutation ticket" at one stop, but a host of other people needed to be moved swiftly around the growing city, too—shoppers and errand boys, factory hands and visitors.

So electrical inventors were spurred to study the problems of horizontal transport first, and some of the most vibrant elevator makers of the 1890s began as streetcar manufacturers in the 1880s. In 1887, Frank Sprague, a brilliant electrical inventor and entrepreneur who had begun by supplying Richmond, Virginia, with a streetcar system, demonstrated a belt elevator powered by a motor of his own design in New York. The Electron Company, another streetcar pioneer, soon moved into elevators. And so, to Otis' everlasting good fortune, did Rudolf Eickemeyer.

The extraordinary chance that had brought both Elisha Otis and Rudolf Eickemeyer to Yonkers in the 1850s had already been exploited, without much success, in an ill-fated harvester project into which Otis plunged in the mid-1870s. Born in Bavaria in 1831, Eickemeyer had fled to the United States after the failure of the 1848 revolutions, brandishing a degree from the Polytechnic Institute of Darmstadt. He soon found himself a draftsman's job in a steam works in Buffalo. In the year of Elisha Otis' first hoist demonstration he moved to Yonkers, where he repaired tools in a hat factory and invented the whip stitch, a mechanical device that revolutionized the hat industry in America. He soon went into business on his own, retooling for the production of small arms during the Civil War, and later devising the differential gear that Otis used on the harvester machine. By the early 1880s he was involved in telephony, and very soon his interests led him toward electric motors.

At the same time, Norton Otis was emerging as the prime mover at Otis, while his brother Charles was burning out. Norton was, by nature and experience, a conciliator, not stiff and difficult like Charles, who roused complaints among his colleagues, and picked battles. He did not resign with Charles in 1890, as he had in 1882. On the contrary, he remained on the board of trustees, something of a corporate and political swell. His relations with William Delaney Baldwin, the real business mind behind Otis in the 1890s, were cordial.*

---

* In 1880 Norton Otis had been elected to the New York State Assembly, and in 1879 to the mayorality of Yonkers; in 1900 he was president of the New York commission at the Universal Exposition in Paris, where he demonstrated the world's first working escalator and was awarded the Legion d'Honneur. In 1903 he reversed an earlier defeat and overturned a Democratic majority when he was elected to the United States Congress, serving less than a term before his death. On his death, an orator at the House of Representatives described his success as one "that came from patient plodding, careful thought, and continuous and unceasing effort." He was remembered, as elsewhere, as affable and dispassionate, a committee man, dependable and thorough and perhaps a little dull. "He made it possible for a whole town to be housed on a small space of ground," a Yonkers neighbor recalled. He was also the author of an astonishingly mean-spirited bill that allowed the police to break up parties of vacationers on excursion.

Norton, and not Charles, had been the first president of the Otis enterprise, actually known as N. P. Otis & Co. until 1867, and afterwards he remained not only a salesman but an inventor, invariably working with others, filing almost as many joint patents as Charles filed on his own. Now he began taking a serious interest in Eickemeyer's work on electricity, which had already made him a pioneer in the field of electric traction and had attracted the attention of Thomas Edison himself.

Working with a fellow luminary of the young electrical sciences, S. D. Field, Eickemeyer had rethought the design of electric motors, treating it as a problem of mechanics rather than pure science. In a development that Edison particularly admired, he simplified the armature by making it serve as the electromagnet itself, and the "direct-connected" motor he produced was adopted first by New York's new elevated railway and then across the field. In 1888, Edison's fledgling General Electric Company, known then as Edison Machine Works, and Otis bought equal shares in Eickemeyer's business.

Edison, of course, was out to encourage anyone who promised to increase electric power consumption and his own profits; and he must have looked with favor on the work Eickemeyer soon began to do with Norton Otis. Elevators, if they could be made to work, were peculiarly well-placed to benefit from, and to encourage, the distribution of electricity throughout a building. As for Otis, it was a technology they could no longer afford to monitor from a distance. Even in the midst of the Eiffel project, with Brown's prolonged absences and Charles' hectic program of factory improvements, Norton, Eickemeyer and R. C. Smith worked in the relative peace of Eickemeyer's shop to apply streetcar technology to the elevator. Together they adapted a two-pole iron-clad streetcar motor to connect directly with an Otis worm-gear elevator machine. Eickemeyer made a number of valuable innovations, reducing construction costs and improving efficiency with the first symmetrical drum armature, while incorporating a mechanical rheostat to alter the resistance of the armature and achieve speed control.

In 1889 two of these machines were installed by Otis in the Demarest Building on 33rd Street and Fifth Avenue in New York. So solid were the principles on which they were designed and the quality with which they were manufactured that over the next 30 years—busy years in the Demarest Building and in electrical science–the elevators continued to give satisfactory performance.

By 1892, Otis Brothers & Co. was not only alive to the potential of electric elevators but also conscious of the increasing specialization in the field. The youth of the science allowed Otis to enter on the ground floor; but it was quick thinking that inspired Otis to do so, and in retrospect it seems remarkable that Otis was connected with at least three of the great electrical pioneers–Edison, Eickemeyer and, in due course, Frank Sprague. In 1892, Otis bought out Eickemeyer's company, with all its patents and manufacturing rights, and recast it as the Otis Electric Company, whose task was to develop and manufacture electric motors, controls and accessories for Otis Brothers & Co.

Eickemeyer, restless as ever, did not survive the shift. Looking around for new heights to conquer, he went off to work for General Electric itself. Otis got to keep many of his staff, however, concentrating their talents firmly on electric elevator development. John Ihlder, Eickemeyer's former assistant, soon worked out a way of replacing the mechanical controls for regulating speed with a series of magnetically operated switches, which gradually and automatically controlled armature resistance instead of relying on brushes moved physically across resistance contacts. Soon car switch operation could do away with the need for a running rope, and the operation of the doors was linked with other elevator operations. By 1892 an automatic push button was operating on residential elevators, where the presence of a full-time human operator was too expensive to consider. By bringing the apartment house within the ambit of the elevator, Otis sold thousands of these units in the 1890s. Contemporary newspaper reports suggest that more than 5,000 apartment elevators were working in New York City alone. To be sure, the push-button device was still too single-minded to appeal to buildings with heavy traffic: it could answer only one call at a time, and then ignored all other calls until the passenger reached his destination.

The mechanics of the electric elevator improved rapidly in the 1890s, reflecting the general advance in manufacturing ability and technology since the days of steam engines, whose basic technology still underpinned the operation of electric elevators. These improvements included new braking systems, better control at higher speeds, a range of more reliable safety devices, including a "slack cable" detector that stopped the motor in the event of entangled hoisting ropes, better winding accuracy, steel T guide rails in place of wood, stranded soft-iron ropes instead of single-strand ropes, and the like. It was in this context that Baldwin could boast of the Otis elevators' improved performance: when the catalog assembled statistics on efficiency and reliability, it was against steam power that electricity was judged, and not against the performance of hydraulics. Hydraulics employed a quite different technology, one that remained far more appropriate to tall buildings until the beginning of the 20th century. It was also an area over which Baldwin had helped establish Otis' strength, and he had no wish to dent its reputation with comparisons to a technology in which, as yet, Otis had a far smaller presence.

Eickemeyer's decision to quit Otis highlighted the inherent fluidity of the infant science of electricity, in which ground remained everywhere to be broken. It also contributed to the realization that electrical engineering had become a specialty. In the 1880s, Hale and Charles had brought Otis to prominence in the market for hydraulic elevators, but the coming of electricity had flung the field wide open once again. New ideas would launch new enterprises, as a host of owner-entrepreneurs sprang up with rival methods of harnessing electricity to the elevator.

It was probably impossible for Otis to keep up with the full range of new ideas flooding into the elevator industry. The brothers had never quite managed the leap into hydraulics, and by the time Hale brought them the vertical hydraulic, Crane had already established an enviable reputation for its alternative, the horizontal, which Otis itself found hard to match. On the day Charles Otis resigned, February 13, 1890, the board of trustees, led by Baldwin and Norton, "decided that the building of horizontal machines by the Stokes shop shall be discontinued, and the horizontal machines required for Otis or Stokes shall be manufactured by Crane."

Now that electricity, an entirely new field of physics, was up for grabs, people all over the country and beyond were at work on improving and redesigning the basic electrical principles laid out by the first pioneers, Eickemeyer among them. Otis had a head start—the governor speed safety device, knowledge of the market, contacts with the construction industry, a large and efficient plant, an established reputation. Otis could make beautiful cars. But it could not be sure of generating the best electrical practice in-house.

In a sense the sheer scale of Otis' operations and its range of distribution entailed an enormous amount of hard capital investment and an incalculable reservoir of goodwill, which had to be protected from rude shocks. But size gave the company considerable leverage to absorb and regulate the surge of 1890s competition, too. It was perfectly true, as Charles had said, that the elevator had become one of the necessities of modern American civilization. It was also true that high quality and high volume were appropriate responses to the rising demand for elevators. But there was a third, possibly easier way for Otis Brothers & Co. to ensure high returns and bring stability to a market that, as Charles himself had been at pains to point out, was as volatile as any in the world. Whatever Charles had said to the contrary, it was in fact possible for Otis "to go down to Egypt and buy its corn."

"Slaughteromania," Charles had called the proliferation of elevator companies and their pricing strategies in the 1880s. In particular, he resented the entry of shoddy workmanship and corner-cutting competition into the industry, almost as much as he disliked the terms on which Otis' management found itself having to compete, going so far as to instruct the sales department in 1888 to sell below cost if "it may be necessary to maintain the position of this Company in the elevator business." The company had made more money selling 333 elevators in 1885 than in selling 568 elevators in 1887. This was the background against which Charles had issued his demands for capital investment.

Hale, Baldwin and Norton Otis saw the possibility of other methods. It would be naive to suppose that Charles disapproved. He liked to identify five major elevator companies in the United States and hinted that "judicious management on the part of those at present in control" would enable them to cover the territory and take the business;[17] but he may have preferred to keep his head down in the machine shop as the struggle grew more fierce. "I am aware that the prevailing fashion is to attempt to meet unsatisfactory results in business by combinations and trusts," he wrote,[18] "but until the materials...are capable of being 'cornered,' and the brains, ability and capital...are no longer available, it will be an open question."

The logic of the elevator trust was fairly irresistible. For one thing, the structure of state laws against operating across state borders lagged well behind the realities of big business. It was perfectly true that as the frontiers of technology, particularly in electrics, broadened, the work became more specialized and expensive. On the back of one single improvement or invention, an entrepreneur could hope to establish a flourishing business, but he risked being soon outstripped by engineers coming up from below, parlaying their new ideas and inventions into business success—the rewards were matched only by the risks. Otis, with hundreds of thousands of dollars invested in plant, with goodwill and large investments to protect, could ill afford to fail. It could, however, afford to approach the new men with near-irresistible offers of cooperation.

The discreet buyouts and alliances of the 1890s were made sometimes outright, for cash, and very often by stock swaps: entrepreneurs tempted to sell out to Otis could judge for themselves the value of stock in a company whose forceful charm they were powerless to resist, and whose market dominion they were helping to enforce. The business could be arranged on a very pleasant footing. The proprietor approached by Otis might take the money and retire, in which case the business was generally run by Otis appointees, though nominally independent. The proprietor might remain at the helm if he preferred, looking for ways to improve his product but perfectly sure of the market share he was ascribed, and able to offer almost any type of product, under his own badge, through the Otis network. To the world at large, all these companies were competing and independent, but in fact market share was being worked out for each region by Otis management, which materially lessened the uncertainties of business. Three ostensibly rival firms normally submitted bids on a project; the bids were worked out at Otis headquarters, and the result afforded few surprises. It was very straightforward price-fixing. In the event of real competition entering the arena, Otis allies would be instructed to take the business at a loss and undercut the legitimate rival.

Aerial view of Yonkers, New York, 1860

Elisha Otis
Company Founder

Elisha Otis' invention, ca. 1861

New York World's Fair, Crystal Palace Exposition, 1853

Otis financials, 1853–55

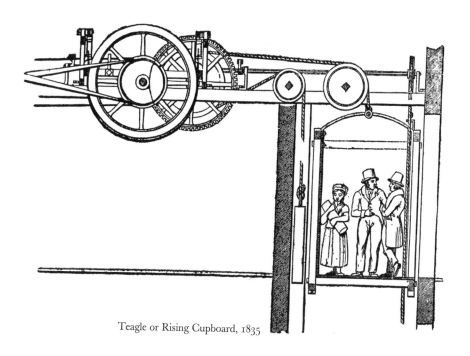

Teagle or Rising Cupboard, 1835

Haughwout building, New York City, ca. 1857
First commercial passenger elevator installed

Norton P. Otis
President, Chairman 1890–1905

Charles Otis
President 1867–82, 1887–90

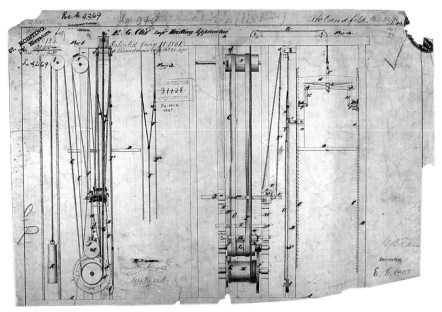

Portion of elevator patent, 1861

Elisha Otis, with hand on artillery piece, was a supporter of Lincoln in the 1860 presidential election. Gun and carriage, valued at $58.65, were received by B. Newhouse as part payment for the first safety elevator in 1853

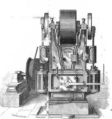

Otis advertisement, 1868

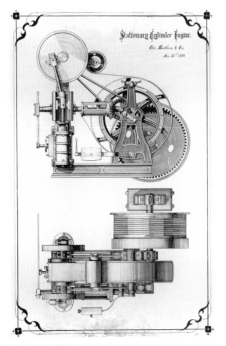

Stationary Cylinder
Engine, 1871

Otis Tufts, ca. 1850

Elisha Otis'
business card

Otis Bros. Factory, Yonkers, ca. 1870

Vol. XLIV.—No. 16.
[NEW SERIES.]

NEW YORK, APRIL 16, 1881.

[$3.20 per Annum.
[POSTAGE PREPAID.

Boreel building exterior, interior, and elevator cab, from *Scientific American*

Mills Building,
New York City, 1882

Washington Monument Elevator Engine, Washington, D.C., 1880

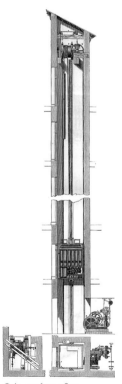

Otis catalog, 1870
(inside front foldout)

Otis Elevator "birdcage" cab design, ca. 1880s

Otis direct-connected
electric elevator,
hand-rope operation,
ca. 1890

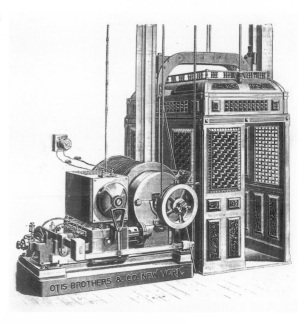

Factory workers inside
elevator, 1862

Stock Certificate, ca. 1867

Yonkers Works engine construction, 1878

⟶⁂THE OTIS⁂⟵

STANDARD

HYDRAULIC ELEVATOR

For Passengers and Freight.

ADOPTED BY U. S. GOVERNMENT,
Upon Report of Eminent Experts appointed by the Secretary of the Treasury.

SAFE, SIMPLE,
ECONOMICAL.

ADAPTED TO USE IN

HOTELS,
  PUBLIC
    BUILDINGS,
STORES,
OFFICE
  BUILDINGS,
FLATS,
  PRIVATE
    HOUSES,
AND FOR
DUMB
  WAITERS,
ALSO IN
WAREHOUSES
AND
FACTORIES.

OPERATED BY

Water Pressure

FROM

STREET MAINS,

OR FROM

A TANK in Upper Story,

or on Roof of Building,

OR

PRESSURE TANK IN BASEMENT

Always Ready for Use,

NIGHT OR DAY.

COSTS NOTHING

WHEN

NOT IN USE.

CAN BE MANAGED

BY ANY

LADY OR YOUTH.

Manufactured by OTIS BROS. & CO., Yonkers, N. Y.

Q. N. EVANS & CO., Agents for New England; also, makers and designers of Steam and Water Heating Apparatus for public and private buildings.

N. Y. Office, 60 DUANE STREET.   Office, 72 SUDBURY STREET, BOSTON.

Advertisement for Standard Vertical Hydraulic Elevator, 1882

Eiffel Tower under construction, ca. 1887

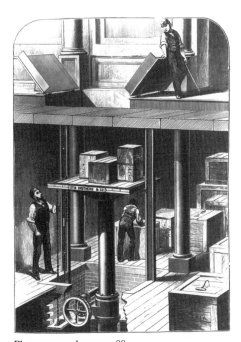

Plunger-type elevator, 1884

Escalator, Paris Exposition, 1900

DON'T FAIL TO SEE THE
OTIS ELECTRIC PUMP.

GROUND PLAN ILLINOIS STATE BUILDING.

OTIS BROTHERS & CO., NEW YORK.
HALE ELEVATOR CO., CHICAGO.

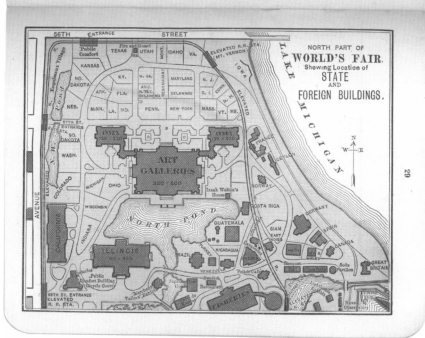

Chicago World's Fair, 1893: Diagram of World's Fair buildings showing location of exhibits (one spread from Otis' complimentary booklet)

Rudolf Eickemeyer, ca. 1895

William D. Baldwin
President, Chairman 1898–1930

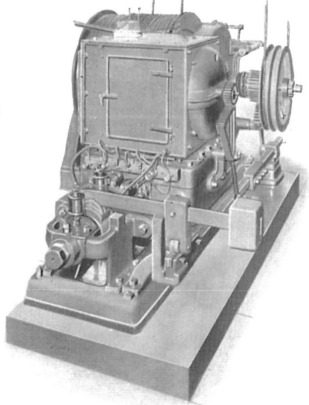

Early Otis electric machine

Otis advertisement, ca. 1905
("Now Grandma—no more
stair climbing")

Otis Double Screw
Electric Elevator, 1890

Norton Otis, we may safely assume, played his part in this Florentine extension of control. The records for the 1890s are disappointingly scant: the archives yield nothing so rich as, say, the letters that Charles and Hale had been obliged to exchange between New York and Illinois on an almost daily basis. Baldwin was a more taciturn speechifier, and his stockholder's reports are brief and to the point. Charles always sought to justify himself, but Baldwin and Norton raised less fuss and consequently left less material; they were princes of industry who kept their own counsel.

Norton was persuasive. By the end of the decade his rank and achievements, not to mention his wealth, spoke for him. His father had been known around New York as "Otis the Safety Man," but toward the end of his career Norton specialized in offering security of another sort. According to R. J. Davies, a San Francisco elevator entrepreneur, Norton approached him in 1901 with a tempting offer to buy a controlling interest in his firm, the Electrical Engineering Company. The attentions of this grandee of politics and business were clearly flattering to Davies. Otis' goal, Norton explained, was to buy up and "retire from business" the local competition. Davies, on the other hand, was to carry on as president of his firm, shielded from the buffets of the market by Otis' broad umbrella. As for the detail of the business, Davies could sort that out with Baldwin in New York.[19]

It did not take Davies long to make up his mind. Norton did not need to spell out the consequences of resisting what was, after all, a palatable offer. Davies went to New York and cut the deal with Baldwin. His company, with others, was placed under the supervision of an Otis regional agent, Samuel Burger. "So far as the public knew," the *New York Sun* was later to report, "they were competing and rival companies, but were managed by one individual [who] directed each company as to what bid it should make on elevator work…. Burger also directed, where no opposition appeared, that these companies bid higher [than Otis itself], and they obtain the contracts at exorbitant prices; that when any real competition appeared one of the purchased companies was made to take the work at a loss…."[20]

Not everyone was quite so open to persuasion as Davies and the others. In tandem with gentle urging, Otis in the 1890s adopted an increasingly strong-armed approach to competition. Speaking of market share in New York City in 1888, Charles Otis had asked: "Can we by any legitimate and satisfactory means obtain a larger proportion?" A few years later satisfactory, if not strictly legitimate, means were being used: the gloves were off–the trustees doubtless argued that tough practices were necessary, and, for most, their way of dealing with competition was relatively welcome. When the company set out with the intention of bringing all its rivals to terms, where money, stocks and the prospect of security did not work, threats and obstructions would do the trick.

It has been suggested that the prime mover here was Ferdinand William Roebling,* a construction man who joined the board in 1887– construction was probably the home of collusive bidding and intimidation. By 1891, Otis Brothers and its allies were using their weight to attack independent firms not only through artificial pricing but by harassment through the courts. An early victim was Alonzo B. See, a former Otis elevator man who had gone independent in 1883 and won a reputation in New York for quality at a good price. In 1888 he maneuvered himself away from small apartments and office buildings into the bigger time by harnessing electricity to his cars.

In 1893, Otis Brothers brought suit against one of See's customers for patent infringement. Knocking the customer was an excellent way of choking a rival off–few people would want the hassle of dealing with a company that brought them elevators and legal difficulties together. In this case the customer made no response to the writ, either ignorant of its weight, or frightened of fighting it, so that Otis stood to win the judgment by default. By purest coincidence, so *Electricity* claimed, Alonzo B. See heard of the matter "just in time to assume the defense." The suit that Otis brought had neither legal nor technical merit, but the court battle, whichever way it went, was costly and time-consuming for the small operator who had to organize his own defense.

Alonzo B. See, as it happened, was a rugged and determined man. It is largely thanks to his persistence and fiery sense of honor that a record of Otis' questionable business methods has come down. With a

---

* Son of John A. Roebling and brother of Washington A. Roebling, designers of the Brooklyn Bridge.

clear, precise writing style, he had a gift for publicity. Long after his run-in with Otis he became something of an overnight celebrity by venting his views on women and education—"all women's colleges should be burned," he remarked, causing readers of the *New York Times* to "hit the ceiling faster than they had ever ascended in one of the See elevators" (though probably not denting his standing much in the manly world of construction).*

So in 1893, See did not give up when Otis threatened him with a suit. He raged in the papers with a number of unflattering Otis stories—tales of rigged bids, fraudulent representations, sharp competitive practices. Among other things, he wrote, "A salesman of the Otis combine would try to learn which way a contract was likely to go, and if it was likely to go to some member of the combine he would simply say 'Well, they build a fine elevator.' But if it was likely to go to one out of the combine, he would say, 'Of course I would like to secure the order myself, but if I cannot I would like to see you have a good elevator' and would advise him not to buy the one he had intended but try to steer him to another one of the combine."

In the eventual lawsuit, Otis charged that the mere use of an electric motor to drive an elevator was covered by a patent the Otises had taken out eight years earlier—for a motor attached to a drum and gear mechanism that was used for simple construction hoists. The court expressed some doubt about whether Otis' patent was valid in itself—it appeared to incorporate features that antedated the Otis motor by at least 10 years. It bore no relation anyway to the technology used by See. It also vindicated See's view that electricity was, per se, generic: its use was no more open to patent control than water or steam, he maintained. Electricity was a power source, and so many different sorts of motors now existed, with so many different applications, that "there could be *no* patent on the mere idea of attaching an electric motor to an elevator."[21]

---

* Enjoying his sudden celebrity as a reactionary bigot, See brushed aside challenges. "I never discuss anything logical with women. They can talk straight for about five minutes and then they go off the handle. They haven't got the reasoning power a man has, and I wouldn't think of debating with any woman on any subject." He also believed that schooling caused diseases of the nerves and eyes. He remained the man that *New York Times* readers loved to hate. In 1936 he changed his mind and threw a dinner for 15 successful women, but his image was fixed, and "attention given to this astonishing about-face was microscopic."

The bad publicity Otis received during the case forced the company to behave with more circumspection in New York for a while; *Electricity* for 1895 damningly concluded that "the Otis Co. and its allies have put themselves without the pale of association with honorable business men whether electrical or non-electrical." But with glorious irony, Otis salesmen actually turned the murky atmosphere to their advantage, confidentially telling at least one contractor not to bother tendering a job with A. B. See, since all See's bids were rigged up at the Otis offices anyway!*

Crane in 1895 borrowed the technique to revenge itself on the Sprague Electric Elevator Company of Philadelphia, which had defeated Crane for a second time running in a head-to-head contest for 14 elevators in the Minneapolis City Hall and Courthouse. As already mentioned, Frank Sprague, who had invented the electric streetcar for Richmond, Virginia,† later followed the logic of transit up the line and began to build elevators in 1892: his high technology product was just the kind of competition Otis most feared. Crane threw a wrench in the works by serving a brief on behalf of an unnamed taxpayer, asking that arguments be heard on the technical merits of hydraulics, which Crane manufactured, over electrics, which it did not. Officers from Otis submitted affidavits on Crane's behalf, and competing engineers debated the relative efficiency of the two systems. It was all very slow and confusing, as Crane intended it should be, but in the end the city commissioners stuck to their original decision and awarded the contract to Sprague by an eight-to-one vote.

To Alonzo See, Otis' moral plunge was easy to explain. He had, like Charles Otis, no particular objection to cooperation among elevator companies, but he was shocked by the more brutish methods that accompanied the alliance drive. "In all the land there was no company conducted in greater honor than was the Otis Company under Mr. E. G. Otis and Mr. Charles R. Otis. But the health of Charles R. seemed

---

* Otis salesmen also used perfectly legitimate sales gimmicks, like the perpetual calendar for 1899, which ran out in 1925, and left space for the recipient to list items of importance easily forgotten, like the size of his cuffs and the number and make of his bicycle.
† "Lincoln Set The Negroes Free! Sprague Has Set The Mule Free!" cried New Orleans trolley aficionados.

undermined, and Charles R. sold out. Then the change came," he recalled in a letter to an Otis director in 1924. He had earlier concluded: "The name-plate on the door of the Otis Company bears the same legend it has borne for many years, but the men who made that company what it was are there no longer."[22]

Norton Otis and William Baldwin were still there, of course—which was just what See meant—and in spite of his bad temper, they typified magnates who were emerging in American industry. It has been said that the best time in history to be rich was the decade preceding World War I, a decade in which the conveniences of modern life—the telephone, railway travel, fast ships, electric lights—co-existed with the conveniences of the Victorian age—servants, deference, and craftsmanship. Baldwin enjoyed the historic moment to the full. He was a member of all the most exclusive New York clubs—the Union League, the Banker's Club, the Adirondack League Club, the Greenwich Country Club and the Indian Harbor Yacht Club. He held a parcel of company directorships in the insurance business. He had a string of glamorous women, and his wife bore his excesses and ill-temper with quiet fortitude.

Baldwin earned his lifestyle by the way he maneuvered Otis from a craft-based firm with a reputation for making quality elevators into a formidable player on the industrial field—if not a giant like General Electric or U.S. Steel, then a leviathan in its arena. To do so, he combined business flair with genuine respect for technology and a determination to be the best.

The defining event in his business career came in 1898, when Baldwin took the company public, incorporating under lenient New Jersey laws that allowed for cross-state holdings and investments. On November 28, lawyers with powers of attorney met in East Orange, New Jersey, to incorporate the Otis Elevator Company with capital of $11 million, more than 10 times that of its predecessor. The capital was divided into 65,000 shares of common and 45,000 shares of preferred stock, at a par value of $100 each; when it was offered to the public, ownership of the company rapidly passed from a close ring of trustees into the hands of distant and dispersed shareholders. Norton Otis was chairman of the new board of directors. Its president was William Delaney Baldwin,

"W.D.," the man who in this decade and the next would do more than anyone to mold the shape of the new century's Otis Elevator Company. Baldwin and his team possessed almost total executive control. Twelve stockholders gathered at the first stockholders meeting, holding proxies for some 300 individual and institutional investors; Baldwin was not a large stockholder himself, but he set the meeting's agenda and year in, year out organized the process by which he and his team were voted to the board of directors.

The level of capitalization put Otis into the big leagues, as far as the elevator industry went, allowing it to draw on a huge pool of funds to finance the research and development needed to stay ahead in a rapidly changing marketplace. Baldwin could raise money to realize long-term goals in a way his predecessors could only have dreamed of. Stock, too, could now form a part of any Otis deal with a rival, helping to complement the spread of Otis-controlled elevator operations around the United States. The basis of Otis' presence in the western United States was forged by a group of Chicago-based companies, including Hale and Crane—Crane Elevator, one of the largest Otis stockholders until 1898, contributed the whole of its assets to the new company in return for cash and a block of stock to the Crane interests. By March 1, 1900, Otis had taken control of 13 significant elevator companies in as many years.

In business terms, Baldwin's timing seemed impeccable. The first stirrings of a merger wave in American industries had been cut off in its infancy by the depression of 1893: only a few railroad and manufacturing firms had taken advantage of the holding-company acts in New Jersey and Delaware. But by 1897 the capital market for new issues of stocks and long-term debt had matured, and the mergers began. Between 1896 and 1904 some 257 corporations, including U.S. Steel, the world's first billion-dollar enterprise, had been consolidated out of some 4,277 companies. While early interpretations of the Sherman Antitrust Act had ruthlessly attacked price-fixing agreements between rivals, the courts seemed as yet unfazed by legal mergers between those same rivals to achieve uniform pricing. In that way law, as well as economics, encouraged this first merger wave in U.S. history, which was bigger in proportion to the size of the country's economy than anything that followed in the 1920s, the 1960s, or even the great polyglot mergers of the 1980s and 1990s. It reflected a shift from owner-entrepreneurs to a new breed of professional managers, of which Baldwin was a typical example. No one but they could master the businesses they ran. Few dared to challenge their authority or judgment. Little wonder that they became known as captains of industry, to whose superior expertise their paying passengers meekly deferred.

Chapter 7

Otis Elevator Incorporated

B ALDWIN REORGANIZED THE COMPANY to achieve specific targets, and in the next decade Otis entered an inventive frenzy that placed it definitively ahead of any conceivable competition. Baldwin also resolved the seesaw between Hale's fondness for business structure and the Otis brothers' passion for factory output, and incidentally paved the way for a corporate rationalization, which took place after 1906.

As the biggest and most predatory company in the business, Otis was able to draw together some of the best talent in elevator technology and set them to work on an overhaul of Otis' product line. The old Otis Electric Company founded in 1892 was dismantled, and its personnel, with that of other subsidiary firms, was moved to two new departments of mechanical and electrical engineering, which were to become components in Otis' drive for rationalization a few years later. The electrical department, already the more glamorous of the two, targeted the cost and efficiency of Otis' geared, drum-winding elevators, resulting in the Type G range, which covered a wide array of duty loads—an ever-widening range, indeed, as the first sizes, 1 to 9, were supplemented by lighter 0, 1/4, 1/2 and 3/4 machines and half sizes all through the range. They embodied all sorts of technical improvements, from strengthened drum stands to the replacement of hardened prisms with ball bearings on the machine thrust bearings. From there, with deliberate effort, the designers moved on to lowering costs, both in production methods and by introducing elements that made the machines easier to fit and put together in the field, resulting in the H and K types. Steel replaced iron in the new S motor, and safety innovations were made to keep up with the increasing rise, lift power and speed of elevator travel.

Yet despite the rapid gains made by electrical traction, electrically powered elevators were still governed by the parameters of the steam age. While Otis was building hydraulics capable of taking buildings to 15 or 20 floors, its electric machines seemed condemned to work by winding rope onto a drum, and so encountered the limitations that had made hydraulics such an improvement over steam. Two hundred feet was the maximum rise, the longest amount of rope that could be safely wound onto a single drum turning no faster than 200 feet a minute. Every new building, though, was wired for electricity, and it was already clear to Baldwin and others that the next great breakthrough would be in high-rise, high-speed electric elevators. It was a market waiting to be supplied.

The race had opened in 1895, when E. M. Fraser of San Francisco patented his duplex-motor-system elevator. By March 1899 he had installed about a dozen of these smooth-running machines in the city, and one of W. D. Baldwin's first moves as president of the newly incorporated Otis was to send George H. Reynolds to San Francisco to see how they worked.

Reynolds was surprised—perhaps unpleasantly—by what he found at the new Wells Fargo building. "These elevators," he said, "run anywhere from about 500 feet a minute down to the minutest movement. You would have to chalk the walls to determine that you are moving at all. The handling of the elevators is absolutely perfect, they have a very simple electrical control, and run just as smooth (*sic*) as the most perfect hydraulic in the world."[23]

Fraser used two motors rotating in opposite directions, fed by an endless rope running over pulleys. Counterweights ensured that any difference between the running speeds of the motors moved the cab—when both motors ran at the same speed, the cab was held steady. To be sure, the conveyance had a tendency to creep away from the landing. Its manila or hemp driving ropes were apt to stretch, and installation was pricey—but it was one of the first attempts to produce a traction elevator, and doubtless its performance would have been improved had it remained longer in production.

The Fraser Electric Elevator Company began to launch out of San Francisco in 1899, starting with a few sales in Chicago and continuing, in June of that year, with a model demonstration made by Mr. Fraser himself at the Waldorf Hotel in New York. This was carrying the war into the enemy camp. Norton and Baldwin asked their new colleague Frank Sprague to go down to the Waldorf and investigate the machine firsthand. Sprague's report, like Reynolds' a few years earlier, was upbeat. With a few minor improvements, he told them, Fraser's elevator could deliver good results for speed and control. Otis was convinced. Fraser never sold his elevator in New York: he sold the whole business to Otis instead, and Otis soon installed the machinery in a building on Broadway.

Half a century later three Fraser-type elevators, built by Otis in 1901, were still running in the Kohl Building in San Francisco, where the building engineer remained "enthusiastic about the equipment," the *Otis Bulletin* reported in 1948. "He still delights in making full-speed reversals to demonstrate the operations of his machines, which, in their time, were the smoothest-riding elevators in the world."

Sprague himself was being generous in his praise for Fraser's invention, because he had his own version of a high-rise electric elevator. The Pratt-Sprague "screw and nut" machine was an ingenious attempt to copy the action of a rope-geared horizontal hydraulic machine, replacing the cylinder with a long screw turned by a motor, and a traveling nut connected to pulleys. Counterweighting was not practicable in this system, so that upward travel of the cab devoured power; the descending cab, on the other hand, drove the nut that turned the screw, which made the motor a dynamo, or generator. The real problem with Sprague's machine, though, was maintaining the bearings on the moving nut.

Otis acquired Sprague's patents in 1898, but almost immediately Baldwin gathered the company's far-flung resources together, raised the cash, and launched all its efforts into developing a gearless, traction elevator for high-rise buildings.

By the turn of the century America considered itself a model of progress. Broadly speaking, Americans gave little thought to the world outside and judged their progress on internal indices—on the growth of the population, the reclaiming of empty prairie, the creation of new cities. Immigrants came to America to better themselves rather than to escape tyranny. Some 1,218,480 arrived in 1914, the second highest figure in American history, and well above the 216,397 passing through Ellis Island in 1897.

The country was feeling unusually self-confident, yet there were signs of a popular disquiet over the form and direction that rapid change had taken in the past quarter-century.

This was often expressed in demands for vigilance and regulation. Questions were everywhere being asked—about unrestricted immigration, unrestricted building, corporate alliances. The little man in America could feel himself surrounded on all sides by mammoth forces he could not control, pushed by processes he could no longer hope to understand.

For many, America's tall buildings were a source of pride. "Our civilization is progressing wonderfully. In New York...we must keep building and we must build upward. Step by step we have advanced from the wooden hut to the 30-story skyscraper...," wrote a builder in 1906, making a familiar and often repeated equation of height with progress. But in the looming new skylines of New York and Chicago some people saw the ordinary man dwarfed by a process that seemed visibly to express its arrogance. George Post, the architect of the first elevatored office block, despaired like Saul of what he had begun, while Otis' own chief engineer seemed ambivalent, at best, when he wrote in 1903 that "this perfection of the lifting service...has altered the restful and classic lines of the architecture of a past age—that pleasing distribution of mass over a large area—and in its place substituted a veritable tower treatment of design where the object is the greatest economy, namely, the largest percentage of net return upon the investment."[24]

The illustration "King's Dream of New York" (1908–09) could be a dream or a nightmare, depending on one's point of view. The illustration shows the Singer Building dwarfed by dozens of other skyscrapers, and the aerial view of Broadway punctuated by sky bridges and elevated railway systems hugging the rooftops. Dirigibles and giant biplanes crowd the skies, while far below, the streets are plunged into gloom, and tunnels and bridges intersecting the thoroughfare suggest the bowels of an underground city.[25]

Daniel Burnham, the distinguished Chicago architect, retorted that modern technology could provide both artificial light and ventilation; still, for everyone who extolled skyscrapers and progress, or described Manhattan as a "tiara of proud towers," there were doom-sayers to deplore sunless canyons, overcrowded streets, the spread of fire and disease—and even impiety after George Post's Pulitzer Building on Park Row surmounted the Gothic spire of Trinity Church in 1892. An article in *American Architecture and Building News* in 1908 argued that "the continued erection of the so-called skyscraper, the excessively tall building, constitutes a menace to public health and safety and an offense which must be stopped.... In the present movement to correct the evil much has been said about shutting out the light of the heavens and circumscribing the air of the streets—to both of which possessions people are entitled, and which, in the pursuit of health, happiness and prosperity, they should demand. This 'canyonising' of the streets is rapidly being accomplished and its baleful results are beginning to forcibly assert themselves."

And what happened, people asked, when at 5 p.m. the elevators discharged the denizens of these vertical cities into the street? An anonymous member of the Committee of Congestion of Population in New York told the *New York Times* what he expected from the Equitable's plans for a 62-story, 909-foot skyscraper on Broadway in 1908. "To accommodate such a crowd the people would have to walk in three layers, one above the other, while the roadway would not hold the delivery wagons, automobiles, and carriages of people going to the structure." As early as 1897, ambitious doctors had begun diagnosing a condition they called "elevator sickness," which afflicted passengers taking express rides of only 20 floors.

Electricity itself was a mysterious change. Never before had power been so silent or so pervasive, never had the sources of power been so remote. Even electrical engineers were still trying to figure out why it worked, as cities worldwide were being laced in copper wire. The power of wind or water to turn machinery was self-evident. A simple kettle could reveal the principles behind the steam engine. Common sense explained hydraulics. But electrical magnetism was different. It really belonged to realms of magic and was one of the curious properties of the physical world that, as they were discovered, could only be demonstrated and not explained.

What increased people's sense of disfranchisement was the distant generation of electricity, which became more common as the century advanced, though many large buildings continued to generate their own in basement vaults. Far away, like priests or politicians, electrical engineers were masterminding the delivery of current along slender wires, using complex science.

Electricity was frightening. Bullets could fly unseen, but bullets had a corporeal reality whereas electricity could deal death from a touch of wire no bigger than a snake's tongue. The debates that raged among electricians themselves inspired little confidence. Edison, for example, had plumped for direct current (DC), arguing that it was safer than alternating current (AC), pioneered by George Westinghouse. AC current was the wave of the future, but Edison fought his turf on scientific grounds. One of his champions actually went out on tour using AC current to execute dogs in front of live audiences. None of this was reassuring.

Electricity plus elevators equaled even more anxiety. If electricity was potentially dangerous, so was gravity-defying transport—as Otis had been telling its customers for years. Electric elevators were utterly beyond the grasp of the janitors and building engineers who used to maintain the hydraulic machines. "When electric elevators were new, and when people were mystified by electricity and a little bit afraid of it, it was not unusual for an Otis man to make a trip of several days to replace a fuse," as the *Otis Bulletin* recalled in 1948.

Even among established experts, the combination of electricity and elevators inspired some fierce, if redundant, criticism. These switches and rheostats on which the operation of an elevator relied functioned, some said, in a cloud of mystery. Their failure rate was unknown, and prominent engineers were prepared to condemn the new technology in public.

When people expressed unease at the invisible power of electricity, or railed against the seemingly unfettered contempt for human scale evinced by the skyscrapers of Chicago and New York, they were thus articulating a response to those enormous dislocating pressures that over the past quarter-century had finally and irretrievably recast the shape of American society.

Until the development of the electric gearless, America had been still, really, in the heroic age, when men like Elisha Otis or Eickemeyer could compel the plaudits of the world for their demonstrable success. "From Log Cabin to White House," the resonant slogan of William Henry Harrison's successful 1840 presidential campaign, still stirred the hearts of millions of Americans. But the frontier was closing. The mythic view of the Wild West, full of heroes and villains and rugged individuals, had long since replaced the vanished reality. In 1890 the value of America's manufacturing production outstripped agriculture for the first time. By 1900, when just two of every five men worked on the farm, the United States was no longer a predominantly farming nation. That year farmers themselves were grouped by at least one naive census taker among the unemployed, because they worked for themselves; and the drift of southern, rural blacks to northern and western cities had already begun.[26]

One of the more disturbing—and exciting—features of the new technological era was its ability to leave critics in the dust. Turn-of-the-century attacks on high-rise buildings and their elevators sounded puny and off the mark after Otis announced the arrival of a new, economical system that promised to take buildings to 30 or 40 stories or higher.

If express elevators reaching 20 floors gave Otis critics elevator sickness, Otis would up the ante, increase the speed, so that people who railed against skyscrapers would now live to hear them contemptuously dismissed as skyscratchers by the coming generation of architects. Otis would bury hydraulics themselves. Those who already lamented, in 1900, the passing of the old rugged self-reliant America would receive instead the glittering sentinels of the New York skyline and the twinkling beacons of Chicago across the Lakes and the Great Plains.

Otis' gearless traction elevator, after four years of costly R&D, was unveiled in 1902. In 1904 its machines were running in the Beaver Building in New York City and the Majestic Building in Chicago. They rendered hydraulics almost instantly obsolete. Architects immediately made plans for a new generation of skyscrapers, beginning with the 612-foot, 46-story Singer Building in New York of 1906–08, followed by the 700-foot Metropolitan Life Tower in 1910 and the 780-foot Woolworth

Building in 1912. All were equipped with new Otis elevator systems, and their performance hushed the critics.

So did their architecture. Many of the early towers that had inspired the backlash were frankly ugly or pedestrian. The seductive new generation of skyscrapers, on the other hand, broke from the box-like mold to embellish both the sidewalk and the skies. The Flatiron Building, though only 14 stories high, had heralded the new aesthetic freedom. Its position made up for its lack of height, and its elegant prow jutting into Madison Square stood at the cutting edge of steel construction. But it was the great new skyscrapers, equipped with Otis gearless elevators, each put up as artwork in its own right, that began to define a truly American, exuberant cityscape.

Unlike most previous advances in elevator technology, the gearless traction was a genuine corporate achievement. Plenty of designers had had a hand in its development, and it rested on foundations laid down as early as the 1870s, when a German engineer recognized the basic principles of rope traction. This Swedish-born engineer, David Lindquist, who had as much right as anyone to claim the electric gearless for himself, actually gave credit to one Duwelius, who supposedly had laid the groundwork. But this odd character was never identified, and one can only suppose that the reference was made tongue in cheek to satisfy the craving of the curious for a namable inventor. The gearless traction system brought together a DC motor, a traction pulley block in place of a winding drum, a brake drum, and an electrically operated brake, mounted on a bed plate at the top of the shaft.

It was simple, little more than the old principle of a bucket in a well. The counterweight was set at between 40 percent and 45 percent of the weight of a duty load, and the directly connected motor had only to turn the drive block in one direction or the other for the cab or the weight to rise. Instead of the old high-speed electric motors, whose moving parts deteriorated quickly, the gearless used a very slow multi-pole, shunt-wound DC motor that was smooth to operate and formidably efficient.

From a safety standpoint, the counterweight all but removed the risk of the car's overrunning its safe upper limit: the counterweight would come to rest in the basement, the ropes would lose traction, and the elevator would automatically stop. Speed governors and wedge-clamp safeties were carried over from drum-winding elevators, but in addition, Otis engineers devised a sequence of switches called a Terminal Shutdown Device to slow and stop the car automatically at either end of the shaft, should the operator fail to do so.

The urbanization of America found expression in government, as in business. Ever-increasing areas of life were to be turned over to the experts: disciplinary expertise, managerial technique and planning could help order and direct the development of the nation. It was a step back from pure democracy, but pure democracy, it was felt, could no longer be relied on to manage the increasingly complex web of relationships among consumers and producers, government and citizens, employers and employees, and between prosperity and security for the many, as for the privileged few. Nineteenth-century America had thrived, indeed, by jungle laws; but people were beginning to appreciate that even the wilderness was susceptible to proper management, as the new national parks demonstrated.

Corporations, which would dominate 20th-century business, were sanctioned by 19th-century America's respect for the principle of laissez-faire, or the right to succeed or fail without government interference, yet the unfettered operation of industrial capitalism had not worked in quite the way that Adam Smith or the Victorians had predicted. Instead of engaging in ceaseless competition and improvement, the first round of victors to emerge from the Darwinian struggle had used their power to set the terms on which newcomers might compete, and altered the rules of the game. Several U.S. magnates were much richer, and more secretive, than any individual state. After the crash of 1907, when he personally held the line against total financial collapse, even J. P. Morgan became frightened of his own influence and power, which handed him responsibilities only the state, in the end, could reliably discharge. All this contributed to the unease Americans felt about their society, which they sometimes vented in attacks on high buildings, or electricity, or elevators.

The unease was partially expressed in the Sherman Antitrust Act of 1890; the vague wording of the act, and the ambivalent response of the courts, left the law as nebulous as the fears it addressed. The Supreme Court began by stepping gingerly from case to case, using common-law precedents. By 1897, though, it had developed a more consistent, free-standing set of criteria by which to interpret the act's prohibition of "every contract, combination... or conspiracy in restraint of trade," criteria which were generally harsher than before and which resulted in judgments against companies that entered into contracts, agreements or combinations perceived to have directly restrained trade and affected interstate commerce, regardless of their reasonableness.

President McKinley's administration was essentially Victorian in outlook, lauding the entrepreneur and expecting the markets to take care of themselves, while favoring philanthropy and individual acts of charity. It was not particularly concerned with antitrust, instead issuing vague pronouncements and enforcing the law sporadically and unenthusiastically. But in September 1901, McKinley was assassinated. Theodore Roosevelt succeeded him with a far more interventionist antitrust program, one that he had already devised as vice president. Almost immediately he instructed the Justice Department to investigate J. P. Morgan and his Northern Securities Company, loudly spurning Morgan's quiet offer to "send your man to my man" to fix things up, and instead creating a piece of grand political theater from which Roosevelt emerged as a trustbuster. In 1903 his stance was vindicated when the Supreme Court narrowly voted to order the dissolution of Northern Securities.

Roosevelt won his second term in 1904 as the people's champion, the president who created Big Government as a counterweight to Big Business, who sought to supervise if not control the "impersonal" forces that increasingly shaped people's lives. Just as finance and manufacturing were staffed by experts in their fields, so, Roosevelt believed, could the mandarin science of government acquire the expertise to manage economic growth and market competition for the public good.

In the 14 years between the passage of the Sherman Act and Roosevelt's re-election in 1904, some 22 antitrust cases had been initiated by the Justice Department; in the next 10 years 130 cases were brought to the courts, culminating in the dissolution of Standard Oil and American Tobacco. On the way to this grand assault on corporations that had achieved market dominance through vertical and horizontal mergers, the Justice Department sharpened its teeth on looser combinations formed by smaller companies in highly competitive industries. Norton, Otis' hotline to the political world, was already dead when in 1906 the Justice Department turned on the elevator trust.

When the Standard Plunger Elevator Company secured one of the biggest-ever elevator contracts in 1904, for 110 hydraulic plunger elevators for the John Wanamaker stores in New York and Philadelphia, Standard's superintendent ventured the prediction "that an elevator suspended by a cable will in 25 years be a thing of ancient history and that the elevator that is pushed up from the bottom and cannot fall and kill people will be in use in all buildings."

The arrival of Otis' gearless traction lift in the same year made a mockery of such hydrophile assertions and goaded that conservative faction into a frenzy of denunciation. Backed by the independent hydraulic-based elevator companies, they pushed their protests to ridiculous extremes, for even before the Singer installation everyone who mattered in the construction industry and beyond could see that the hydraulic age was over. Only the Worcester plunger elevator, the "lollipop on a stick," maintained some residual appeal in the market for high-rise buildings up to 300 feet. It was not just that the gearless traction elevator system was infallible in principle; it also mattered that it came backed by Otis' reputation for quality and safety. Carp as they might, the hydraulic firms had to either develop their own electrical technology or wind up their affairs, leaving Otis streets ahead of every competitor and now unquestionably the greatest elevator manufacturer in the world.

In one area only did Otis look weak to industry insiders. From the boardroom's point of view, the means by which Otis had achieved dominance in the elevator business in America—insofar as they went beyond merely producing what America wanted to buy—belonged to the practice of the day, combination, and had been launched on a sea of goodwill and understanding. The late Norton Otis, who had sponsored many of these deals, was an upright man of the people, representative of a decent East Coast constituency. William Baldwin, the company president, was a man of such strict moral rectitude that he had embraced Christian Science and figured high on the list of Yonkers benefactors. If price-fixing and market-share agreements had been made with other companies, and if some of those companies in fact worked for Otis' head office in New York, it was only in an effort to bring some sort of stability to a market that was notoriously volatile, and to blunt some of the rougher consequences of unbridled competition. Heaven forbid that Otis should engender job losses and the collapse of the proverbial widow's stocks. Were elevator prices twice as high, the board might well reason, the developers would pay them cheerfully enough. Surely there was enough slack in the system to provide for stability, and Otis' charges were invariably fair, Otis' technology invariably superior. By then Otis tended to view itself not just as a business but as a kind of public service, underwriting the safety of its passengers around America in contrast to the "slaughteromaniacal" behavior of its more disreputable rivals.

But Otis' stranglehold on the electric wave of the future was a step too far. Twenty-eight elevator companies were indicted together by the U.S. Attorney for the Northern District of California on March 7, 1906. Otis figured at the head of the list, and the rest followed in alphabetical order. Between them the indicted companies were responsible for at least 80 percent of all elevator business west of the Rockies. Otis had a controlling interest in all of them. All the same, these were small potatoes by the standards of the Justice Department, and it seems obvious that Otis' technological leapfrog had pushed some disgruntled competitor to press Justice into action.

None of the arguments that Otis' top brass liked to entertain cut much ice with the drafters of the charges, who were bound to regard the matter in a purely commercial light. Rather than merge the businesses, they claimed, Otis had fostered "an unlawful combination, trust and conspiracy... to fix and maintain high and oppressive prices," driving all but three independent companies out of the region by a mix of deception and intimidation.

Although the case was heard in California, Otis' activities were not confined to the West Coast. *Electricity* had charged the company four years earlier with corruption of the Philadelphia elevator inspector, who tended to reject any elevator not equipped with the Otis air-cushion safety (Otis Tufts' memorable hole in the ground). A. B. See, too, was available to remind the lawyers of Otis' anti-competitive practices in New York in the 1890s.

Otis' lawyers spent five weeks convincing Baldwin that the company could not win the case, while a battle would generate an enormous amount of adverse publicity and probably lead to a dissolution of the company's extensive holdings. Baldwin was reluctantly persuaded of the lesser evil, and at last Otis and its co-defendants entered a consent decree.

On June 1, 1906, the decree was finally issued by the court. Otis escaped any explicit charges: for the record, the company merely declared it had done no wrong and promised not to do it again. The decree told Otis exactly what sort of behavior it should avoid—dividing territories, arranging bids or setting prices by the merest whisper. The defendants were to do nothing in violation of the Sherman Act or, for good measure, article 73 of an 1894 federal import-tax law against conspirators in restraint of trade. Without forcing Otis to sell its stakes in other concerns, the decree ordered that those concerns would have to "be managed, controlled and directed as separate, distinct corporations," with no personnel overlap.

In the opinion of Otis' counsel, "the Government is at any time in the future at liberty to take proceedings in this suit or institute another suit to test any of the points not covered by said order," powerfully suggesting to Otis management that its actions would be under perpetual scrutiny from now on. Yet the decree was in fact much less alarming than Otis had any right to expect. There were no fines, no damages, and the problem of clearing up its pattern of co-ownership and coordination could be left, as it turned out, to the principle of a merger.[27]

Chapter 8

The Otis Elevator Industry

B Y A CURIOUS IRONY, the verdict of the court proved to be the making of Otis. Convenient as it might appear to control the markets by
subterfuge and deceit, the cartel or trust in fact tended to promote inefficiency and waste–duplicate plant, parallel sales organizations, a
confusing plethora of different products. By 1906 it was probably impossible for the most scrupulous salesman to know which of the elevators the
Otis group produced to recommend, while apportioning orders and their
profits had become a Florentine sub-industry in itself.

Meanwhile America was entering the branded age, as market leaders became household words. Ford, Hoover, Ajax, Coca-Cola and others
could take advantage of the spread of communications, the sophistication
of advertising and economies of scale in a mass society. Otis as yet had
been unable to follow their example, or at least not to the extent it might
have wished. The Otis name had been forced to jostle for position with
27 other firms while the trust lasted. Well-founded suspicions in the construction trade had probably caused orders to be lost. Otis was now a
domestic giant, with $15.7 million in annual revenues and seven factories
around America, all of them wholly owned, and an eighth in Canada.
Within a decade, Otis bought two more factories and built two more, in
Buffalo and Harrison, New York. This posed an obvious risk of over-
capacity as well as a confusion of management styles, roles and

specifications, the result of inbred traditions that had grown up in Otis' erstwhile competitors' officers and preserved more or less intact through the years of alliance and cooperation.

Prodded by the government, Otis now set about liquidating the firms under its control, bringing more rational corporate management to the whole business and learning to market the products of its various factories under one name. One name meant one style, one standard of quality and an awareness of the ever-pressing need to maintain cost-effective development and production to counter competition.

The year of the court ruling, 1906, happened to be the year in which Frederick W. Taylor delivered a series of lectures to the American Society of Mechanical Engineers on the principles of "scientific management." When he looked for examples of industrial inefficiency, he might have been paraphrasing Otis' own early history: "the remedy for this inefficiency lies in systematic management, rather than in searching for some unusual or extraordinary man." His message that "the best management is a true science, resting upon clearly defined laws, rules and principles" found an echo in the post-trust, fully merged Otis company.

Of course, it was not Taylor or antitrust that prompted Otis' rationalization program. The term scientific management may have been coined by Taylor, but its precepts were already in the air. In 1898, in his bid for technological superiority, Baldwin had established specialized mechanical and electrical engineering departments at corporate headquarters—in part the old Otis Electric Company under new auspices, maintaining its program of R&D—and this organization at the core of the Otis empire became the model of centralization that the company now sought to follow. As rivals were folded in, their most talented employees were brought to headquarters, where everyone's experience contributed to the evolution of excellence. Here, too, production methods and specifications were worked out for each factory—more standardization of basic components for economies of scale, better factory layouts, dedicated machine tools.

Not that Otis ever achieved anything like the standardization of mass-production industries. It was impossible for Otis to follow down the road soon to be pioneered by Ford, because while every family had some use for a cheap, standard car that was famously black, every building, every architect, and every client came to Otis with different needs. Compared with products in other burgeoning sectors of American industry, Otis products remained to some extent craft-based—individually designed and produced by human skill. It was only within the elevator industry itself that Otis could outperform its rivals by embracing modern production and management techniques.

The Otis Elevator Company's capacity for survival was extraordinary by the standards of any age. It has always been the rule rather than the exception for companies to fold as swiftly as they are created, out of step with changing demand, outstripped by evolving technologies, underfunded or overstretched. By the time Otis sought to incorporate, it had achieved a miracle in business terms—still thriving after 40 years in the hothouse of development and competition. Every year it went from strength to strength, with higher profits, increased turnover and market-winning products. Although it had long since stopped being a family firm, Norton Otis was still chairman, very active and effective up to his death in 1902, and the family name still stuck to the business. In one sense, the Otis Elevator Company was already like one of those very old, dignified, craft-based firms one expects to find in out-of-the-way corners of London or Boston, turning out hats, or weighing tea, suppliers to the gentry since 1726.

But only in one sense. Otis by 1900 was a name for most of the American elevator industry. By virtue of mergers and acquisitions, its history was no longer only, or even primarily, the story of Elisha Otis, his sons and colleagues. It included the history of Frank Sprague, the Elektron Elevator Company, Davies' Electric Elevator, the history of the 27 or more companies it had taken over, along with the hundreds of individuals who by force of circumstance now found themselves working for the single corporation. Away from the engineering departments, a host of different practices and traditions, different impulses, uneven goals divided them, however much their bids had been coordinated or their products passed off as the work of another firm. Incorporation, and then the events of 1906, might give them all one name, but a name alone did not make a company.

The delay in implementing rational reforms—the kind of reforms that would mark Otis' evolution from an East Coast concern into a genuinely national company—had been due to a suspicion that profits were helped, at least in the short term, by customer confusion, as well as by a natural reluctance to fight turf wars throughout the company. It was a situation that would recur almost to the letter 70 years later, as Otis moved from operating at a national level to a multinational one. The 1906 court judgment, though, not only prodded Baldwin into action; it gave him the tools to stifle internal opposition.

Ironically, little is known about the man who guided the policy of the Otis Elevator Company for almost 50 years. At the top of the Otis tree, William Delaney Baldwin was the very model of a corporate CEO. When Otis moved into a new corporate headquarters in New York, Baldwin masterminded the company's progress every step of the way, outlined its strategic goals and decided how Otis' money should be spent, all from his wood-paneled, carpeted office on the top, seventh floor. In the evenings he went home to a grand house in Westchester.

We know Baldwin had a rather vain obsession with his family roots, and that as his status rose his desire to obtain a pedigree equal to his rank increased. "I think I have struck the line that will land you in the *Mayflower*," a professional genealogist wrote him in December 1905, and he bequeathed to the Otis archives a host of materials on medieval Baldwins in France and England—Baldwins on crusade, family coats of arms, images of old manor houses and feats of derring-do.

He was a staunch supporter of his church, and a donor to charity, and was a profound believer in the principles of noblesse oblige, who took his duties very seriously. It could not have been easy for a man in his position and with such strong convictions to embrace the newfangled faith of Christian Science, as he and Mrs. Baldwin did in 1900—his motives can only have been sincere. In line with these private preoccupations, Baldwin set the tone for a benevolent paternalism in Otis' business operations.

In a speech to mark the opening of Otis' plant in Quincy, Illinois, in 1910, Baldwin spelled out something of his management philosophy—a philosophy of excellence and high expectations that he could have heard articulated, in slightly different terms, by his old boss Charles Otis.

He began and ended with a recognition of the principles behind what has come to be called good corporate citizenship: he wanted Otis and Quincy to prosper together. He would provide jobs; Quincy might like to consider how to provide housing for the workers. He would provide growth; Quincy would provide the original plant, which Otis bought, land for future expansion, and a fine shipping point. Under the heading "Believe in High Wages," Otis' in-house *The Indicator* reported Baldwin's ideas on labor:

> *We maintain union shops and non-union shops, open shops and closed shops, and endeavor to deal with each situation as it arises, having in mind the conditions prevailing in each particular locality, with proper regard for our neighbors employing labor and their views. We do require in our business a high grade of mechanics. We do believe in high wages rather than low. We believe we get better men and a larger production, and in every way better results. We believe in no place can the Golden Rule be applied to better advantage than in dealing with our workmen.*

Only a man with Baldwin's drive and vision could have steered Otis through the upheavals of the early 20th century. Always firm in his convictions, he saw to it that the company was organized to carry out his wishes. One can see his influence not only in the intensive R&D that went into perfecting the electric gearless and the whole range of electric drum-winding machines in the early 1900s, but also in the company's persistence in developing the escalator.

Nowhere was Otis' ability to fuse the best ideas and developments of the age into a single product better demonstrated than in the escalator, although the project had to be launched against the protests of a number of Otis' personnel, who pointed out that costs, rather than stairs, were escalating wildly. Some $7,000 earmarked for one project, for example, proved to be only the first installment of a $32,000 investment. The battle over the escalator was sufficiently acrid to be remembered 10 years later, and even mentioned discreetly in an issue of *The Indicator*. The market was, of course, untried. The overruns were horrendous. The final product was a huge success.

Ideas for a moving staircase had been around since at least 1859, but nothing practical had been achieved until two inventors, working independently in the 1890s, came up with one-half of the modern escalator apiece. George H. Wheeler thought up a loop hung with flat steps which ceaselessly revolved, along with a moving handrail, and patented his idea in 1892. In Wheeler's contraption, passengers stepped on and off the staircase from landings to one side. Plagued with financial worries, Wheeler in 1898 sold his idea to a rival inventor, Charles Seeburger. Seeburger introduced the machine to Otis, and the $32,000 started to get spent.

There was a small but steady demand for the product from department stores and subway stations. The first machine was installed in the elevated train station at Sixth Avenue and 23rd Street in New York in 1899. Lyman Bloomingdale put one in his store in 1901 and never looked back—it immediately opened up all his floors to through traffic. At Otis, increased production taught the company something about costs and how to hold them down. Gimbels took a machine—the very design which Norton Otis had assembled at the Paris Exposition of 1900 and which had won it the Grand Prix. At Herald Square, Macy's responded by buying a bank of moving stairs to link all the floors of the store.

Seeburger surrendered his license to Otis in 1910, when the company bought his patents as well as the copyright to the word he had coined, *escalator,* to describe the machine. Ironically, the U.S. Patent Office had refused to recognize *escalator* as a noun, and forced Seeburger to register it as a trademark. Fifty years later the decision was reversed, to Otis' dismay, and the company lost its exclusive rights to the term.

With Seeburger's escalator in hand, Otis was now in a position to go after its chief rival in the field, which it did in time-honored fashion, buying out Jesse Reno in 1911. Reno, like Wheeler, had hit on his half of the escalator in the 1890s. What he built was a sort of inclined walkway, without the steps but with ridged hardwood cleats set on a flexible loop that were swept top and bottom by iron combs, setting the passenger directly onto the floor ahead.

Not until World War I ended did Baldwin feel strong enough to begin the process of combining the two half-inventions into the escalator we know today, adding Reno's hardwood cleats to Seeburger's steps. In 1922 the "L"-type inaugurated metal platforms and two drive chains, one on each side of the steps. The company would sell about 30 of these every year until the end of World War II.

The escalator proved a triumph for Baldwin's judgment and resolve, but Otis' foray into automobile manufacture, the Sultan sedan venture, bears the hallmarks of a Baldwin infatuation. On one level, the idea of importing from France a complete design for a car—blueprints, patents, dies and all—was not a bad one; and it was reasonable to suppose that Otis should have an interest in the car business as it stood around 1906, when entry barriers were low and the industry was dominated, amazingly, by distant European manufacturers. Otis, after all, was in the transportation business. Moreover, the links between elevators and streetcars were historically and technologically very close. What could be more natural, then, than to take the next step into a new and clearly growing field of enterprise?

Otis began to manufacture the Sultan at its factory in Springfield, Massachusetts; handmade bodywork was fitted to the chassis in Newark, New Jersey or New York. Most Sultans were equipped as cars or taxicabs; a few were made with truck bodies. The engineering was good for the period—six bolts held the transmission; leaf springs provided the suspension; and a four-cylinder engine generated speeds of 30 mph at 16 miles to the gallon. The car could "turn around on a manhole cover." Later models built around 1910 boasted carbide gas lamps instead of oil lamps, and even a glass windshield. One filled up with oil every time one stopped for gas, because the oil was on a one-way drip, and most of it wound up on the road. After about 2,000 miles the tires had to be replaced for around $250 each. At that price the cost of tires could soon match the cost of the car itself, a near-impossible $3,500.[28]

Otis itself needed cars and trucks. "We Are at Your Service Days, Nights, Sundays and Holidays," one ad proclaimed, with an illustration of a Sultan promoting "Otis Automobile Service for Expediting Delivery of Needed Parts." Otis construction workers needed vehicles to cover their territory, too. But building the Sultan must have seemed more natural to Baldwin than to his employees. Otis' expertise was in a quite revolutionary area of mass transport: elevators were unusual in that they catered to all classes at once, from the haughtiest CEO to the humblest clerk. Baldwin rode the office elevator like everyone else, but he did not come to work in a streetcar, any more than his employees would dream of commuting, as he did, in a motor car. Cars in 1906, cars like the Sultan, were still for the rich.

The whole Sultan project was bedeviled by one vast source of trouble. The car came from France, where Baldwin had spent five years of his early business career. His enthusiasm for the country, and his well-placed regard for French engineering, must have outweighed the fairly obvious snag that the Sultan was engineered using metrics. That made it impossible for ordinary American mechanics to repair, even though spare parts were available from Otis' regional elevator service centers.

Baldwin can hardly be blamed, though, for not foreseeing Henry Ford. Otis was in an industry that required craftsmanship. The Sultan was irreproachably lovely to look at, but cars rolled off the production line at the rate of one a week. Baldwin fell in love with the Sultan, and the best testament to his skills as an administrator is that he cured himself of his affliction by 1910, and cut his losses in good time.

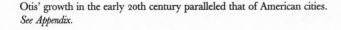

Otis' growth in the early 20th century paralleled that of American cities. *See Appendix.*

Chapter 9

Abroad Again

O TIS' APPROACH TO FOREIGN MARKETS was cautiously opportunistic. In Europe, which always held out the promise of richest pickings, the American Elevator Company that Hale had launched to sell Hale and Otis elevators was retired in 1893, and the company had instead become known as the Otis Elevator Company—five years before it changed its name in the United States. European offices were maintained in London, Berlin, Amsterdam, Rome, Stockholm, Paris and Brussels. Brazil, Argentina, Spain, Chile and Mexico were covered by agencies, as was Australia after the collapse of the Austral-Otis Company in 1893.

But the competitive climate sharpened as electricity drew new players into the field abroad as at home, and the number of foreign shipments—about 250 a year in 1900—did not represent as large a market share as it might have been. Until 1907, when the first foreign department was organized, foreign sales were handled by New York's domestic sales department. It was in New York, after all, that most of the trading companies who worked as Otis agents around the world had their own headquarters.

By citing single installations, Otis could be said to cover the globe, from southern Africa to the frozen north, Petrograd and Scandinavia. In reality, the business was heavily tilted toward Britain, Australia and Argentina. In 1907, when sales on 445 machines sent abroad grossed the company $408,000, well over half were sent to England and

Australia. Argentina split the difference with the rest of the world, 75 machines apiece.

All the same, Otis had established a name after 40 years' foreign trading. Some of the swankiest installations in the world were Otis elevators. In 1909 the Otis company could boast that the Forbidden City in Beijing had Otis equipment, as did the Mikado Palace in Japan. When the emperor of Austria-Hungary paid a visit to his royal palace in Budapest, everything in the building except the two passenger elevators from Yonkers was Hungarian-made. In India both the governor in Delhi and the maharajah of Mysore rode Otis elevators, as did innumerable dukes and marquises in Spain and the Emperor Nicholas II himself. *The Indicator* for July 1909 enthusiastically reported that "While such installations attract the attention of the engineering world, it is the constant recurrence of the name Otis in the elevators of the hotels and buildings of interest throughout the civilized world which attracts quite as much attention from the restless American traveling abroad, and perhaps gives him the feeling that he is not out of touch with his home country."[29]

As well as persuading foreign grandees into its elevators, Otis was exporting them on the back of American *style*. "Single buildings abroad, as a rule, do not include as many elevators as do some of the large installations in the United States," the company reported in 1909, but the American tradition of massive hotels and department stores was spreading. "It may be an inspiration to know that there is never a day and never an hour in which there are not Otis elevators on the water en route to some foreign country," the report continued, and Baldwin was referring regularly to foreign sales in his addresses to shareholders.

The rising volume of foreign work put Otis in a virtuous circle. As it became involved in a growing number of prestige projects around the world, so its opportunities widened. Its name was familiar in more than a dozen countries. Americans traveling abroad stepped into Otis elevators with a sense of coming home, so foreign sales made for good home publicity, too.

Already, however, Otis had begun responding to local pressures to form alliances with foreign companies. The first of these mergers was made in the most promising market of all, Britain, which by way of its empire fed other markets around the world.

Queen Victoria, the "née plus ultra" of foreign royalty, had balked at traveling in a common lift; but Waygood, the company that would soon merge with Otis in the British Empire, was permitted to provide her with a small, hand-operated royal lift in Balmoral Castle.

The idea of an alliance with one of Britain's leading manufacturers had been floated as early as 1888. Ten years later negotiations were renewed, and in 1902, Waygood & Otis Limited was formed, with the announcement that the company would be in a position to offer elevators manufactured in either Britain or America. This boast, as the head of Otis' overseas division remarked dryly in 1960, "does not seem to have been as good a sales point as it was supposed to be." The merger was dissolved only a year later, and in 1904 it was the Otis Elevator Company of America that received the world's largest elevator contract to date, an order worth $2 million from the London Underground. (Technically, this huge contract, for 175 elevators, was won by Frank Sprague, who turned to Otis as the only manufacturer in a position to deliver.)

With the mysterious collapse of Otis' alliance with Waygood, Otis' foray into Canada proved to be more lasting. Baldwin himself masterminded the operation, from an idea that occurred to him at the end of a fishing holiday in Quebec. Otis' Canadian agent, Watson Jack, persuaded Baldwin and his fishing companion, Henry P. Douglas, that Otis was missing out on a rising tide of business. Douglas went back to investigate in 1902 and suggested that Otis open a Canadian company with its own manufacturing plant. In August 1902, Otis incorporated in Canada and began work on a factory in the industrial city of Hamilton, Ontario, under Henry Douglas as general manager.

The market for elevators in Canada was expanding as Canada followed the United States' lead into tall buildings, and Otis faced major local competition from the Fensom Elevator Company of Toronto, a concern that had begun life as a general machine shop but had been making elevators exclusively since 1885. By the turn of the century the founder's son had opened an office on the West Coast and employed more than 100 workers; in 1905, like so many entrepreneurs before him, he acceded to an offer of a merger with Otis.

Baldwin's grasp of rational corporate style was now unmatched: the erection of a new, state-of-the-art factory in Hamilton reflected all the best techniques devised at Yonkers and elsewhere. Automatic machinery was used "in all cases where at all possible," and eight buildings, including an administrative block, were erected from scratch in Hamilton in such a way "that all parts, from the raw materials to the finished equipment, go through a straight course without unnecessary or waste handling." The 12,000-square-foot factory was even provided with a test tower with two shafts, in which any type of elevator could be tested at heights up to 80 feet. This "special feature" was probably not used for research but rather to cut down installation times. Understanding the need to co-opt tradition, Baldwin put George Fensom in charge of the new company. Douglas worked briefly for Otis in New York but soon resigned and returned to Montreal with his family to work for a construction firm. His relations with Baldwin, however, remained cordial, and 50 years later his son Percy would emerge as the architect of Otis' worldwide reconstruction after World War II.

The failed merger with Waygood in Britain was compensated by Otis-Fensom in Canada. Canada was a special case: closer to and more like the United States than any other country. For all intents and purposes, Otis-Fensom could be run much like any other North American subsidiary. Everywhere else the prospect was more clouded, although Otis worked hard to increase its foreign business in the years leading up to World War I. There was too much goodwill at stake to throw away, even when the added costs of shipping Otis elevators and installing them at a distance seemed to put the company at a disadvantage.

Various factors were at work, however, to compound the disadvantage as the century turned. Sometimes Otis' products were probably too sophisticated for foreign markets: electricity, for instance, got off to a slower start in most countries than in America. Often Otis faced sophisticated competition. More significantly, the nations of the industrialized world tended to be jealous of foreign competition and prided themselves on the superiority of their domestic manufactures. Foreign manufacturers might learn from Otis, but they would not yield to it. Nor is it hard to imagine the difficulties that customs men and local engineers could impose on a foreign firm poaching in their markets.

Japan, where protectionism seemed to be as much a cultural disposition as a political choice, was on the face of it one of Otis' most unlikely markets. When Elisha Otis invented his safety hoist, foreigners who dared to enter Japan faced a death sentence.[30] The year Otis exhibited his device at the New York World's Fair, Commodore Perry forced the Japanese to end their 220-year-old policy of isolation.

Under the ensuing oligarchic Meiji regime, from 1868 to 1912, Japan flung itself into a program of industrialization and modernization that by 1905, the year the Japanese defeated the Russians in the Russo-Japanese War, had turned the country into a formidable power. The old isolationism, such as it was, was now maintained by the Japanese determination to catch up with the West through their own efforts. Japanese businesses grew on capital raised by thrift, not foreign loans, and aimed at complete self-sufficiency in those areas of industry–steel and transportation–that formed the basis of Western "industrial might."

Coordinating national efforts to achieve these goals, and on the way reinforcing the kinship patterns of earlier times, the Meiji oligarchs had little time to worry about elevators. Their buildings, for the most part, were small. When, however, demand arose at the beginning of the 1890s, they were untroubled by the prospect of buying foreign-made machines in what appeared to them a nonessential industry. The Central Bank of Japan in Tokyo bought four Otis hydraulics in 1891 and another in 1894 for its Yokohama branch.

Otis–and Waygood–continued to find a market for their elevators in Japan as the century turned, Otis relying on an American agent, the American Trading Company, which had links across eastern Asia. Meanwhile Japan had already begun its search for raw materials, invading Korea and Taiwan. By the outbreak of World War I, in which Japan, as an ally of Britain, acted against German colonies in the Far East, Japan was a regional power; by the war's end, the country was one of the Big Five that went to Versailles to map out a new world order.

Otis' involvement in foreign ventures was unusual among U.S. firms, and the reason was obvious. Otis' increasingly sophisticated elevators could not be pushed over the counter ready to run, and it was in the company's interest to see that they were installed correctly. The kind of confusion that reigned over even domestic installation procedures, with bits and pieces arriving on site in haphazard order needing to be sorted by an experienced hand, could prove a nightmare.

Otis had built up a long backlog of goodwill around the world, when only Otis could be relied on to provide, say, the Eiffel Tower's inclined elevator, or the great lifts at work in the Glasgow Harbour Tunnel. Foreigners were attracted by the breadth as much as the length of Otis' experience in the industry, for Americans made more elevators than the rest of the world put together, and one company made more in America than any other. Otis' elevators were, so far, expensive; but the demand was there.

To Baldwin, too, "abroad" was not foreign. Home-grown corporate leaders scarcely had the time to acquaint themselves with the world beyond. Corporatism was an American invention, which had come about in order to satisfy huge domestic appetites, and there was no foreign input into either its revolutionary rationale or its personnel. Baldwin, on the other hand, had joined Otis from a stint in Paris, and he often traveled abroad. On the testimony of his granddaughter, he at least once, after a marital row, calmly left the house and went to Europe to cool off. In Europe, he seemed to be saying, "I will be at home, but you can't follow me!"

In 1899 an alliance had been made with a footling engineering firm in Paris, Atelier Abel-Pifre, whereby Abel-Pifre would act as Otis' French agents and also produce elevators at its Bezons factory under the Otis name. Otis invested around $300,000 in the deal, seeing it as a way to sidestep the cultural and political chauvinism of the French market, which seemed unmoved by Otis' herculean efforts to win its spurs on the Eiffel Tower.* Progress was very slow. The market was small, dominated by two major French concerns, and the arrangement with Pifre, which did sell to Spain, Portugal and the French colonies, seems to have wavered: at least the company was not listed as an Otis agent in 1910, 1911 or 1912. In 1913, however, the companies merged formally.

There was not, as yet, an articulated foreign policy, nor the people or institutions to figure it out and drive it home, only a very powerful president dealing with reports as they came in, from people relatively low down on the corporate ladder. In 1910 Germany—soon to lose a bitter

---

* Otis' contribution, anyway, was scrapped in 1902, when a domestic rival refurbished the legs of the tower, and it took Otis another 67 years to get the work back.

four-year war in Europe—was clearly a country to reckon with, and so Otis launched an assault on the German market.

At the same time, another kind of pull affected Otis' decisions to invest abroad. Local agents or ambitious personnel hoped to persuade the company of the opportunities that were being missed, in order to become empire-builders of their own. In Germany, the man who had been responsible for Otis' sales throughout southeastern Europe, Italy and Switzerland since 1890, Hans von Andelson, had been content with a small number of sales, mostly of low-powered machines. It was his death in 1910 that triggered the clamor for investment. Otis' London office created a German subsidiary, Otis Elevator GmbH, in 1910.

As in Canada, Otis rapidly moved from agency to a brand-new, state-of-the-art, built-for-the-purpose factory close to Berlin, with a sales office in the city and others soon appearing in Dusseldorf, Budapest and Vienna. At 32,000 square feet, the Berlin factory dwarfed the Hamilton enterprise: the plan was to launch Otis aggressively on the European market. By 1913 all the elements were in place, but it was not a very good moment to launch a European enterprise.

The same trouble, of course, dogged Otis' foray into the largest established market for elevators outside the United States, the British Empire, leaving the company awkwardly straddling the divide between belligerents. Otis' advance on the empire market was complicated by other factors, too. For years, Otis and Waygood had been exploring the prospect of an alliance between the foremost elevator enterprises in America and the rest of the English-speaking world. In England mergers were relatively rare—the smaller scale of business in the country had not provoked the kind of antitrust legislation Americans were familiar with, and cartels were more common in British markets. The 1903 merger, unusual in itself, may have failed because Waygood was not yet ready to allow Otis to act as the stronger financial party in the relationship.

Otis' organizational flair plainly alarmed the Waygood old guard in a country whose industrial culture was notoriously old-fashioned. As the world's first industrializing nation, Britain had never had to face the competition that made other countries organize their enterprises more rationally from the start, and the strongest traditions in manufacturing were for small, family-owned enterprises with low levels of capitalization and investment. Waygood had begun as a country-town affair in the 1830s. The move to London was accomplished in the 1840s; and in 1863, Richard Waygood had built his factory on the present site of the Otis works on the Falmouth Road, London.

Not until the 1870s, following Richard Waygood's retirement, did the company move out of general engineering to start focusing on lifts, but its progress was rapid after that. The factory was constantly expanding to cope with rising orders: "Factory was added to factory, office to office," as Henry C. Walker, the managing director, recalled, and Waygood never experienced the sort of all-out rationalization that Otis periodically had to undergo. When R. Waygood and Co. incorporated in 1897, the company was already, by American standards, small, informal and paternalistic in its methods. To its employees, though, it seemed almost ruthlessly efficient. "The old hands...were gradually absorbed in the growing crowd," Walker recalled with naive regret, "whilst the sphere of each one's work became specialized into narrower channels." It is hardly surprising that Waygood found Otis' very American methods alarming.

Yet the race, as people of the day were prone to observe, is to the swift, and by 1913, after several years of collaboration, Waygood's managers faced the inevitable and agreed that the company should become a subsidiary of Otis. It was actually Baldwin, having spent the summer in England, who proved initially reluctant to amalgamate the two businesses: the cultural differences that made Waygood managers suspicious of their American partner must have exasperated the organizationally minded Baldwin. But if Waygood's production methods seemed out of date, there was no denying the strength of the company's sales organization, which not only covered the whole of Britain but by 1911 had offices and agencies in India, South Africa, Burma, Singapore and Australia, and a strong presence in Egypt, Belgium, Portugal, Russia, Brazil and Ecuador. In years to come, the majority of Otis' overseas ventures would be managed from the London hub.

Chapter 10

The Indicator Years

A RECENT PRESIDENT OF OTIS, Hubert Faure, has remarked that it takes at least 10 years to change the company's attitudes and goals. Baldwin had already been trying to weld his elevator empire together for 10 years when he licensed production of *The Indicator*. The first issue of Otis' in-house journal rolled off the Chicago presses in 1908.

The Indicator was one of the channels by which Otis' central management communicated its goals to everyone down the line—to factory hands in Buffalo, sales representatives in California, inspectors in Moline—all members of a 5,000-strong enterprise scattered across the United States, England, Germany, Japan, Hong Kong, Argentina and Canada. It was one of the first "in-house" journals produced by an American corporation. Professionally put together, printed on high-quality paper that has withstood the passage of a century with barely a mark of discoloration, *The Indicator* was an offshoot of the new stationery department based in Chicago, a department increasingly central to the process of imposing system and clarity onto what had been a ragbag of styles and traditions.

Though the department wasn't responsible for analyzing problems like waste, weakness or time losses—that task was left to the Taylorites, with their clipboards and time-and-motion studies—it expanded rapidly to assist in implementing solutions. *The Indicator* belonged between the standard forms and the officially sanctioned office stationery. In 1911 the whole department was moved to Yonkers, closer to corporate headquarters in New York City, an integral part of the way Otis was reinventing itself for a new age.

The magazine was issued in a brown card folder, its title set off handsomely against a background of burnished bronze. The December 1910 issue portrayed an elevator invitingly half open, its operator peering through the colonnades that framed the picture, the date laid out in mosaic on the floor in the elegant Art Nouveau style of the day, like a classy welcome mat. From the masthead down, it imparted a sense of unflagging confidence and drive. A fancy dial set at 39 on the first 1908 edition indicated the highest floor that Otis elevators currently served. *The Indicator* was published, so the blazon ran, "In the Interests of the OTIS ELEVATOR INDUSTRY." As the journal pointed out, the company slogan "Otis Elevators–The Standard of the World" was designed to "so fix in the minds of the people the name of the Company that one could not think 'Elevator' without thinking 'Otis.'"

Otis operations were continental in scope. Canada was already well within the Otis fold, and although its operations were treated technically as foreign, "we have lost much of the idea of considering it as a foreign country." The legal ruling of 1906 that produced a unified Otis organization provoked a well-founded desire to streamline all company operations and to make each individual in the great machine better aware of its operation at large and of his contribution to its continued smooth running or, as the masthead put it, "to give to the co-workers of the Otis Elevator Company a more comprehensive knowledge of the industry, to encourage individual effort and to unite in closer co-operation all those actively engaged in promoting the growth of the Company."

The stationery department used it to explain the latest assault on sloppy practices, and to make employees conform to the dictates of what was then tenderly referred to as "bureaucracy," a program to render office activities transparent and uniform. One of the beauties of embracing "systems" was that no element in it could appear too small for attention: everything transparently built toward the perfect efficiency of the whole. Sometimes a word was needed to nudge people in the right direction: "Our offices are requested to exercise care in the use of the new standard envelopes, it is found that much larger envelopes are being used than is necessary...," *The Indicator* finger-wagged in May 1909. But on the same page the company was pleased to report that it "has standardized three styles of paper fasteners, or clips, to be known as follows..." Indeed, the overhaul of Otis' stationery department in these years, with its general office stationery numbered 401–999 (including, as random examples, special #572 stock paper, quadrille ruled, for sketches),* and its special office paper, such as letterhead, numbered from 1001, its new in-house printing service in Chicago, its different colored notepaper for every zone, all this, so automatically assumed as the birthright, and sometimes the bugbear, of the modern corporation, not only was perfectly new but reflected what was happening to the company as a whole. In sales and dispatch, in production and development and customer relations *The Indicator* disseminated a whole bevy of rules, forms, best practices and evaluated methods across what it chose to call the entire Otis Industry.

A thrilling undertaking down to the last paper clip, it marked on a wider scale a shift from an America which, through abundant material, fertile imagination and unlimited enterprise, had raised itself into an industrial powerhouse, to an America which was shaking up the very principles of industry, recasting them according to the precepts of mass production and mass consumption, an America which was already exporting a style that came to be known as the American Way.

The Indicator embodied the guiding belief that all the disparate traditions and people who made up the Otis Elevator Company could be welded into a supremely rational, seamless whole. In part this could be achieved, as Taylor and others had prescribed, by examining best practices in one branch of the industry and methodically extending them to all the rest, saving time, cutting costs and raising quality and output. *The Indicator* had its part to play in this, explaining the importance of a precise knowledge of costs; or noting how the streamlined movement of pig iron had been achieved at the Yonkers Works; or trying to persuade people of the difference between economy, which was good, and parsimony, which lost the company customers.

---

* Within a few months a stock standard typewriter #687 was already on the list, with #688 for pencil work.

Beyond this, *The Indicator* became an agent for fostering what would nowadays be called a corporate culture. Old-time Otis had been kept together by respect for the boss—when Baldwin took over the presidency, it was said that he knew all his employees by sight. New Otis was necessarily more impersonal, bound together by an implicit understanding of the company's aims, its corporate style. In cultural terms, among others, the center sought to export its vision to the periphery and to heal the divisions that perhaps still lurked there after the consolidations of 1898 and 1906. The journal offered instruction in salesmanship, installations, manufacturing processes and technicalities of the company's current product, but in far more general terms it told each employee what the company expected from him.

The Indicator had a very distinctive tone in addressing its readership: a pedagogic, purposeful and insistently moral tone. He who "makes use of his energy and ability... not only advances the interest of such business but individually benefits in the broadening of his own powers—and these are the men who naturally are selected to positions of trust," the journal counseled. Each issue was spangled with uplifting mottoes and admonitory aphorisms. Under the heading "Why He Was Not Promoted" the reader was told that "He did not learn that the best part of his salary was not in the pay envelope."

"Any Bee which loses sight of the spirit of the Hive, and works only for private good, is considered sick, criminally insane and the community no longer allows him to take up good space" was a representative, unforgiving epigram quoted from *The Fra* in July 1910. In the same issue a passage from the *Denver Times* exhorted people to "sweep out the dust from the floor of your mind that your lot in life is harder than the other man's.... The most fortunate of men...will show you that he has a battle on that very minute.... Who of us would exchange life with anyone we know.... You are yourself. You can only live your own life, and, thank God, you really can do that. It is your inalienable right (*sic*). You will live it. Your back is fitted for just your load. You may shift from one shoulder to the other. You may lighten or increase your load, but it is yours; you and the load constitute personality."

Part of *The Indicator*'s uplifting tone was derived from the culture of night schools and self-help. In this spirit, the journal offered sensibly written articles on subjects not remotely relevant to elevator production, like the origin of salt or the state of the nation's timber resources. There were not enough of these articles to make up an actual education, but there was enough to tie the journal into a broader agenda of self-improvement, which had a powerful grip on Americans at the beginning of the 20th century.

The Indicator was part of Otis' effort to give local gossip and local pride a nationwide circulation, and so stamp the entire company with a sense of unified character. Sometimes it simply peddled hot tips, doing for the entire workforce what word of mouth might otherwise do for just a small portion of it, telling draftsmen, for example, how to stop blueprints from fading in sunlight. Sometimes it repeated jokes and told tall stories about old ladies standing impatiently in telephone booths waiting for the lifts to ascend, or about hicks stepping gingerly into elevators for the first time. More directly, in 1910 it reported on the first-ever conference of sales representatives drawn from Canada and the United States, who met in New York and were given an introduction of the works, tours of the city and its monuments, and a formal dinner.

Otis' latest achievements were proudly flagged in articles describing some of the new wonders of the age—from New York's Metropolitan Life Building down to the giant stores and hotels across America, Australia and Hawaii. Credit was tactfully distributed in all those articles to architects and engineers involved, and the local communities came in for generous praise, too.

But there can be no character without history, and *The Indicator* was chiefly responsible for giving the company a past. The history of hydraulic elevators was being written up by *The Indicator* at a time when no one gave hydraulics a second thought, the point being not to give practical information but rather to illustrate the invisible links that bound together the Otis of the day. The founders of the company were pictured as possessing near-mythical status, and were held up with mottoes and exhortations as examples of all the virtues that the company promoted—hard work, constancy and imagination as opposed to fancy.

The Indicator's short, five-year run was actually a measure of its success. Otis, after all, was not in the business of publishing for fun, and by 1913, when the last issue rolled from the press, top management could feel confident that the turmoil of the previous decade had settled down, and that for the most part Otis—standard of the world—was working as a corporation should.

In an age when dislocation fed personal insecurity, even the frostily paternalistic tone of *The Indicator* must have inspired some confidence. The world, like the gigantic new Otis corporation, was an unpredictably lonely place, but *The Indicator* told its readers not to be afraid; so long as they approached their work in the proper spirit, Otis would see them through. *The Indicator's* writers occasionally drew on imagery from the military, to which people unfamiliar with the new science of management could perhaps more easily relate. The Otis corporation, they maintained, was very like an army, and twice *The Indicator* repeated the story about an ensign who had taken letters to Garcia in the recent Spanish-American War without stopping to ask where Garcia might be found—the point being that he displayed both the ingenuity and obedience to duty that Otis wished to find in its employees.

Martial imagery, however, was quite secondary to the Darwinian notion of survival of the fittest. Otis and its management team leaped at Darwinism, and *The Indicator* promulgated the current view that the world was a cockpit of struggle and endeavor in which the race was to the fleet and the fight to the fair.*

Above all, *The Indicator* put its faith in scientific method. Charles Otis' management strictures of 25 years earlier seem homely in comparison with the new "scientific" outlook of the journal. Charles had been given to using farming terms—of organic growth, nurture, even buying corn—in an effort to cajole people to take the leap into the technological unknown. By 1908, however, no one at Otis doubted the technology per se; they placed their faith in its scientific rationale. "In business, as in biology, it is a question of survival of the fittest," as *The Indicator* put it, emphasizing the need for organization, efficiency, equipment, magnitude and capital. Darwin was very much in vogue.

---

* Ironically, *The Indicator* later undermined its own argument by lifting from the *New York Times* an article about the 1911 *Titanic* disaster and the noble behavior of the ship's engineers, who had stuck to their posts and kept the lights burning until the ship went down, and had gone unsung amid the elitist breast-beating that surrounded the disaster. No one seemed to notice how the episode brutally contradicted Darwinian logic: the best, the fittest captains of industry and the engineers, all drowned.

One thoroughly Darwinian feature of the new technology crowding in on the world in 1910 was its ability suddenly to break free of the constraints that had hitherto governed its application, and leave the opposition tilting at windmills. No sooner had the Neanderthals begun to rail against the 12-story monsters that supposedly blacked out light and flung their denizens all at once into the streets at night, than the builders began to construct edifices 30, 40, 50 stories high. In April 1910, about 30 years after its feature on Otis' Yonkers Works, *Scientific American* ran a cover showing Otis' elevators—electric gearless—being installed in the Metropolitan Life Tower, the "eighth wonder of the world." The elevators had been selected, according to *The Indicator,* after the "equipment was subjected to a more searching inquiry than all of the other apparatus" and the Otis product had emerged as the clear winner. The elevator dial on the masthead of *The Indicator* moved subtly around from 40, where the Singer Building had taken it in 1908, to 44; the height of elevator travel had risen to 586 feet.

Chicago and New York had been the first cities to impose height restrictions on buildings, but the restrictions were not consistent and their application waxed and waned in the early part of the century. When the *Springfield* (Massachusetts) *Republican* called for a 100-foot limit on the height of Springfield's buildings in 1906, it claimed that "New York and Chicago would be far handsomer and healthier without 'the skyscrapers.'" The *New York Times* ridiculed the notion. Something should be done, it agreed, to bring the skyscraper under the rule of law, but big buildings were an apt reflection of burgeoning capitalism, and restricting such buildings would be tantamount to restricting the businesses they housed.

Still, restraint of some form or other did seem desirable, especially after the erection in 1915 of what T. Coleman du Pont, its owner, called the du Pont "cottage." The Equitable Building was striking not because it was tall—at 39 stories it was only the third-tallest structure in New York— but because it was so unbelievably greedy. It contained a total floor area more than 30 times the size of its footprint, gobbling up an entire city block without a single set-back. Its through-block vaulted lobby resembled a city street. Unpopular with the public, it glutted the real estate market with empty office space. In 1916 the nation's first zoning ordinance laid down limits that would prevent another Equitable; buildings would go higher, but never with such naked determination to cram as many offices as possible into a patch of city sky.

Otis elevated the Equitable, but in spite of the company's gung-ho rhetoric, *The Indicator* years were relatively dull in business terms. Revenues failed to ignite: between 1898 and 1906 the value of U.S. construction had doubled, but 1907 brought an economic squeeze that slashed the company's value by a third, and between 1908 and 1916 the value of the construction market as a whole rose by only 8 percent. Three-story buildings had lined Broadway within living memory, and there was a limit to how much growth a country could absorb now that the street boasted dozens of buildings 10, 15, 20 stories high.

Otis' revenues and profits remained stable. Preferred shareholders got their 6 percent on the dot, and the company continued to invest earnings in expanding manufacture and R&D. The time was spent consolidating. As Baldwin put it to the stockholders in 1909, "the reduced volume of business has given the opportunity to further improve the efficiency of all branches of your Company's organization, and to put it in position to handle even more successfully than heretofore any future demands that may be made on it."

New York, of course, was still headquarters. In August 1912, *The Indicator* ran an article exploring Otis' new headquarters on Eleventh Avenue and 26th Street, a seven-story building that covered a whole city block and was designed, so the architects explained, after "the modern French phase of Renaissance architecture with an adaptation of other styles appropriate to modern American commercial requirements." In other words, it was a typical speculative office block of the period, with few real aesthetic pretensions, and Otis managers were pleased at the arrangement by which they leased the building. The building had its own water and a network of pneumatic tubes for internal correspondence. Downstairs, departments for sales, service, construction, drafting, manufacturing, orders, traffic, purchasing and stationery ran Otis' largest regional market. On the three upper floors were all the departments that formed Otis' centralized bureaucracy—the legal department, accounting, advertising, general sales. On the seventh floor, where Baldwin had his sober offices, the chief electrical engineer watched over departments for engineering and drafting, and patents.

Much of this work involved rationalizing the company's field and factory operations. Soon the United States was divided into five regional zones, each with its own production facilities, run from offices in New York, Chicago, St. Louis, Houston and San Francisco. A certain amount of specialized work was carried out by each factory: Quincy, Illinois, for small elevators; Chicago for hydraulics and larger electric machines; San Francisco, established after the 1906 earthquake, for low-level general machine work. Buffalo, which took its power from Niagara Falls; Harrison, New Jersey; and Yonkers were all big, all-purpose works, with most of the new designs being made at Yonkers. Moline and Peru, both of them acquired before 1906, were closed down.

Chapter 11

⟨⏸⟩

The Search for Control

ΤHE SHORT AMERICAN INVOLVEMENT in World War I did the company no harm. In 1917, Otis took its place in the command economy, diverting production to military hardware—screws for gun lathes, worm gears for gun mounts, truck wheels, steam steering mechanisms and windlasses for the navy, recoil mechanisms for French howitzers, hydraulic valves for explosives manufacturers and, of course, heavy-duty elevators for seagoing vessels. It developed a leveling hoist for the Navy, much to the relief of gunners as they wheeled live shells across the gunnels. At least the books were balanced, and higher profits compensated for the relatively brief disruption.

Moving out of the recession that followed the Armistice, Otis was caught up in the frenzy of economic activity that characterized the '20s. The Crash of 1929, which brought the frenzy to an end, unmasked a speculative boom; but the boom itself had solid roots—mostly in sales of consumer electronics and the automobile. Meanwhile, elevator technology advanced in fits and starts.

Many years earlier, Otis' hydraulic lifts had put pressure on architects and engineers to come up with a building that could economically exploit the elevator's vertical reach. Discarding traditional masonry construction, they had turned to steel as a construction material that offered potentially limitless thrusts. The challenge was thrown back to the elevator men, and Otis responded with the electric gearless. But in practice the new heights that were achieved served only to magnify the limitations of elevator technology from another angle. Just as masonry had imposed limits on building height in the 1880s, so did the proliferation of elevator shafts in the 1920s.

By today's standards prewar skyscrapers were amazingly over-elevatored. To ensure smooth traffic flow and ensure that every passenger was on his way within 30 seconds of calling the elevator, a building like the Empire State Building–completed in 1931, but essentially a belated product of the '20s–had to be equipped with 58 passenger elevators using 119 miles of rope to serve 102 floors.* Calculations made by the American Institute of Steel Construction in 1929 demonstrated that, with existing technology, the optimum height for a midtown Manhattan building would be around 63 stories; above that, shaft space would eat into rental space with diminishing returns until, at 132 stories, profit would vanish altogether. Not that the more flamboyant builders really cared: their magnificent constructions, from the Woolworth on, were really outsize billboards for their products.

The Empire State Building nevertheless embodied the results of over 20 years' intensive study and development under the direction of the brilliant Swedish-born engineer David Lindquist. Even in the elevator industry, even after the invention of the gearless electrical machine that seemed capable of scaling immeasurable heights, and even though, from a mechanical standpoint, almost everything in elevators that exists today existed in, say, 1910–the safeties, the rise, the speed, the configuration of ropes and the relationship of gears–the elevator still awaited major breakthroughs in technology. Indeed, from a purely business standpoint, Otis had barely scratched the surface. On the one hand, elevator controls remained primitive; on the other, the growing maturity of the market–the sheer number of elevators already installed and the increasing acceptance of them by the public–would lead to development of a branch of the industry that at times would sustain work on new installations: maintenance and upgrading.

---

* Rental activity in the Depression was so slow that the building was dubbed the Empty State Building.

Lindquist had joined Otis just in time to have a catalytic influence on the development of the gearless traction elevator: his 1:1 motor of 1905 brought the invention to a state of high efficiency and reliability. "The only limitation to car speed then," Al Saxer, who ran Otis' elevator-modernization program in the 1980s, once remarked, "was how fast the operator could read the numbers." Lindquist soon set out to remove it.

Lindquist was 28 when he sailed from Sweden to America in 1902. A graduate of a Stockholm technical school, with three years' experience of work at the Swedish General Electric Company, he had completed graduate studies in Germany and Switzerland before he began to hanker for the land of Edison and steel pylons. Soon after his arrival in New York he accepted a job with Otis, dropping his original interest in high-power transmission in favor of solving the problems of bringing electrical power to high-speed, high-rise elevators.

By 1911, Lindquist was Otis' chief electrical engineer. When he retired in 1944, after 43 years at Otis, it was he, rather than any architect, who was known in construction circles as the father of the American skyline. It was he who masterminded Otis' technological progress through the first half of the 20th century, who perfected ways of leveling cars, automating controls and connecting high-rise elevators to electricity. Under his charismatic leadership, Otis' electrical department became a generator of new ideas and a magnet for talented young graduates: Otis' old practice of scouting for available technology, and then developing it, ceased when he became chief engineer. From then on, the company was entitled to make all its developments in-house.

Lindquist taught his staff to set great store by empirical observation. "The importance of visualizing realities and facing facts," he wrote, "too often is overlooked by engineers. Theories have limitations: actual conditions do not always conform to those which are assumed, and there is often extreme variability in factors which are usually considered constant."

He himself analyzed the qualities the traveling public wanted from elevators. "Safety, speed, and silence are the three factors in elevator design, and the biggest element in the whole problem is human behavior." He spent time and energy examining the parameters of human expectations. "Smooth silent operation," he reported, "is paramount for the peace of mind of the passenger. Yet people complain about a sense of 'imprisonment' in closed elevator cars, and others who meekly tolerate the bangs and screeches of the subway will report a squeak in 'the lift.' Such is the task confronting the designers of elevators."[31]

For all his exasperation with the antediluvian instincts of elevator passengers, Lindquist used all methods imaginable to fathom them. The solution was to test products exhaustively. Paper solutions threw up practical problems, as he could illustrate. Otis had managed to reduce one source of noise by exchanging the gearing in the elevator drive for a cable drum mounted directly on the motor armature. It looked like an elegant solution, but this "apparent simplification gave rise to a number of perplexing engineering problems" associated with the increased load on the armature shaft. Each of these required, in turn, to be discovered, analyzed and resolved. Testing under real conditions was the only way forward.

Like Elisha Otis many years earlier, Lindquist could not conceive of a machine without itching to improve it. Even after the electric gearless had established Otis' dominance in the industry, Lindquist ensured that the company was always pushing at the boundaries of technology. Competitors were forced either to follow in Otis' wake with copies of the latest technology at a lower price, as A. B. See and Haughton sometimes did, or to move to the sidelines, to the low-rise, small-profit jobs that Otis shunned.

Lindquist was a man of pure science: he possessed a profound faith in the power of science to accomplish anything, and a lofty contempt for people who would hold it back. His faith was consonant with his time, when everyone turned to science, daubing their theories with a scientific imprimatur, even if the label seemed inappropriate—scientific socialism, Christian Science, management science, the social sciences. Art embraced the new catholicism: vorticism, futurism and its paler, popular refraction in the ubiquitous Art Deco style, which gave everything from ashtrays to skyscrapers a wind-brushed, high-velocity look, best captured architecturally in the gleaming chromium spire of the Chrysler Building in New York. Lindquist carved, in consequence, a rather dashing figure in the world of electrical engineering and attracted recruits of high caliber to Otis.

What he taught them could come as a surprise. Elevator science was limited only by the public's want of education. This was, in part, an echo of Norton Otis' perception half a century earlier that the public had to learn to "think" elevators, which he carried into effect by traveling the country to teach potential customers the benefits of the elevator. But it was perhaps more strongly an echo of Charles Otis' exasperation with the one random and unpredictable factor in all his attempts to rationalize the business in the 1880s: human beings. Charles had fantasized about a productive machine; Lindquist dreamed of the perfect passenger, who would allow Otis to whisk him up higher and faster in an elevator than ordinary people could have believed possible.

Ordinary people, Lindquist lamented, were hopelessly governed by their prejudices. They were poor judges of what they needed, prone to feel more uncomfortable than they really were. "The development of the modern elevator," he taught, "is 10 percent technique and 90 percent psychology." Again and again, Lindquist's hard-won efforts to improve by various means the speed and reliability of the elevator, his attempts to clip journey times and response times and his innovations to save on shaft space were baffled by the reluctance of the traveling public and, speaking for them, the building contractors, to accept speeds greater than the 1,400-feet-per-minute standard accepted by the mid-1930s, or double-deckers, or even the principle of synchronized cars operating in a single hoistway.

The list of Otis' installations in the interwar years nonetheless reads like the roll call of architectural Americana.

Each new project seemed to call for new approaches from the engineering team. In 1921, thanks to setback codes, the Standard Oil Building could find room for only six gearless traction elevators, too few at current performance levels to make the building economically viable. The solution was to improve performance. Otis went back to a project it had undertaken three years earlier, when it devised efficiencies for a four-unit gearless elevator system to suit the capacity of an in-house power plant at the Astor Hotel in New York. The result was GMV, or Group Multi-Voltage control, which replaced the traditional DC-based method of controlling motor speed by altering resistance to the electrical circuit with a system of voltage regulation. This cut the consumption of power by more than half. From four steps of voltage, Lindquist soon began experimenting with 12: higher speeds, greater efficiency.

For Standard Oil, GMV was combined with push buttons in the cars and in the halls; a central relay control panel, which took calls and assigned them to the nearest car heading in the right direction; and a selector device on each elevator that organized starting, accelerating, slowing and stopping. The entire package was known as Signal Control, and Standard Oil thought it was magical—"absolutely human," according to the *New York Times*. But for the presence of an operator to close the doors, it was as automatic as any modern elevator; and because all the devices were housed in a central control room over the hoistway, it was easier to operate and maintain.

With power plants transferring to AC current, GMV became the even more sophisticated UMV, or Unit-Multi-Voltage Control, which offered reduced wear on moving parts and a smoother ride. Soon the main elevator machine could level each lift, doing away with the separate micro-leveling devices; electric doors replaced pneumatic; "collective control" automatic return features were installed for nighttime, when operators were off-duty; and elevators could even be made to stop automatically at a certain floor, such as the exit level from a store at closing time.

Hardest of all was organizing dispatch at peak traffic times. Otis' first effort was called Automatic Sequence Dispatching. Just after World War I the company introduced a timing device that released cars from terminal floors in numerical order. But if the first lift moved slowly from floor to floor, all the rest were held up behind it. In 1927, Otis stood the old solution on its head. Non-sequence Dispatching allowed any car to answer a call, which did save on waiting times. Cutting the wait, of course, was the paramount target: the sooner elevators answered a call, the higher the carrying capacity of the whole system over a given time.

Schedule Timing soon followed. The time intervals between cars leaving their terminal points could be varied to meet traffic conditions. Later, in 1933, Schedule Timing was replaced by Highest Return Call, a system that at last allowed elevators to reverse direction before they reached their terminals. All these represented incremental changes. Not until 1937 were the rules overturned and a new system introduced that eliminated the human starter's role altogether.

The Empire State Building can hardly be called typical for the period, but Lindquist's approach to the problems it raised was certainly typical of his methods. No doubt he was pleasantly surprised that New York agreed to revise its safety codes to allow speeds of up to 1,000 feet per minute from the old 700-feet-per-minute ordinance. It must have looked to him like a rare instance of engineering outwitting psychology, for it was entirely due to the automation of speed controls that the advance was possible, 700 feet per minute being the maximum speed that a human operator could safely control. Because the cars were laden with new technology, however, they weighed 3,500 pounds apiece, and this entailed an overhaul of the hoisting machine, better roping and improved safety features. As always, Lindquist moved methodically and experimentally from one adaptation to the next, testing and testing again.

While four buildings, of which the Empire State was only the last and largest, captured the New York headlines and skylines between 1929 and 1931, Otis did not neglect its commitment to less startling work. The medium-rise building continued to be the company's bread and butter, particularly as the idea of elevatoring reasonably low-rise buildings had already taken hold. Climbing the stairs began to look old hat, and even small towns wanted this status symbol of modernity as eagerly as their larger cousins. By the end of the 1920s, even geared elevators could come with UMV controls.

William Baldwin meanwhile viewed the business as an unbroken run of astonishing successes, not without reason. Looking about him in his later years, he saw a world that had borne out all of Charles' rosy predictions and bore testimony to his own Christian Science beliefs. America's economy in the 1920s had given almost everyone work to do. Recessions had been weathered and a war fought in Europe, and America was actually richer than ever before. Nearly everyone's income had spiked sharply upward in the 1920s. The things that people wanted had grown cheaper—cheaper food, attainable luxuries, mass-produced cars, radio sets, refrigerators. The country was no longer predominantly rural, and its people no longer had to struggle with the penalties of rural life, the poverty, the cold, the mind-numbing uncertainties of harvest and the weather. America was Babbitty, bourgeois, well-insulated. Baldwin himself had had something to do with all that.

The world looked to the United States with a mixture of envy and wonder. When Le Corbusier came to New York and made his famous remark that its skyscrapers were too small, the outrageousness of the joke was lost on his audience: everyone else came to New York to be dazzled, crowding the rails of the great transatlantic liners, whose interiors resembled the best Park Avenue hotels, and boggling at the promise of "bootleg gin and backseat sin," skyscraper canyons, tickertape, Tin Pan Alley and jazz—a black response to urbanization. Everyone knew America was immensely rich, a towering creditor among the nations, a refuge for foreign money which there would grow and grow, a breeding ground for tales of rags-to-riches. *The Indicator* in 1912 had poked gentle fun at the country that invented the elevator as "a sort of human skyrocket, [and] also produced the quick-lunch counter, the revolver and other time savers," but by the 1920s speed and efficiency were indelibly linked with the United States. The rest of the world was getting used to department stores, elevators, escalators, big hotels and office blocks, as to other manifestations of the American Way—cheap cars, telephones and refrigerators. Whatever America did today, domestic pundits liked to say, the world would do tomorrow.

On the economic front, at least, that much proved grimly true in the early 1930s. W. D. Baldwin, stepping onto one of those fine transatlantic liners in the spring of 1930, told reporters he was looking forward to "a prosperous year." Tightening conditions would be reversed, he felt sure, by an "easing of the money rates." Construction would bounce back. Construction always did.

After slowing during the World War I years, Otis' sales resumed their rapid growth. *See Appendix.*

Chapter 12

The Great Depression

IN 1926 THE *MAGAZINE OF WALL STREET* had taken a look at the prospects for Otis stock at $70 a share, and daringly observed that "straws which show the way the wind is blowing indicate that the peak will soon be reached and passed." That same year the new-housing market decelerated. The housing market was oversupplied.

When construction gets a cold, the saying goes, economies sneeze, but despite the downward trend in new construction, the years 1926, 1927, 1928 and 1929 were record ones for Otis. Nationwide, business still prospered, and Otis harvested the contracts. The year 1926 saw Ford's Tin Lizzie, the old Model-T, knocked from its number-one position by General Motors—and in the following year, while Ford was considering its response, Chrysler launched the first Plymouth. By 1929 the Detroit Big Three dwarfed U.S. Steel, the largest prewar corporation, and employed half a million people, turning out cars that were bought on the installment plan. The American dream of mobility seemed about to be realized; the American tide of consumerism seemed set to produce a cycle of prosperity. Baldwin was still addressing his stockholders bullishly in March 1930, when the company had more cash in hand than ever before, and was paying out generous dividends on stock. Three years after the *Magazine of Wall Street* had said its piece, Otis stock, which had moved steadily upward, stood at $450 a share.

Over the decade, Otis' real fortunes had soared. In 1922 the company employed about 8,000 people, but constant expansion had brought the figure to near 19,500 by 1929. Returns on common stock averaged $11.50 a share. Dividends on preferred churned out a regular 1.5 percent per quarter. When everyone in the company was paid, around half the annual profit remained to be reinvested in the business. A ten-year bond issue of $3.6 million in 1920 was to be Otis' last visit to the bond markets for almost half a century, and plant expansions, as well as the 1928 acquisition of two manufacturers of "accessories," were financed by earnings—$8.3 million in 1929 on turnover of $63.5 million.

But as Baldwin sailed away to his European vacation, neither the figures in America nor the actions of the money men supported his blithe assertion that construction would recover. Too much had been built in the 1920s: the real estate market was oversupplied, and the rate of population growth was falling.

Worst of all, the 1920s had not been quite the decade of dizzy prosperity that everyone recalled. Like many booms, it had been fueled by credit while interest rates were kept artificially low. Between 1919 and 1929, output per worker in the manufacturing sector rose 43 percent and capital investment increased by 6.4 percent a year. Enormous productive gains, however, had not been reflected in lower prices. Real wages had not risen. Workers ultimately found themselves unable to buy the alluring products they were turning out in ever-increasing volume.

Until 1928 stock prices matched industrial performance. After 1928 the relationship became significantly, then alarmingly, unstuck. No harm seemed to come of it, though, which was the problem. The dream of riches began to look solid, and many people believed that they had discovered a new law: money begetting money.

It came to an end on Black Thursday—October 24, 1929—when a record 12.9 million shares of stock were sold on Wall Street. A consortium of banks prevented wholesale collapse, but the first investor suicide occurred at the close of business that day. The weekend passed; on Monday trading grew more desperate as the day wore on. It was still the frothy, unsupported shares that were tumbling; but on Black Tuesday 650,000 shares of U.S. Steel, the bluest of blue chips, were shed in the first three minutes as people rushed for the liquidity they needed.

Pandemonium erupted. The brokers roared and clawed like beasts to sell, sell, sell. Radio collapsed. General Electric collapsed. Timkin Roller Bearing and Anaconda Copper collapsed. Mail order collapsed. Woolworth collapsed. Twice the amount of currency in circulation in the entire country at the time, $10 billion, was wiped off the Exchange by the close of business at 3 p.m. Some $50 billion was gone by the end of the month, and it seemed that the entire fabric of American business and industry had simply caught fire.

The Crash was institutionalized by the reaction of government. Individual enterprises, of course, consolidated their business, shedding staff and reducing the scale of their activity; but that was to be expected and did not necessarily betoken more than a brief recession. What was new was the scale of government reaction. Rather than let the downturn clear out unsound business, as Hoover's treasury secretary, Andrew Mellon, advised, Hoover "agreed to take on the business cycle and stamp it flat with all the resources of government."[32] The Federal Reserve pumped up credit in late October. Corporate America was forced to promise that wages would not be cut—Hoover still believed that high wages were the key to maintaining the boom. Taxes went down, spending went up, and when Hoover pressured the banks not to foreclose on bankrupts, people not unnaturally lost confidence in the banks.

The deflationary pressures ganged up. Depression spread to Europe, still recovering from World War I on the back of the U.S. economy, and washed back again; all parts of the world economy had become sensitive to the levers which, in the hands of relatively few experts, worked the machine. To most people in 1930, though, it came as a surprise. People were still being told to stand on their own two feet as months of deflation turned into years, and the nation, then the world, lurched into the Great Depression.

By 1930 the language of commerce was clipped, all business. No effort was made to characterize the business climate any longer, as none was needed; and no forecast was made at Otis, either. Instead, President Jesse Van Alstyne paid a solemn tribute to William Delaney Baldwin, who passed away on September 9, 1930: Baldwin's "many years of experience and intimate knowledge of the business, his broadmindedness and sound judgment, contributed to the signal and outstanding success he had achieved; and his indomitable yet kindly spirit was an inspiration to his associates."

But however much Baldwin was missed, he could have offered little by way of first-hand experience of the kind of downturn that was taking place. Unemployment in the United States stood at 1.5 million in 1929, at 5 million a year later, and at 13 million at the end of 1932. A huge new oilfield discovered in eastern Texas destroyed the price of oil. Montana wheat rotted in the fields. In Oregon, sheep were slaughtered on the hoof because farmers could no longer afford to feed or ship them. By 1932 the Red Cross was so stretched that it could afford to give each impoverished family only 75 cents a week, and Herbert Hoover was icily commemorated in the tarpaper Hoovervilles that sprang up around big cities, and by the Hoover blankets—newspapers—that their miserable denizens slept under at night. Banks went broke; speakeasies closed; veterans marched on the White House and were dispersed by tanks, guns and tear gas.

Otis did everything it could to protect its multi-talented staff from cutbacks, still hoping for an upswing that would call for their skills again. Managers pressed salary reductions, shorter work weeks and work-sharing agreements on employees to stave off massive job losses, but the upswing never materialized. Conditions in the country only grew worse. For a while the company was able to maintain itself with various monumental construction projects taken on before the Crash, but by 1933 even these had come to an end. There was simply no more work. The entire construction business had shrunk 90 percent. Major job losses occurred at Otis in 1935, across the board.

President Van Alstyne was certainly unlucky to come to the job when he did; yet temperamentally, he was just the man to manage seemingly endless decline, rather as Baldwin's exuberant faith had jibed with conditions of seemingly endless growth. Van Alstyne came from the same background as Elisha Otis: as a boy, he had lived and worked on a New York farm, and in 1889, at the age of 17, he took a job in canal construction, as foreman. "Different lines of engineering" brought him to Sprague, and then to Otis, once Sprague had been absorbed. He was one of the clever young men brought into central operations in the early part of the century. He possessed a kind of old Dutch phlegmatism, and without formal engineering training, he was known for his "unusual capacity for mastering details."

It can be argued that conservatives make the most effective radicals, that when they embrace change under pressure of events, their initial reluctance gives way to the greater determination. Van Alstyne's methods were painstaking and innately unshowy, but he managed Otis smoothly through an unprecedented era of contraction and oversaw a dramatic shift in the direction of Otis' business. Van Alstyne learned to recognize the benefits of long-term relationships in the market and to rate the solidity of service revenues over the mercurial satisfactions of pure sales.

The Depression taught him that. Sales slumped in 1930, the year he made his first report to shareholders, and in 1931 revenues fell by almost half. In 1933 the company registered its first book loss, a deficit repeated in 1934, though on a smaller scale. Almost half of Otis' 19,000 employees were laid off in the period, while Otis' common-stock dividends collapsed from $8 a share to 60 cents. Van Alstyne, as a new recruit remembered him, liked to play poker in smoke-filled rooms. He was very steady.

The Depression forced Otis to act out of character, and the experience scarred those who held their jobs almost as much as those who lost them. When Joe Mastroberte arrived at Otis as a mechanical engineer in 1926, he had rapidly learned that "Otis was like a family, and once you got in there and you kept your nose clean, why, you were one of the family." The history of Otis' labor relations bore out the impression that this was a remarkably happy family, too. There had been no strikes at all at the company before it incorporated in 1898, and only a handful in the field afterwards, before a strike by Yonkers machinists over pay and hours in 1910. This was a tiff, not a feud. Baldwin's paternalistic approach to the workforce showed that, on the whole, as he said, he liked to give good pay for good service. The International Union of Elevator Constructors, or IUEC, was formed at the beginning of the century, but Otis could afford to appear generous in response to union demands.

In 1921 the union and various elevator companies reached agreement on union recognition and collective bargaining. A wage formula was worked out to cover the entire country, with the exception of New York, where Local No. 1 insisted on pegging members' wages to those of the other city building trades. One reason for the amicable relations between union and employers can be found in the turf wars the union had to fight with other affiliates of the American Federation of Labor. For IUEC members were very broadly qualified. In the cramped space of an elevator shaft, where only two men could work at the same time, and where time was always of the essence, elevator workers had to master an astonishing range of skills. If they had to know how to wire an electrical machine, they had to know how to lay bricks, too, and the IUEC was forever fighting off attacks launched by the Machinists, the Plumbers and Steam Fitters, and even the International Brotherhood of Electrical Workers. More than most labor organizations, it recognized its own fortunes were heavily dependent on the viability of the industry as a whole. From 1922 until the depths of the Depression, with the AFL's consent, it extended its jurisdiction over the more militant ranks of elevator starters and operators, bringing stability to a notoriously volatile section of the industry.

The union's reasonable attitude seemed to justify the elevator manufacturers' willingness to recognize its right to collective bargaining. Otis itself made patently honest efforts to mitigate the effects of the Depression: management "tried to keep everyone on," as Joe Mastroberte recalled. This mutual understanding, amid the numbing realities of the downturn, saved both sides from entering into serious conflict as the program of staff reductions kicked in.

Otis gave the unions a further advantage. Van Alstyne was looking about for ways to cut costs during the recessionary years, but he never tried to address the traditional and expensive work practices that the IUEC maintained, in particular the union's insistence that all equipment be broken down at the factory and delivered to the installation site in pieces, for reassembly. If Otis men were jacks of all trades, that was one of the reasons why; and of course the union meant it to be so. Management chose to target other important but less thorny problems from the mid-1930s onward—estimating costs, accountancy, inventory controls. Management of the company's overseas operations was improved and streamlined. By the late 1930s, Otis had recovered at least the old operating ratios, if nothing like the old volume.

As for growth, it was due to come from a hitherto unsuspected direction.

The Great Depression didn't spare Otis, as the company experienced its first prolonged profit shortfall. The rebound came slowly in the pre-World War II years. *See Appendix.*

Chapter 13

Service

O TIS PUBLISHED A COMPANY-SPONSORED BOOK in 1936 which ordained a policy shift that circumstances had forced on its operations. The following anecdote served as introduction.

HOW WAS THE FIRST BRIDGE BUILT ACROSS THE NIAGARA?

First they flew a Kite across.

Next they attached a stronger cord to the kite string and pulled that over.

Then in turn they pulled over a light rope, a heavier rope, and finally a wire cable. After that the real work began.

This book came about in much the same way.

First we collected all the available Maintenance data. Next we wrote a summary of the subject. Then a salesman asked for a carbon copy, a Zone Service Manager asked for a number of copies, and finally it was decided to print the entire story.

After that...well, here it is—the when, what and why of Otis Maintenance....

"This book" was *The Maintaineer,* published in a snappy, black-jacketed volume. Its title was avowedly heroic—something between musketeer and mountaineer—and it was also very apt, for the secrets that *The Maintaineer* dispensed, and the business it represented, really did maintain the Otis Elevator Company through the Depression and into the decades beyond.

The idea that Otis might have anything to do with its elevators after they were built and installed had been a long time coming. Charles Otis seemed to have had an inkling of it back in 1861, when he contracted with a storekeeper "to assume the entire charge and responsibility connected with the care of Hoisting Machinery now being erected in your store... for one year... for the sum of Seven Hundred and Eighty Dollars ($780.00) to be paid in equal monthly payments." But strangely, this entirely logical and intrinsically profitable development was a one-time arrangement.

For the next quarter-century, Otis confined its after-sales service to the provision of spare parts. Public demand for some sort of safety inspections led to Otis' forming its own inspectorate in New York in 1885, but the job really needed to be carried out by an independent body to satisfy public building officials and insurance firms. After a vigorous campaign waged by the newspapers, municipalities and states issued their own codes and sent out their own inspectors.

Otis inspectors, however, still found themselves busy. In the 1890s, as electric elevators grew popular, Otis began to sell routine "inspections and reports" so that customers could plan for replacements ahead of breakdowns. The busier, more complicated installations required inspections weekly, while far-flung cities received an inspector perhaps once a year. "This inspection service had one drawback," as *The Maintaineer* put it. "All that the Otis inspector ever brought the owner was bad news." He diagnosed faults, then walked away. On top of that, he charged for the visit. Owners felt they were paying twice.

In 1915, Otis figuratively flew its kite across the Niagara, adding adjustment, lubrication and small parts replacement to the inspector's job. These POG (parts, oil and grease) contracts were far more popular and became even more so when they were extended to include callbacks in the event of a failure, making Otis visibly responsible for the quality of its own inspections. For this visibility, as it were, contracts were sold at a higher price—"and the contracts sold better!" (*The Maintaineer*).

The popularity of these contracts did not last: as soon as a major repair was called for, Otis billed the customer, who tended to think that Otis should have prevented any need for major repair. According to *The Maintaineer,* it was the customer who then "went one step farther. He demanded a contract service that would relieve him of any but a fixed monthly expense."

The author of *The Maintaineer* was not, as it happened, an unassuming scribe. Cecil Jackson almost single-handedly launched Otis' maintenance business, although he appeared so unusually self-effacing in *The Maintaineer* as to be unrecognizable. To Jackson nevertheless was owed the tone of remorseless logic that underpins the entire narrative. When Jackson wrote that the customer went one step further, he really meant that Otis did; and if he meant Otis, he really meant Cecil Jackson.

Sometime during the First World War, Jackson had been a commission agent for the company in Springfield, Illinois. This was the city whose plans for a 100-foot height limit had drawn the scorn of the *New York Times* a few years earlier. But Springfield was actually a burgeoning market for elevators, and Jackson was a consummate salesman. When he heard customers complain about the costs of repairs and the slow response of Chicago repairmen, he saw an opportunity.

"I'm the only guy in town who can take care of your equipment," he announced, and so successfully did he gather up Springfield's service accounts that his policy reached the notice of the Chicago Zone managers. They decided to take the program on themselves, on an experimental basis, and brought in Cecil Jackson to run it. Once he was a member of the corporate staff, Jackson never left. The experiment was not allowed to end.

To build up the business, Jackson had to take an actuary's look at almost every piece of equipment Otis had ever produced. One well-known Otis story concerned an elevator shipped to Cuba, whose operator solemnly informed a curious Otis employee that "oil was shipped with the elevator some eight years ago, and that so far as he knew no oil had been used since." Jackson had to work with averages. "No one seemed to know whether a worm and gear lasted five years or 20," he recalled. "Armatures for the same motors apparently needed replacing every eight years, 15 years, or never. Ropes were easier. Anyone could guess rope life and not be more than 50 percent off."

To assess the averages, Otis Maintenance was sent out cautiously across several regions to speed up the production of useful data. About 500 customers with traditionally high repair bills were offered "POG service, plus major repairs, at a fixed monthly sum." Sometimes, Jackson sweetly said, their costs dropped. But lower repair costs were secondary to the convenience when trouble got dealt with in advance, and the budgeting was simple. Jackson's system, such as it was, appeared to work, and when at last, in 1924, the figures were in place for a wide variety of machines, Maintenance got the go-ahead to launch itself nationwide. By the end of 1925 some 1,407 elevators were under Maintenance contracts in North America.*

Jackson probably already thought of himself and his men as Maintaineers, buccaneering types blazing their way through the static traditionalism of a mature corporation. But the real challenge for Jackson was to sustain Maintenance in the face of company indifference, not to mention hostility. His department was *very* small potatoes. At best, Maintenance was the garnish on a dish called Service, which most people in the business had learned to avoid. Service's demand for engineers to take repair calls irritated elevator construction managers as much as Service's demand for money had once irritated customers. Elevator salesmen had a specific complaint against Jackson and his Maintaineers, too: Jackson's outfit could claim an average revenue of $300,000 a year between 1921 and 1927, while sales accounted for $41 million. Yet here was Jackson busily letting every Otis customer know that his lift was going to cost him between $25 and $40 a month for the rest of its working life.

To make matters worse, Jackson was flashy; he seldom allowed facts to stand in his way when he had a proposition to make. Years later a future Otis CEO, Ralph Weller, remembered that "Cecil would go around on all the large maintenance contracts, also go into the local offices preaching his message. And he had the same habit as a lot of old-time contractors, writing with a stub of a pencil, and making all kinds of notes, here, there and the other place." An old-timer had told Weller that his first job at Otis "was to pick up all of Jackson's notes, because he'd

---

* There is a persistent rumor abroad that Otis' first maintenance contracts were devised in France. Given that Jackson had to work on a large scale to achieve the averages he needed to formulate prices, this seems unlikely; but with France and Otis, anything is possible.

add up numbers and prove that you couldn't afford to do it any other way, and his arithmetic was very convenient at best and maybe just bad arithmetic. So I picked up all those papers so nobody could get them, and destroyed them."

Bad arithmetic or just convenient–Jackson was always promising new figures, arguing for time, working the sums. He launched his creative presentations on doubting colleagues as often as on clients. Both, it seems, were faintly bamboozled in the years he was building up an indispensable raft of cost data, "which could be tabulated by classes and analyzed from an actuarial standpoint." Whether the data were valid or not, Jackson's hunch seemed to be paying off. The Service Department promptly clothed itself in the garb of corporate respectability by setting up a network of national service districts under centralized control, so that at the very least it looked less like an operation that flew by the seat of its pants. The department started to issue schedules for routine inspections. It formulated programs of mechanical and electrical adjustments. It set standards, at the very least, of cleanliness. Jackson was empire-building.

Jackson's diplomatic talent can be seen at work in a single paragraph in *The Maintaineer,* written in 1936 when Maintenance had proved itself, at long last, as one of the mainstays of the business in a depression: "Possibly because more new elevators were being sold than ever before," he wrote of the year 1929–30, "possibly because of the rapid development of automatic control, possibly because of increased quality of Maintenance–most likely because of all three–Maintenance contracts increased to 9,227 in 1929, and to 10,081 at the close of 1930."

Much as they might resent or mistrust Jackson, who could object to this description? Not the salesmen; not the technical crowd, their ranks anyway decimated by events of the early 1930s. Everyone was generously allowed to have contributed to his department's success. And Jackson in 1936 had a message for them, as they faced up to a world in which all their business had withered on the vine.

"Oh yes, the depression...," he wrote. "To get off to a flying start, a recount showed that we had about 400 less elevators under maintenance than our records had previously indicated." We may imagine the grim smiles this recount produced: Jackson had fiddled the figures again. No doubt he had been made to look a fool, or worse. But here he was, five years after the event, taking the bull by the horns and actually making it work for him. "Then came 1932, perhaps the worst year that real estate activity has ever seen. Maintenance cancellations approximated 1,500. But over 1,000 new contracts were sold, and the total billing dropped off only 2 percent from the peak! Almost all cancellations affected small machines in small speculative buildings where existing ownership could not survive, while larger buildings with large machines retained or increased their service—more impressed than ever with the desirability or necessity of Otis Maintenance."

Jackson was alluding to a debate about pricing that had raged in the face of the worst depression anyone had ever known. Full Maintenance sold at a premium, in return for the promise of quality service. In a depression, some argued, prices should drop to stimulate demand. As the 1,500 cancellations of 1932 rolled in, this argument must have gathered strength. Rival operators, after all, were prepared to take over Otis' maintenance contracts at substantially lower prices. Desperate pricing was in the air.

Jackson's team foresaw another outcome. Lowering prices, they argued, would lower the quality of service. If anything, costs should rise, and with them the standards of maintenance. And they were right. When times were hard it was something to be able to say that the elevators ran well. People were prepared to pay for credible maintenance—for at least one link, perhaps, to the good times when the elevator had been commissioned, for some certainty in a crazy world. Meanwhile, many building owners were doing without janitors to save money, and needed someone to keep an eye on the elevator. As for Jackson's Maintaineers, they knew they were lucky to have a job at all, and if this did not make them go the extra mile for their clients, Jackson's training served to remind them. He told his people how to sell a deal, and how to answer the more familiar objections to the Maintenance package. But once they were in there, once the job was theirs, he taught them to make a total commitment to quality and reliability, and give the customer what he wanted.

The postscript to Jackson's little history in *The Maintaineer* was illustrated by a diagrammatic worker striking a test-your-strength machine with a sledgehammer and ringing up the figure 11,347—the number of contracts out, "at least a thousand more than we had at the previous peak. You can tell a great deal about a product or service by watching how it is affected by adverse times. Any service that can ride through six lean years and come out better than it started—*that service had to be good!*"

Nervous, punchy, all sales, Jackson had managed to work his division from the ugly sister into Otis' fairy godmother. The company's annual reports began commenting on the performance of Maintenance in 1932, the year the value of service bookings first outstripped the value of escalator and elevator sales combined. The company continued to earn more from its Service Department than from new sales until 1946.

Not all Service work was Jackson's Maintenance: indeed, the major portion came in the form of Modernization, and it was the Modernization Department that kept the factories and fieldworkers busy through the Depression. Modernization sold in hard times just as Maintenance did, as the real estate market discovered that buildings could be refurbished effectively far more cheaply than they could be replaced. As Otis declared in 1934, "The Company's Modernization Service is helping to solve the obsolescence problems of building owners in this and foreign countries. Because of the sound manner in which the Company's products are designed and manufactured, the older types of Otis elevators can usually be modernized to today's standards.... Otis Modernization has aided in solving rental problems, and in maintaining or increasing occupancy." This was a brave boast in the midst of the Great Depression, but it was certainly true that old hydraulic machines could be scrapped in favor of electric models, while electric elevators could be upgraded for automatic controls and smoother rides. They could be brought up-to-date aesthetically, too, and all without losing much of the old framework or machinery.

Indeed, with new sales devastated (bookings in 1932 were a bare 8 percent of the peak figure for 1929), the whole concept of new and old was undergoing a revision. In 1934, Otis Vice President J. C. Knapp publicly tore into the assumption that buildings were deteriorating investments, like "a horse or a suit of clothes." This, he said, was "a fantastic notion," adding: "We have been growing so fast, and have become so accustomed to seeing old buildings pulled down and then replaced by newer ones, that we take the attitude that this pulling down and building-up process is an evidence of American progress. My own belief is that it is not any evidence of progress at all; it is merely an evidence of instability...."

Knapp was being too gloomy when he predicted that the American demand for new buildings would soon fall to European levels—a significant reversal of the rhetoric of the 1920s, when everyone seemed set to follow America's lead. But all through the 1930s, and well into World War II, the value of updating and maintaining Otis elevators eclipsed new sales. In straitened circumstances, Otis seemed to have found the solution to Charles Otis' complaint that the elevator industry was a rollercoaster of boom and bust, and solved a problem that affected almost every other industry in the world. Gradually the sheer reliability of service contract revenues began to alter attitudes toward new sales. A fresh sale came to be regarded as a means to a maintenance contract: that was the prize, and the sale price could be adjusted to reflect the fact.

Yet in some indefinable sense, service remained the country cousin; for elegance, glamour and fast-track promotions, new sales was still the business to be in. As Al Saxer, the head of Modernization, recalled, "Selling a new automobile is a prestigious position, but working on it to repair it is not, and that has spilled over into Otis." As far back as the early 1900s, while mechanics peddled oil and grease, the salesmen of Chicago, at least, went about in shiny top hats and silk scarves.

When Jackson wrote *The Maintaineer* in 1936, the Great Depression was by no means over in real terms. But the government had waded in at last, and the New Deal was beginning to alter the psychology of a country shocked by the depths into which it had fallen. At Otis, those who had survived at least knew they were the survivors, and not merely tomorrow's victims. After several years of enforced idleness, uncertainty and near despair, hard work seemed likely to bring results again. That was the message of *The Hub,* a little journal put out by the Chicago Zone at the end of the decade.

PEP IT UP. IT'S 1939!

And nobody complained.

Endnotes (Part One)

1   Ref. 'Because of Iron'

2   *The Annals of Vertical Transportation,* Donald Shannon, February 15, 1869

3   *The Annals of Vertical Transportation,* Donald Shannon, August 4, 1882

4   President's Report to the Board of Trustees, 1887, Otis Archives

5   W. E. Hale to Charles R. Otis, February 18, 1888, Otis Archives

6   W. E. Hale to Charles R. Otis, March 5, 1888, Otis Archives

7   W. E. Hale to Charles R. Otis, March 23, 1888, Otis Archives

8   President's Report to Board of Trustees, New York, November 14, 1888, Otis Archives

9   Ibid., November 14, 1888

10 Charles R. Otis to W. D. Baldwin, July 17, 1889, Otis Archives

11 J. M. Short to Otis Brothers & Co, July 13, 1867, and July 20, 1867, Otis Archives

12 W. Frank Hall, Interview in Pall Mall Gazette, quotes in "The Engineering and Building Record and the Sanitary Engineer," May 25, 1889, Vol. 19, p. 345, taken from *Elevator Systems of the Eiffel Tower 1889* by Robert M. Vogel

13 United States National Museum Bulletin, 228, Washington, D.C., 1961

14 W. E. Hale to Charles R. Otis, March 3, 1888, Shannon Files, Otis Archives

15 President's Report to Stockholders, February 14, 1889

16 W. D. Baldwin to Charles R. Otis, London, November 20, 1889, Otis Archives

17 Charles R. Otis to Stockholders, February 14, 1889, Otis Archives

18 Ibid., February 13, 1890

19 Affidavit by R. J. Davies, U.S. and Otis Elevator Co. et. al, 1906, Otis Archives

20 "After the Elevator Trust," *The New York Sun,* in circular No. 2, April 10, 1906, Shannon Files, Otis Archives

21 "Statement of Facts, Number 9 by the A. B. See Manufacturing Company, Relating to the Suit Brought by Otis Brothers & Co.," Alonzo B. See and Walker L. Tyler, June 10, 1896, copy in Wilkie, Farr legal files, in Shannon Files, Otis Archives

22 "Circular No. 2," Shannon Files: Alonzo B. See, "A Copy of a Letter Sent to a Director of the Otis Elevator Company," November 22, 1924, Otis Archives

23 "The Fraser Elevator" article in the *Otis Bulletin,* January 1948, pp. 7–9

24 Thomas E. Brown, "Notes for History of Otis Elevator Company" typescript, Shannon Files, Otis Archives

25 "King's Dream of New York" by Harry M. Pettit, in *King's Views of New York,* 1908–09

26 *Secrets of the Temple* by William Greider, 1987

27 Letter, opinion of counsel, April 1906, in Wilkie, Farr legal files (see endnote 21)

28 *Otis Bulletin,* June–July 1950, pp. 20–21

29 *The Indicator,* Vol. 2, No. 7, July 1909, p. 52

30 For much of the information here and later on I am indebted to Steven Fossoy's Historical report No. 49, Carrier and Otis in Japan, 1891–1979

31 Otis Elevator Company, "Unusual Experiences in Designing Machine Elements: an Interview with David Lindquist," *Product Engineering,* reprint 1931

32 *A History of the American People,* Paul Johnson (Weiderfeld & Nicolson, 1997), p. 617

Part Two

Chapter 14

⟨I⟩

International

WHILE THE OTIS ELEVATOR COMPANY in America contended with the wreck of the Depression, in much of the rest of the world it was still seeking to recover from the economic and political fallout of World War I.

Not that the company ever admitted as much, at least before the reforms to its overseas business that Van Alstyne introduced in 1934. Otis' overseas ventures followed a pattern, more than a policy–a pattern that unfolded only gradually as a result of the determination expressed by Charles Otis as early as the 1880s that Otis should seek to become the standard of the world. Not until the end of World War II did Otis view its foreign operations as anything more than an insurance policy, a hedge against hard times at home.

True, Otis had lodged serious bids for supremacy in England and Germany immediately before the war broke out in August 1914, and had devised the beginnings, at least, of a strategy that would bring France, Spain and the Austro-Hungarian Empire up to the Standard of the World. But it looked more like policy in retrospect. At the time, it seemed to be brought about by ad hoc responses to pressure, usually on the ground, for Otis to boost the fortunes of its local representatives.

Whatever coherence the strategy appeared to possess was in any event shattered when the European nations fell to fighting. After a few months their economies were placed on a war footing as the demands of this new, "total" war, unimaginably costly in terms of life, began to register.

On either side of the struggle, Otis factories were effectively requisitioned by the military. Waygood in Britain turned to making guns and shells. In France one Pifre factory retooled for the production of artillery shells; the other was bombed out. In Germany, where the war aims of the economy were realized most efficiently, Otis' brand new factory in Berlin became first a producer of war materiel and then, of course, an enemy target once the United States, suffering from German U-boat raids in the North Atlantic, was drawn conclusively into the war in 1917.

The year 1917 was the year of the Russian Revolution, which, by removing Russia from the war, allowed Germany to make a final burst through the defenses of the Allies in France. When this was checked and reversed, with the aid of 2 million U.S. soldiers, Germany and Austria sued for peace. An Armistice was signed, and President Woodrow Wilson arrived in Europe to rearrange the map.

"The lights have gone out all over Europe," Britain's Foreign Secretary, Lord Grey, had said when the war broke out; in its aftermath they glittered only fitfully back to life. Postwar Europe was quite unlike the Europe that had gone before.

In Russia the Bolshevik Revolution gradually lowered the curtain and, as far as the rest of the world was concerned, dimmed the lights for the next 70 years. This was a pity for Otis, which had actually established offices in Moscow and St. Petersburg in 1915. Another go-go American firm, Singer, had ordered Otis machines for its headquarters in St. Petersburg, which were blessed by priests on their inauguration in 1904. More blessed still were the Kremlin elevators, one of which—a standard No 1K electric machine—reposed in the tsar's private apartments.

When in November 1917 the Bolsheviks took power and repudiated all former contracts, Otis and International Harvester were the only two American manufacturers capitalized in Russia—Singer was listed as a trading company—and Otis consequently lost $274,000, a claim the company was still pursuing in 1958.

But Otis' approach to Soviet Russia remained phlegmatic. It advertised in certain specialist journals in the late 1920s and early 1930s, and at the same time installed 30 skip-and-bell hoists, several in Stalin's brave new city of Magnitogorsk, others in Kuznetsk, which was soon renamed Stalinsk. During World War II the U.S. Treasury sent more of these to Russia under Lend-Lease. They were the biggest machines Otis made during the war.

Meanwhile, the end of World War I had brought half a dozen new nations into being, but circumstances ensured that they remained bitterly poor. For the defeated nations, the bitterness was compounded by territorial losses not contemplated when the Armistice was brokered but inflicted in the treaty negotiations that followed (when wiser leaders, Wilson in particular, were recklessly outmaneuvered) and institutionalized by the staggering reparations that the victors demanded. The scale of the disaster—the sheer destruction of European wealth—is perhaps best illustrated by the fact that Britain, a nominal victor in the struggle and by far the most robust participant at war's end, had converted its total U.S. investments of $3 billion into a debt of the same amount.

To pay their debts, Britain and France relied on the war reparations from Germany. Ultimately, thanks to an American fad for investing dollars in Germany, they were enabled to begin repayments with "German dollars." It was this high-strung, four-cornered operation that came disastrously unstuck when Wall Street crashed in 1929. Britain (and her Empire) was forced off the gold standard, but in Germany and other countries the effects were notoriously far worse.

In the 1920s, meanwhile, Otis had sought ways to adapt to the new circumstances. London had not suffered much physical damage in the war, and Waygood-Otis soon resumed normal service, selling a considerable number of lifts not only at home but also throughout the Empire, where a manufacturing plant was at last re-established in Australia after a gap of 30 years. Britain's position as a financial center, an imperial power and a major industrial nation ensured a steady demand for elevators, but its low-wage economy ensured that the 1920s were bleak for employees.

In France the little Pifre concern had to cope with the destruction of its factory at Albert, the reconversion of a factory at Bezons and the lack of any genuine demand for elevators caused partly by the generally slow recovery and partly by the French resistance to big business. The big government contracts invariably went to "French" firms, and 90 percent of Pifre's sales were to small apartment buildings, which wanted only cheap, no-frills machines.

Germany, racked by the costs of war and defeat, was a hyper-inflationary basket case; Belgium was a decent small market; Italy, though poor, was inescapably stylish. Since its unification in 1871, it had experienced rapid but uneven industrialization, and a German engineer, Augusto Stigler, who had made the first elevator in the country for the Costanzi Hotel in Rome, had effectively captured the elevator market in that country. He exported to Eastern Europe and South America, and by the 1920s his company had made more than 20,000 elevators and moved into mass production.

This bright spot in the general Continental catalog of gloom naturally attracted Otis' attention, not least because under the founder's son, Stigler's products had become both racy and successful. Stigler made elevators of glass. It made inclined elevators—a technology Otis rather liked to think was its own. Its electric elevators were powered by compact driving units that combined all the electro-mechanical gears together, a solution as neat as it was unusual. Even today the quality of Italian engineers is matched only by the effervescence of Italian style. In the 1920s the effervescence of its politics was solved by Mussolini, but Stigler was hampered by the patchy progress of industry. Vigorously looking for foreign markets, Stigler, or his name, was almost as well-known in Europe as Otis.

Otis struck where Stigler was weak: at his base. In 1921, Otis Ascensorie Montecarichi (escalators) was incorporated with the grand capital of 1 million lira, worth exactly $48,498. It was a sum that allowed the company—without taking profits—to have fun at Stigler's expense, doubling its capitalization in 1923 and again in 1927, as Stigler was forced to react to the challenge to its small home market.

It remained a peculiar market, too. Fierce local patriotism in a country united only 50 years earlier, and the Italian flair for small engineering operations, made Italy a collection of local markets still. It was very hard for centralized producers to penetrate distant communities with their own personnel, so they relied on local "concessionaires" to perform most of their installation and maintenance. Otis was at a disadvantage, being doubly foreign. Meanwhile, in the 1930s, a manufacturing company called Sabiem expanded into elevators and used its close ties to the

Mussolini government to batter Stigler into financial difficulties. Then Mussolini invaded Ethiopia, and the League of Nations imposed sanctions, which, cutting Italy off from supplies of copper, tin and nickel, forced the country to develop its own aluminum industry. This soon set a distinctive Italian taste: Sabiem was the first company to make elegant aluminum panels with no visible fastenings for the cabins and fronts, which became general in the country after World War II.

Mussolini's fascism demanded a mix of private (corporate) enterprise and government supervision. Stigler, Otis and Sabiem were swept into a cartel in 1938, the first time Otis' operations in Italy began to show profits, on the back of an allocated market share of 22.1 percent. The cartel restored Stigler's fortunes, under the ownership of the Meridiolani Railway Company, but a year later, Italy was at war.

The picture for Otis outside Europe was far rosier in the interwar years, and economic growth in Argentina, South Africa and Australia more nearly reflected conditions in America. Waygood-Otis' sales network across the British Empire was unrivaled, and the company remained determined to export. In Australia, Waygood began to revive and consolidate the various agents and local elevator firms that had been handling its business since the 1890s, when its first investment in the country collapsed. So internecine had those arrangements been that Waygood-Otis in Sydney competed with the firm of Johns and Waygood and the firm Standard Waygood. It was all rather confusing.

Australia had suffered many casualties in the war, but with the return of peace it could offer a standard of living that far outstripped anything England had to offer. It must have been something of an experience for Waygood personnel to leave the dank, Dickensian headquarters of the company in the Falmouth Road for Australian sunshine and optimism. Australian cities were splendidly laid out and had more than their fair share of civic institutions—parks and museums, libraries and court houses—while none of them was very large. By 1923, Waygood had set up a manufacturing facility in Sydney, from where it could ship its best products instead of the "primitive machines" it had been sending from the United Kingdom.

Management took a while to shake down, and building inspectors, as well as the public, took some convincing of the virtues of gearless machines. In 1923 the company had to run trip and "full-load" tests for the benefit of inspectors to secure its first gearless order in Sydney. "Everybody was waiting for the test to begin," H. C. Bradbrook, the first Waygood-Otis managing director in Australia, wrote. We "borrowed an inspector's watch, placed it on top of the oil buffer in the pit, and then ordered the drop test to commence. The inspector's face, as the car fell, was a picture. Of course we Otis people were relieved when the safety acted normally...."

The 1920s saw rapid development in Australia. Immigration soared; construction boomed; hydroelectric plants were built; Carnegie steel was driven out by a domestic producer; railways and bridges were erected; and Ford began to manufacture automobiles. In 1926, Waygood-Otis installed 28 gearless lifts in a Sydney department store, and 12 of them grouped together formed the largest elevator bank in the British Empire. As for the Depression, the country's first escalators were installed in Melbourne in 1932, and crowds poured in for weeks to give them a go.

Escalators were to dominate the market in another Pacific country, Japan, for reasons of safety. Japan was earthquake country. It had emerged from World War I as one of the Big Five victor nations, and by 1927, Otis' business prospects there looked so encouraging that the old agency agreement with American Trading was torn up and Otis allied with the Mitsui Trading Company to run branch offices throughout Japan and its new empire. Mitsui was one of the great Zaibatsu houses, one of those vast, family-dominated financial and industrial conglomerates that had done the heavy lifting in the Meiji period and now had a commanding role in the Japanese economy. Quite apart from Mitsui's financial strength, the Zaibatsu's cultural influence in the market made the tie-in look better to Otis than reliance on another American firm. The Japanese liked to buy from their own.

Competition was rising, not only from American rivals like A. B. See, Houghton, Warner and Wadsworth, but also from domestic rivals. By allying with Mitsui, Otis was introduced throughout Mitsui's interlocking business interests, Mitsui taking 40 percent of the net profit and 0.5 percent of sales. The elevators were imported from the States.

No doubt this situation would have changed even without the powerful pressure that the Japanese authorities brought to bear on imports in order to encourage domestic manufactures. In 1930 a long-serving Otis official, Charles Grandgerard, New York's export manager,* was sent to Tokyo as Far Eastern manager, initially to organize the Toyo-Otis manufacturing joint venture with Mitsui. "Eastern Seas Good Elevator" was 60 percent Otis-owned, and once the factory had been built in the Kamata district of Tokyo only special orders were executed in America. Toyo-Otis moved to capture 40 percent of the elevator business in Japan and its dependencies.

Nevertheless, the details of the Mitsui deal were less impressive than first appeared: Otis provided 60 percent of the capital, and all the design and production expertise, but codicils in the contract gave Mitsui effective control over policy. Edward Sims, Otis' legal counsel in Japan, gave Grandgerard a warning that Mitsui might well simply take over Otis' technology for its own sake. Grandgerard didn't think so.

Grandgerard's confidence seemed well placed when, after a few short years, Mitsui's sales force had bolstered Toyo-Otis' new equipment revenues ninefold and its service revenues by six, and turned net losses of almost $30,000 into profits of $102,862. In 1937 the company began paying dividends to Otis Maine, the holding company which, for tax reasons, parented most of Otis' foreign enterprises.

But Otis' happy commercial trajectory in Japan began gradually to encounter political difficulties. From the end of World War I, Japan had been moving to the right, with an authoritarian government at home, aggressive imperialism abroad and rising militarism. America's desire to maintain the status quo in China increasingly clashed with Japan's perceived need for Chinese raw materials, labor and perhaps adventure. So while America and Japan grew ever more distant, Toyo-Otis was forced into further cooperation with the Japanese authorities to keep up its supply of preferential contracts.

Grandgerard was still at the helm as managing director of Toyo-Otis, where he worked with an all-Japanese staff save for a chief manufacturing technician and an office manager, whose role was to keep Toyo-Otis' practices in line with New York's. His position in Japan fitted in fairly

---

* He began work in New York as a translator in 1907, made his first foreign trip to Puerto Rico in 1918 and subsequently visited every major Otis office in the world.

comfortably with the Japanese outlook on the western Pacific: from Japan, Grandgerard acted as manager of the Far Eastern Region, set up in 1930, which included Otis offices in Shanghai, Hong Kong, Manila and Singapore. He held court in Tokyo, and in 10 years succeeded in becoming "very Japanese." He spoke the language fluently, and–a rare honor for a foreigner–was inducted into the exclusive Hodogaya Golf Club, where he cultivated important friendships with Japanese company presidents. Not surprisingly, he became protective of "the Japanese Way" of doing business: indeed, from the Japanese point of view, the baffled awe with which foreigners held "the Japanese Way" was one of its major side benefits. The more it eluded them, the more nervously they bowed to it. A brief Japanese history of the Otis company quotes, with every sign of approval, Grandgerard's own confession, back in 1932:

> *I don't think I can do the Japanese management style because I don't know much about it. For example, I don't know how to manage the welfare for the employees in the Japanese style. Therefore, I would like to make it up by paying more salary than the other Japanese companies. I am thinking to pay twice as much.*

Of course, there was an element of shrewdness in Grandgerard's policy, but it was underscored to a degree by what modern commentators call cultural cringe. Overall, Grandgerard's efforts to keep Toyo-Otis in line with the "Japanese Way" did unfortunately mean keeping in with the militarists who were currently defining it, and some of his commercial decisions caused disquiet among Waygood-Otis colleagues in Hong Kong and Singapore.

In any case it proved a waste of effort. In 1937, Japan began a war of annihilation in China. Wartime rationing and anti-Western feeling made Toyo-Otis' position untenable. Taxes rose; men were conscripted; production was diverted to army needs. The entire venture from 1930 to 1941 proved an enormous waste of funds–the cost of simply training joint-venture employees exceeded all the dividends received by the parent company in America. The last American ship to leave Japan before Pearl Harbor carried Charles Grandgerard back to New York, a decade's work in shreds.

Otis' foreign policy received little oversight in the 1920s as long as a boom lasted in the United States. The company continued to enter any foreign market that showed a demand for elevators. Usually it moved in by first appointing an agent to handle orders; only if the business grew large enough would it then open an office and in rare instances begin manufacturing. Otis' principal aim—which has scarcely changed over the century—was to be recognized worldwide and to have a presence in every market that seemed likely to develop toward American norms. Before World War II, Otis never pulled out of any country for economic reasons.

This is all the more remarkable given the poor performance record of many of Otis' overseas operations. Enterprises that turned a profit were seldom able to contribute to Otis' bottom line, because in the uncertain economic climate earnings abroad were difficult to repatriate. On the whole, it was hard for the parent company to understand what was going on abroad. Since 1907 a Foreign Department had shared offices and staff with the New York Domestic Sales Department. Not until the early 1920s were two divisions established, one—the Foreign Department—to oversee South America and the Far East, the other everything else. The latter department, significantly, never had a name. The two departments reported separately to an Operating Board of the company's senior executives.

By the late 1920s, Otis' operations on the continent of Europe were losing money so badly that a vice president was moved to Paris, where he set up a third headquarters. His work improved results but, as William Reid, a vice president, recalled, "with the growth of the elevator business throughout the world, our foreign operations were no longer a simple sales problem but represented a sizable octopus with three separate bodies. No one person knew or even saw the entire picture. Conflicting policies could not be avoided and overall planning for development purposes was impossible without a single operating head."[1]

Reid was simplifying for the benefit of his audience when he spoke of only three bodies without a head. Managers of local Otis offices, or even factories, had complete control over their own activities. Roving managers were sent from New York to transact deals abroad, but they, too, enjoyed enormous freedom, and could report to New York as much or as little as they wished. While the scale of foreign operations remained small, this seemed a reasonable state of affairs, and the business could be run on trust. Baldwin, typically, considered putting all foreign operations under a single subsidiary, Otis International, in 1925, but it never happened.

The problem of accountability received no further attention until the crisis of the Depression forced Otis to look more carefully at its foreign dealings. Who was doing the business? What deals were being struck? What sort of machinery was being sold, and where did the money go? As the Depression became worldwide, governments threw up a bewildering variety of currency controls, barter agreements and market share allocations. Was Otis exploiting its opportunities fully?

The new, centralized International Division that Van Alstyne established at Otis in 1934 was a product of the "new management." Otis' overseas empire had grown as traditional empires always did, by piecemeal additions, by a desire to satisfy demand and through the energy of local empire builders—Grandgerard in Tokyo fitted the mold. It would have been hard for Otis not to have developed considerable foreign holdings: it was the world's best, richest, perhaps most reliable elevator company, and the famous remark made to explain Britain's Indian empire—acquired "in a fit of absent-mindedness"—applied to Otis, too.

By the 1930s, Otis not only needed to ensure greater accountability; it also had the power to do it. Modern telephone communications had wired the globe. The transatlantic crossing had been whittled down from seven days in 1900 to a bare three aboard one of the elegant liners of the 1920s. When the new head of the International Division sent Leversee Lansing Van Schoonhoven to find out what was going on in Rio in 1936, Van Schoonhoven spent only two days getting there, in a fragile splint of an aircraft. Once he had arrived, he could discuss his discoveries with Fred Town on the telephone, 2,000 miles away.

So Otis acquired the mantle of the multinational corporation long before it became the American norm. Van Schoonhoven himself never looked back, and when he retired 30 years later he had circled the globe many times as Otis' chief sales officer for international operations. At the time, he was grateful simply to escape the tedium of domestic sales.

The International Division was not an immediate, flying success. Fred Town, picked to head it by Van Alstyne, may have been overpromoted; contemporaries remember him as a sinecurist who liked to travel the world in a haze of cigar smoke punctuated by visits to foreign golf courses. In New York, Van Schoonhoven recalled, Town was careful never to let his superiors see him take lunch, and would "fly like a bullet" upstairs to the chairman's office when a summons came. But the agreeable atmosphere of International attracted talented men, and Percy Douglas, Henry P. Douglas' son, established a small office on Eleventh Avenue, surrounding himself with a small staff of engineers, draftsmen and clerks.

Centralization also revealed problems that had hitherto been obscured by the Byzantine system of divided responsibilities. Otis' quality standards were all over the place, and nowhere overseas mirrored standards in the United States–bringing the risk of associating the company name with poor products. In the United Kingdom, Waygood was still turning out the old machinery it had brought to the merger in 1914–the best in Europe, perhaps, but produced by old-fashioned methods which in no way resembled Otis' manufacturing philosophies in the United States. In the mid-1930s, Waygood engineers never worked to the tolerances and specifications targeted by American factories, and the Drawing Office had exhausting responsibilities for every job that came in. "You would take the job on from the time it was sold," Arthur Mawson recalled, "and you would go on the site, you would do survey... and then you would specify what we used to call 'alter' material in the factory. You'd do any detailed drawings. You'd do layout drawings."[2]

Of course, the market itself was less sophisticated. Waygood did not produce an elevator without a folding gate until 1936, and even London was without skyscrapers. Hard as the overpressed firm tried to keep up with developments in American technology, it could not overcome its own built-in resistance to mass-production methods, at odds with Britain's craft-based, small-business culture.

Elsewhere, International faced diplomatic difficulties in trying to organize market divisions. Waygood offices in Malaya and Hong Kong, for instance, resented Toyo-Otis shipments to Korea, Formosa and Manchuria. And efforts to "extend the policies and procedures of the domestic company to foreign offices with whatever modifications... necessary to conform to local conditions [and] to produce in our plants abroad equipment identical, insofar as the competitive situation will permit, to that manufactured in the United States"[3] were never realized. In certain Far Eastern offices, Reid reported, "suggested reductions in the normal work week were refused by the employees." In others, the system of jobs-for-life made it impossible to provide pensions.

Pensions, turf wars, synchronicity—none of Otis International's troubles, of course, mattered very much when the world disintegrated once more into war.

Chapter 15

World War II

ORPORATE AMERICA WAS THE WORK of a people who did not contemplate going to war, and whose products—elevators, harvesters, automobiles, refrigerators and radios—were engineered for a world at peace. Perhaps their blood-lust was satisfied by their own corporate battles, or perhaps they looked to the bottom line and saw war as a write-off. But perhaps, having grown responsible as private citizens and then as a nation for the lives and prosperity of their fellow human beings, they also could not credit that nations sometimes do not solve their differences in the way businesses solve theirs.

Andrew Carnegie, the world's richest man and founder of U.S. Steel, engineered two conferences, in 1899 and 1907, that established the International Court of Arbitration at the Hague; he also gave away much of his fortune and said that "the man who dies rich dies disgraced." Henry Ford sent a Peace Ship to Europe during World War I, with instructions to bring back peace by Christmas. He was laughed at by skeptics, and, of course, his mission was a failure.

But war does seem, from the vantage point of the historian of a business, a ludicrous and grotesque interruption, a period of bewilderment and misrule. The Second World War was no exception, although in the long term in the United States it made the link between industry and the military permanent and explicit. Kermit Kraus, who had spent two years at Toyo-Otis, spent a further three in a Japanese prisoner-of-war camp. Arthur Mawson spent several years of his professional life dodging into old tunnels under the factory in the Falmouth Road when the air raid warnings sounded. In France, Otis Pifre's two factories were divided between Germany and Vichy; the manager of the Vichy plant lost 30 of his workers to forced labor programs in Germany, and had to plead with the local overseer to save the remaining 1,000.

Around the globe, Otis colleagues were conscripted to fight one another. Otis' construction manger in Hong Kong died defending the colony from the Japanese, whose own Otis people suffered devastating raids from B29s in 1945. The Red Army dismantled Otis Berlin. Around the world, hundreds of Otis personnel died or were wounded in the conflict.

In 1940, Franklin Roosevelt, like Woodrow Wilson before him, was elected on a peace ticket and almost immediately led America into war. One effect, at least, was to slay the serpent of the Depression, and in that sense World War II was the culmination of the New Deal, returning America to full employment and healthy profits. Otis' Harrison Works, for instance, was transformed "from a convalescent elevator factory just getting over the depression to a surging, straining war plant"[4] that had to find 1,000 new workers on top of the 500 it already employed, and recruited many women. Overtime became the norm. Sundays and holidays were ignored.

Business understood that it could best serve peace by winning the war, and with emergency-level funding it proceeded to do just that. Henry Kaiser's shipyards built their first "Liberty Ship" in 196 days; soon the time was down to 27 days, and by 1943, Kaiser was sending a new boat down the slips every 10.3 hours. In 1942 General Electric raised its production of marine turbines from $1 million worth to $300 million. One reason why America won the Battle of Midway in the Pacific in June 1942 was that the three-month repair job on the war-damaged carrier *Yorktown* was completed in 48 hours, using 1,200 technicians working around the clock. With more than 15 million men in uniform, the United States still managed to build 296,000 planes, 102,000 tanks and 88,000 ships and landing craft.

Otis' own impressive war record, then, was not unusual, although the book the company published to commemorate its war effort in 1945 was a proud reflection of Otis' unusual worldwide commitment. In Canada, Australia, Britain and the United States, Otis personnel had turned their attentions from elevators and used their multifarious skills—at science, engineering, factory management, production—to supply the tools that led to victory.

In the United States, Otis factories and design teams worked in ordnance, aircraft, ships, machine tools and various production services; Otis engineers designed and drafted special hoists for the Navy and organized the construction of war plants. As John Magee, a quality-control engineer, recalled, employees "of an outfit that didn't know anything other than elevators almost overnight were up to their ears in 96 different projects. It was unbelievable."[5] Otis-Fensom in Canada took over production of the Bofors guns and worked in radar equipment, mounts and trailers among a host of other new specialties. In Australia the Sydney factory turned out depth-charge launchers, machine tools and naval equipment. In every case new procedures had to be learned, new technology absorbed, and new production records set. In Britain the company had to contend with relentless bomber raids, which targeted the semi-industrial area of south London where the factory stood. The plant received six direct hits, and a V-2 "buzz bomb" unguided missile killed 11 employees and wounded 60 more in June 1944.

The last Otis plant to be taken into war production was, ironically, in Berlin. The Nazis did not seize the factory until 1942, when Louis Scheel, who was managing it, was one of the last Americans out of Berlin. Its fate was to be part of the territory overrun by Russian troops in 1945. What remained of its plant was shipped to the Soviet Union, and its employees were scattered.

Annual sales more than doubled during World War II, as Otis lent some of its manufacturing capacity to the war effort. *See Appendix.*

Chapter 16

Postwar America

AMERICAN INDUSTRY SURGED after World War II. Pent-up demand for new goods and services, along with wartime destruction of overseas competitors, aborted the postwar downturn the Jeremiahs had predicted and eased millions of returning servicemen into full-time productive jobs. For the first time, it seemed, everyone in the country could be middle-class. People who made refrigerators and cars and toasters could afford to buy them, and the more they bought, the more buoyant was the demand for new elevators. Production soared. Almost every factory and office building required them. Elevators were needed for the new hotels being built for salesmen, and by the banks that managed all the money that was being made. New bookings set a record in 1946. By 1951 the company grossed $120 million in sales, a third for maintenance and modernization services. By 1955 those two items accounted for 43 percent. Profits at Otis were deliciously rich, a 15 percent return on equity year after year, margins as wide as a '53 Studebaker with fins.

Otis, in this happy postwar circumstance, was out front by a comfortable margin. Its capabilities, like its profits, seemed limitless. When production had readjusted to the demands of peace, Leroy Petersen, who had taken over as president in 1945–of a firm that had demonstrated a capacity to embrace a whole host of machine-based industries–proudly observed the way Otis switched back to making elevators in 1945 at "a rate…substantially in excess of our prewar normal…." But in his own mind Petersen considered Otis' elevator business to be one strand in an apparently seamless industrial web.

And what Petersen thought mattered, given the power conferred on U.S. captains of industry at the time. Petersen was not an engineer by training, but when Van Alstyne died in 1944, Petersen had been considered the inevitable choice, a man who understood perfectly how Otis should be run as a war machine—and who proved, in later years, reluctant to change. Like most CEOs', his decisions went unchallenged by either shareholders or captive boards.

The outbreak of the Korean War handed him the diversification he sought on a plate. Very reasonably, he saw Otis earning its share of the vast investment Cold War America would make in the interests of national defense. In 1953 he steered Otis into acquiring a company producing T2A bomber trainers, paying out $365,000 in stock for a company with over $800,000 in awarded contracts. Within two years it had become Otis' "Electronic Division," moving through the production of military radar and electronic controls to missile guidance test equipment and missile electronics by the end of the decade.

Meanwhile the elevator business was forging ahead as never before. In 1947 there were 17 billion elevator rides made in the United States, taking people a total of 241 million miles.[6] Otis could generate more profit than was necessary to please shareholders and more than even the new R&D department could spend, with a range of elevators and escalators that got better every year. Their quality improved. Their design was refined. Otis' elevators became simpler to make, and cheaper, too.

The pent-up demand from the war years led to, among other things, a huge growth in "retrofitting": Otis' increasingly refined elevator controls actually allowed customers to reduce the number of lifts they ran, saving shaft space as well as energy. The main technological advances were to make elevators more responsive. With a series of new lifts, redolent of 1950s America and its discovery of gadgetry, Otis rapidly did away with the need for elevator operators. There were some 90,000 of them in the country in 1950. Within a few years an entire culture disappeared, and soon elevator attendants were retained only by a handful of very conservative apartment buildings and grand hotels, where they maintained an illusion of bygone courtesies and Old World charm.

This was faintly ironic and had more to do with the $7,000-a-year wages that prestigious addresses could still afford to pay for elevator attendants than with the real needs of the traveling public. Otis had absolutely no trouble selling operatorless elevators—they were a huge success for Otis' Modernization department. "Operatorless elevators didn't have anybody getting sick, didn't take vacations, didn't get it to the top of the house and have a smoke and just sit around," as Mike DiZio, vice president of customer service, recalls.[7] Time is the great healer, and nostalgia lent elevator operators an air of cozy warmth they seldom achieved in practice. W. F. Miksch crystallized suspicions in a piece he wrote for *The Saturday Evening Post:*

"Well, well, Johnson, so you want to run an elevator?"

"Yes, sir. Mr. Botkins said to see you. Mr. Botkins said you were the best in his store."

"He did? Well. Then suppose we start you off with a little adaptability test."

"I'll be glad to try, sir."

"Suppose you've just slammed the cage door on a lady's package. What do you say?"

"Er... Excuse me?*"*

"Johnson! Don't ever say that! Puts you on the defensive right away. Just say, Yay wash adore.*"*

"Yay wash adore. Like that, sir?"

"Uh-huh, but with a little more feeling. Now then, let's run through your floor calls."

"*Oh, like:* Mezzanine, ladies' suits and dresses?"

"*No, Johnson. It's* Mezzy, lazy suzy dressy. *Try it from there up.*"

"*Okay.* Mezzy, lazy suzy dressy. *Third floor.*"

"*That's* Thuffle."

"*Sorry.* Thuffle, lamps and lights."

"Lambs and lice."

"*Oh, yes.* Lambs and lice. Going up."

"*Not* Going up! Gun hop. Gun hop. *Don't let the passengers read your mind, Johnson.*"

"Gun hop. Pains and horrors."

"*Um-m-h-m-m...* Paints and hardware... *Very good, Johnson. Then what do you do?*"

"*Then I stop the elevator a good ten inches above floor level and say,* Washest upup. Gun hop. Yay wash adore. Fuffle, hoe furshin."

"*Swell, Johnson. You'll do.*"

"Fuffle, spore goose."

"*That's enough. Report to Car Eight tomorrow.*"

"Gun hop. Porsh hairs, glires, tabby rays. Yay wash adore."

The year 1948 saw the introduction of the Autotronic Elevator, in which electro-mechanical relay switches processed information from call buttons in the lift and in the lobbies. Now the elevator could travel entirely unattended, although someone had to set the schedules mechanically, at different times of day, to meet changing traffic flows.

By the late 1950s, with introduction of the automatic response indicator, electronic programming even surpassed the capacities of a human operator; Otis' "Autotronic Unlimited" elevators lurked wherever they were likely to be most needed up and down the shaft. They knew the pattern of the building's traffic—up in the mornings, down in the evenings—and would whiz back to their predetermined stations as soon as the last passenger was disgorged. Elevator attendants—rascally, amorous, taciturn or delightful, whose peculiarities had belonged to the American morning as surely as had hot coffee and late trains—were replaced by automata that operated like genies from a bottle, summoned not by furious rubbing, or even the punch of a button, but by a waft of the fingers over a piece of plastic.

Automation was much appreciated by the people who placed an order, but it had some unexpected consequences. More fundamentally, elevators had a worrying habit of bobbing up and down, if only fractionally, when they were resting at a floor. An attendant could have thrown the mechanism out of gear and held the lift steady; but once elevators were unmanned the cars experienced this unsettling phenomenon.

The crucial elements in an unmanned car were the sliding doors and the electronic eye. Since 1931 a monstrous DC motor, gearbox and electric brake had been mounted on the roof of the cab, and in the late 1950s Otis was able to fit the 6970A, a high-speed mechanism driven by a fractional horsepower DC motor. The elevator, meanwhile, had to "see" what people were doing as they went in and out. True to form, Otis developed a mechanism—involving expensive transformers, a preamplifier and antennae running off vacuum tubes—and fitted it to its high-end elevators; for cheaper cars the company tended to use light-ray detectors available on the open market, which proved desperately hard to mount in such a way that they could detect someone entering or leaving a lift from every angle. Short people, quick people, people who managed to launch themselves into or out of a lift from an awkward corner, all could evade the eye.

There was a particular peril, too, in being the company that led the market. Popular expectations were raised by an Otis machine. Informed purchasers were always eager for the newest development, and at the first rumor of a rabbit would demand that Otis pull it out of the hat. At least twice, in 1951 and in 1982, the company was pushed into installing new elevator systems whose performance had not been extensively evaluated. But if on these occasions the designs failed to meet expectations, engineers were still constantly refining the performance of geared and gearless machines. By the 1960s they were tighter and lighter than older models, using barely half as many parts, cheaper to make, and easier to install. And thanks to the attention paid to the design of "public spaces" in hotels and office buildings, they were even better-looking.

But the cost benefit, given the heady prosperity of the time, was practically incidental. It was not on price that Otis competed with its chief U.S. rival, Westinghouse. Margins were wide, while the salesmen concentrated their pitches on things like superior performance, the latest technological innovation and the reliability and efficiency of service. An unspoken law of general contractors reflecting the equity of the two giants ordained that they split their projects roughly 60/40 in Otis' favor. Elevators were a second-rank concern with Westinghouse, and all that really held Otis back from taking a larger market share was the general contractor's fear of Otis dominance.

In 1960, F.B.I. agents broke what was to become known as the Great Electrical Scandal. The immediate target of the investigation, and the legal action that followed, was a bevy of middle-ranking executives in the electronics industry, who were brought to trial, humiliated, convicted and, in some cases, sent to jail for pursuing what they believed to be normal business practices and the government deemed to be price-fixing. But the narrow target, once hit, had wider repercussions in the management of corporate America. The sort of coziness that had sustained big business in the country since the war, and which had encouraged firms like Otis to compete on technical specifications, delivery and maintenance while downplaying price, would no longer be tolerated by a watchful government.

The effect on Otis, which had had nothing to do with the scandal—which had mainly involved Westinghouse and General Electric—was indirect but deep. Westinghouse's non-elevator divisions had been implicated in the scandal, and its senior managers now put out blanket instructions to avoid even the appearance of antitrust-sensitive activity. The elevator wing of the corporation was caught up in the fire; bang went the atmosphere of collegial goodwill that existed at the sharp end of the business—among the salesmen in the field. There was no more 60/40, and when Westinghouse's operatives became more aggressive, Otis' salesmen followed suit. Inevitably prices fell. By the late 1960s the company's profit margins as a return on equity had dropped from well over 15 percent to less than 10 percent.

But like the Cold War itself, the contest was still a game between two players. Some 300 independents gamboled at the giants' feet—mostly local firms concentrating on the type of elevator business that could be brokered among friends. However, Otis did not compete with them. Aside from the two majors, there was one other national elevator company, Haughton & Armor, but it was in terminal decline. Competition, such as it was, also involved two regional players, the hopefully named U.S. Elevator, which captured a substantial slice of the low-end market on the West Coast, and Warner Elevator of Cincinnati, capable of building up a good business in Ohio as far north as Cleveland, but utterly unable to compete with the two majors beyond its own backyard—two hundred miles out and the cost disadvantages became prohibitive.

Otis was content, in the main, to ignore small fry—to ignore their technology, based on oil hydraulics; to ignore their market activity, which was small, even in the aggregate; and to ignore, with lofty disdain, their efforts to pool resources in the National Association of Elevator Contractors. This had been founded in 1950, and although it never became, as its members hoped, a springboard for coordinating sales, it functioned well as a resource of ideas and know-how, and managed to bring in two companies which were to have the largest effect on the U.S. elevator market in the years to come.

Dover and Montgomery were both manufacturers and suppliers of components and complete machines to the small independents, who installed and serviced them. Dover had begun as the Rotary Lift Company in 1925, a small Midwestern producer of hydraulic automotive repair-lifts, and had turned its rather basic technology to passenger use during the Depression. In the 1950s it introduced a line of oil-plunger machines. For owners of small buildings, oil hydraulics were an attractive option. They needed no penthouses built for pulleys and motors, no hoist cables or car safeties, no counterweights; they were space saving and cost-effective. Installers reaped high margins on these machines, which were simple to make and relatively easy to assemble, and required very short lead-times.

But Otis did not consider that the millions it spent on R&D were justified by a descent into the slum of creaking hydraulics, employing a technology from which the company had escaped when it invented the electrical gearless machine at the beginning of the century. As a salesman recalled, "I would go out to an architect or a builder and say, 'Why do you want one of these noisy, smelly, dirty, crummy hydros when I can sell you a geared elevator for a little bit more money, [that] will do the job and do it better?'"[8] He answered his own question: hydraulics were cheap and did the job well enough for the people who bought them.

On the back of sales, Dover was busy reinventing itself as the model for a national elevator producer. Beginning in the mid-1950s it started to acquire some of the local independents, elevator installers with whom it already had established business. They were given virtual independence within Dover's decentralized operating structure, and so shared with Dover the advantage of local community ties—their managers invariably members of local civic organizations, charity boards and business associations with a history of cooperation with local contractors and small businesses. Though Dover grew quickly, it retained what one analyst called "intimacy," with the result that its manufacturing operations had to compete for the favor of its own installers. Unlike Otis, whose products ranged from the most complex, custom-made elevator to the simple gearless, Dover's product line began to grow from the bottom up. The company spent almost nothing on R&D, content to follow technology and proving itself to be a good copier; and it took Otis a while to realize that entry into the low-rise market, at a national level, could be used over the longer term as leverage to enter elevator markets at higher levels. "We were very stupid," the salesman recalls, "because once Dover sold that hydraulic elevator in an area, then they'd put people there to maintain it, then they were able to sell geared elevators too because, hell, they had a presence."

By the time Otis realized what was happening and responded with its own low-priced hydros, Dover's position in the low-rise market was supreme; and by 1970 oil hydraulics employing a single plunger outsold gearless machines in the United States. Dover had kept its corporate overhead low and standardized product lines, using modular designs over specially crafted lifts. The company entered the Canadian and British markets by acquisition and expanded its product line from hydros to geared and then low-rise gearless machines.

Montgomery, too, expanded at Otis' expense without performing much R&D of its own. In the mid-1960s the family-owned Illinois firm began importing German escalators for sale across the United States. The machines arrived complete, but union rules demanded that each escalator be broken down and then reassembled for installation. Before long, reverse engineering had shown Montgomery how to manufacture its own components, including the entire machine, leading to a full line of escalators produced and marketed in the United States. In the years to 1975, Otis' share of the new-equipment market, in unit terms, fell from around 45 percent to 31 percent, with a pass-along effect on the growth of its service base, the grail of profit in a maturing market.

Competing on price with Westinghouse's newly aggressive salesmen, and challenged for market share by the surprise arrival of new national companies, Otis in the 1960s found itself hard-pressed to respond. Tendencies that had emerged in the previous decade were beginning to smother Otis' capacity to react.

One of these tendencies could be described as an exaggerated respect for the "Otis Way," the accumulated methods and morals that had established Otis' postwar leadership in the first place. The Otis Way was not a written code but a shadowy imperative in the individual imagination, an elusive rationale tinged with an element of fantasy, collusive and undeclared.

There was nothing much *wrong* with Otis' elevator technology in the period—so that Harry Gray, who brought it to an end, could at least reflect that he had never been stuck in an Otis elevator. But it lacked the consideration it deserved.

If Otis' elevator technology steadily set the pace in the postwar years, the drive toward diversification begun by Petersen almost on a

THE COSMOPOLIS OF THE FUTURE. The city in 1930 as imagined in about 1908, with the Singer and Met Life Buildings overshadowed by 1,000-foot-high structures bridged above tiered sidewalks. "Airships" connect the metropolis with the world.

Receipt for $21,875 received from N. P. Otis,
signed by W. D. Baldwin, August 6, 1890

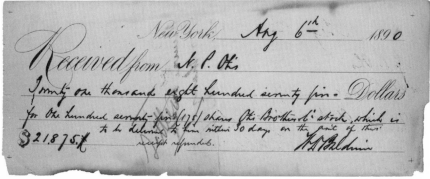

Otis Elevator Works, Yonkers, New York, ca. 1908

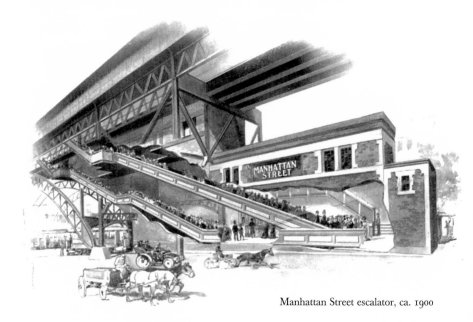

Manhattan Street escalator, ca. 1900

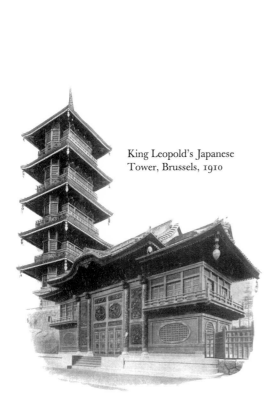

King Leopold's Japanese
Tower, Brussels, 1910

Richard Waygood, ca. 1870

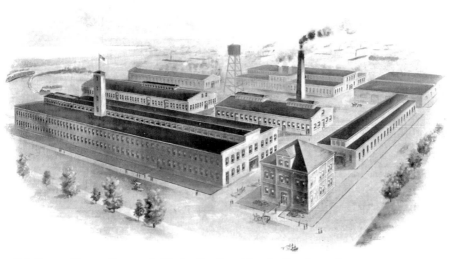

Otis-Fensom Elevator Company's Works, Hamilton, Ontario, Canada, 1926

THE INDICATOR

VOLUME 1 ✦ **1908**

OTIS ELEVATOR COMPANY

Cover of *The Indicator,* 1908

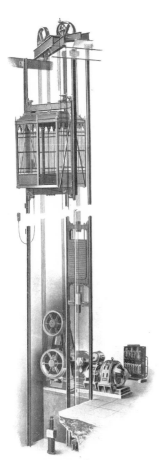

Otis Alternating Current
Double Screw Geared
Traction Machine for
basement installations

Machine repair shop, Yonkers, 1912

Otis Building, New York City, 1912

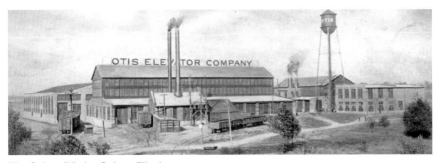

The Quincy Works, Quincy, Illinois, 1913

SCIENTIFIC AMERICAN

[Entered at the Post Office of New York, N. Y., as Second Class Matter. Copyright, 1910, by Munn & Co., Inc.]

A POPULAR ILLUSTRATED WEEKLY OF THE WORLD'S PROGRESS

Vol. CII.—No. 18.] ★   NEW YORK, APRIL 30, 1910.   ★ [10 CENTS A COPY. $3.00 A YEAR.

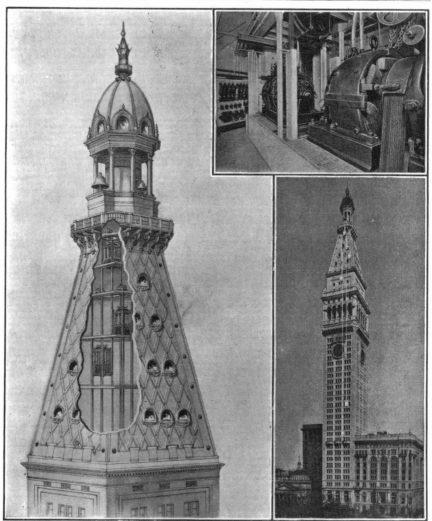

The upper ends of the elevator shafts.   Motors installed at top of tower.   Position of elevators in shafts.

HOW THE PROBLEM OF INSTALLING THE ELEVATORS OF THE METROPOLITAN TOWER WAS SOLVED.—[See page 358.]

April 1910 *Scientific American* cover: Elevators going into Metropolitan Life Tower

David L. Lindquist
Chief Engineer 1911–40

Empire State Building,
New York City, 1931

First signal
control
elevator
installation,
in Standard
Oil Building,
New York
City, 1924

Men working on elevator engine, ca. 1930

Jesse Van Alstyne
President 1923–44

Photo for *Elevator Constructor*, March 1937

First State Trust & Savings Bank,
Form 123
202 So. 5th St., Springfield, Ill.

OTIS ELEVATOR COMPANY

CT6060

(736)

First State Trust & Savings Bank,   Springfield, Ill. March 11, 192

202 So. 5th St.

We propose to furnish OTIS-SERVICE on Two (2) Otis Electric Passenger Elevators

elevators located at 202 So. 5th Street,

from April 1st 192 and thereafter until this agreement is terminated in writing by either of the parties thereto.

For the sum of Eighty and no/100----- DOLLARS 80.00 PER MONTH PAYABLE MONTHLY.

This service to consist of a weekly examination of the elevator, excepting signal devices, including oiling and cleaning machine, motor and controller; greasing or oiling bearings and guides; necessary minor adjustments; call back service during regular working hours of regular working days; and furnishing the following specified supplies: All carbon and copper contacts, contact insulations and contact springs, motor brushes, copper braids, oils, greases, rope preservatives, and cotton waste, wire ropes and all windings, except new armatures.
This agreement is subject to the terms and conditions printed on the back hereof which are expressly made a part of this agreement.

Respectfully submitted

OTIS ELEVATOR COMPANY

BY Cecil Jackson

First State Trust and Savings Bank

Machine No. 76767-8

Signed and Accepted
in Duplicate

John George
Vice Pres & Manager

Approved:
Tracey F. Beggs

3-11   192

Otis maintenance contract, First State Trust & Savings Bank,
Springfield, Illinois, March 11, 1921

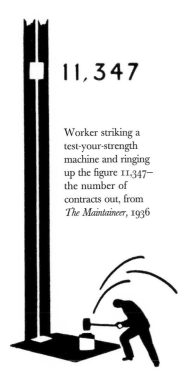

11,347

Worker striking a
test-your-strength
machine and ringing
up the figure 11,347–
the number of
contracts out, from
The Maintaineer, 1936

Otis maintenance uniform,
first used in Philadelphia, 1932

John T. Finnerty at the Empire State Building, New York City, 1948

Waygood-Otis Works, Sydney, Australia, ca. 1926

Escalator in Manchester
Unity Building, Melbourne,
Australia, 1933

P. J. Kessel, Service, USA; H. E. Hertz, Valuation Engineer, USA; D. N. Carpenter, Sales
Manager, USA; F. C. Munn, General Manager, USA; E. O. Mather, Shorthand & Type, UK;
E. H. Walker, Vice-General Manager, USA; Lengotlety, Finance, Germany; Devlengly, General
Affairs, Germany, in front of Otis offices at 935 Beijing Road, Shanghai, ca. 1935 or 1940

Otis factory, Tokyo, Japan, ca. 1958

Aeronautical Division, Harrison, New Jersey, 1942

Leveling socket for 4.7 A.A. Gun, rear view, 1942

World War II ruins of Ascenseurs Otis offices in Albert, Somme, France, ca. 1942

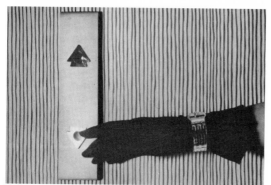

Electronic signal control elevator button with hand showing that by simply touching the plastic arrow one can call an elevator, 1950

Airplane elevator, picture taken from a carrier's "island"

Leroy A. Petersen (President, Chairman 1945–66) reenacts Elisha Graves Otis'
original demonstration of first safe elevator in Crystal Palace, 1953

Otis Escalators sign used to identify Otis equipment in transit

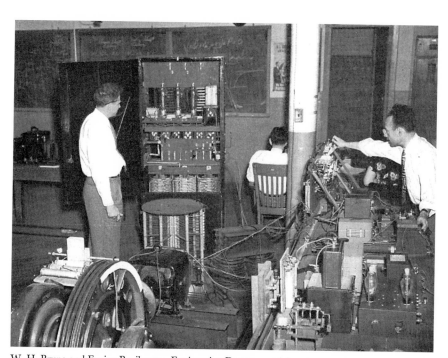

W. H. Bruns and Enrico Bevilacqua, Engineering Department laboratory, 1947

Sales engineers view new "32-R" escalator in production: S. G. Margles (back to camera) points out details of machine assembly at Yonkers Works

Otis Mechanic John R. Pach, Jr. (right) checks 32-R escalator track alignment while Frank W. Kraus casts critical eye on special pin gauge. Site is 308 Madison Avenue, New York City, 1952

Type "O" escalator in the William Hengerer Company Store, Buffalo, New York, 1948

whim was growing stronger by the year. Partly as a response to Otis' relatively declining fortunes in elevator operations, it continued long after Otis stopped earning the easy money that made such purchases seem like good investments. By the mid-1950s, under Petersen's command, top management was carving out a justification for Otis as a short-distance mover of goods and people—a policy aim almost immediately clouded by a freakish foray into pin-setter machinery for bowling alleys, which opened with a set of roaring profits and closed, three years later, with ignominious losses in a speedily saturated market.

Other areas of investment were not so strange or immediately disappointing, with the downside that they became more difficult to throw off when, in the end, they looked like a case of throwing good money after bad. In 1954, in line with management's vision of Otis as a short-distance mover, Petersen arranged to buy the Baker-Raulang Company of Cleveland, which made forklifts and short-haul industrial trucks. The decision was based on the CEO's hunch that Otis could wed its business and marketing expertise to Baker's electric and gas-powered vehicles, expand lines, upgrade quality and push its products through 266 established elevator branch sales offices. The analysis of the deal, and its effect on Otis' established business, was thrashed out on the back of an envelope.

But that was the least of it. Through the 1930s, America's civilian economy had been on hold—car ownership, for instance, which had grown in the 1920s to 15 million, did not reach that level again until 1947. Television, although invented in the early 1930s, did not become affordable until the end of the war. With the postwar consumer boom, however, mobility and independence were the watchwords. The car gave ordinary Americans the freedom of the huge road network built as a Depression relief measure in the 1930s.

Meanwhile the war itself had altered the demographic map beyond recognition. Henry Kaiser with his Liberty Ships was one of the new champions of the West, and during the war a vast amount of industry and business had been drawn there, where land was abundant and cheap. After almost exactly a century, America was going horizontal once again. The suburbs had been growing around cities ever since the skyscraper forced real-estate values up beyond what ordinary people could afford to pay for housing, but postwar America, with its cheap mobility, introduced industry into the suburbs, alongside the new malls. There was still business to be done amid congestion, but easy, lateral movement was the order of the day. There was an appreciable lull in skyscraper construction between the completion of the Empire State Building in 1931 and the beginning of Chicago's Sears Tower in the 1970s.

In that period Las Vegas, Los Angeles and even Phoenix arguably did the job of Chicago and New York a generation earlier in crystallizing the direction of the American city. Phoenix grew geographically faster than its population grew: from 17 square miles with 107,000 inhabitants in 1950, to 248 square miles with half a million inhabitants in 1970.

William Shannon, who edited Otis' new in-house magazine, the *Otis Bulletin,* in the postwar years, was repeatedly struck by what this extraordinary historical circumstance meant for Otis. Whenever short a story, he fell back on the astonishing contrast between America's present expansiveness and its older, jammed-up cities.* "What Kind of Otis District Would You Like?" he asked in October 1949. "HORIZONTAL, replied E. O. Janke of Salt Lake City. VERTICAL, responded F. P. Wingate of New York City." Janke's territory covered 212,000 square miles in four states, and a photo accompanying his reply showed his car receding along a thin black road in Lincoln County, Nevada. Wingate looked after 3.5 square miles, jammed with traffic.

The new American cities of the South and West lay halfway between these two extremes, and what distinguished them was not only their profligate use of land but their reliance on modern transport. Los Angeles had cut its teeth on the railroad, but by the 1950s the rail network had been ripped up and replaced by a network of highways, following the old rail lines. Airports accelerated the seismic shift from density and height to lateral spread. The railway station, made redundant by the car, was replaced by the airport.

In manufacturing and distribution, too, the trend was to spread and keep closer to the ground. With the proliferation of consumer goods and reliable transport, warehouses grew larger and larger. Industries relocating or expanding into the West—the process was less pronounced in the

---

* At the start of the 20th century, parts of New York's Lower East Side, for example, had a density of 478,080 people per square mile.

South–no longer had to contend with either the cramping patterns of land ownership or the availability of transport that had dictated, for example, the layout of Otis' Yonkers Works, hogging its acres, its railway siding and its access to the river. Factories, even warehouses, could be almost anywhere. Registration of trucks rose from 6,000 in 1946 to 19,000 in 1970, and the power of the Teamsters' Union came to be one of the barometers of U.S. industrial success.

It was in this context that Baker's profile, and Otis' contribution to it, became the model for two decades of diversification. Baker had begun its manufacturing existence with the Baker Electric automobile, an elegant confection of the 1920s that weighed two tons and had a range, at a maximum speed of 40 miles an hour, of some 25 miles–one of many early automotive projects long since consigned to the junkyard by the triumph of the internal combustion engine. Yet in its short-haul vehicles, Baker's battery technology impressed Petersen and the Otis directors; they even hoped that Otis' engineering expertise might power it to some kind of breakthrough in the urban transportation market. In any event, the limits of the electric storage battery baffled Otis as much as they baffled everyone else before and since.

Unfortunately, the perfectly adequate market analysis that encouraged Otis to pursue Baker did not work through to Otis' core activity: the logic that favored Baker might also have suggested that cheap, short-rise elevators would be in demand. Instead, Otis left this booming segment of the market to rivals like Dover, who established themselves strongly in the West and South. What made Baker an especially awkward partner, though, was its size. While Otis was a giant in its field, Baker had rather less than 5 percent of the forklift market. Otis effectively priced its own industry, while Baker had to battle in a crowded market. The cost of upgrading Baker's products in the hope of improving a 5 percent market share never really worked out, for although Otis put a marketing executive in charge in the early 1960s, and the company turned a profit for a few years thereafter, nothing could really justify the sums Otis spent on it.

Many years later that executive, Robert Bry, pointed to a link between all the companies Otis acquired in these years–and the common denominator was not that all of them were involved in short-distance carriage. They were the products, as he said, of a single entrepreneur. "Each company really was founded or run by the person from whom we bought it, ranging in age from a high of 70 to a low of 30 years old.... All of them bore the imprint of the president or the chairman of it. While we bought the brains and hopefully the assets, there was no case where we had a successful management transformation. Even if we institutionalized it minimally—put in a controller, put in an engineer—we began to load it with overhead and lost this magic momentum that the entrepreneurial business had."

In a rash of acquisitions between 1965 and 1967, Otis' initial purchase, Reflectone (electronics for military training equipment), suggested just how far the passion for divestment and acquisition had penetrated Otis and U.S. industries in general. Reflectone suited Otis only slightly better than it had suited its original parent, the Universal Match Company of Stamford, Connecticut. Undeterred, Otis next acquired the York Company of West Memphis, Arkansas, manufacturer of pneumatic-tire lifting equipment for earth-moving operations. Moto-Truc of Cleveland, maker of narrow-aisle forklifts, and the Allied-Superb Bronze Company of Long Island City, New York, whose products—balustrades and fixtures for escalators—at least related to Otis' core activity and fitted the traditional policy favoring in-house production of components, were acquired next.

After a pause for breath, the purchasing pressed on, growing ever more futuristic, its outcome ever less predictable. What could long-term shareholders have made of the 1970 annual report's declaration that Otis was "the largest manufacturer of electric-powered vehicles in the United States"? Otis had by then acquired Euclid Crane and Hoist Company and the West Coast Manufacturing Company, which made golf carts. It now announced plans to move into auto parking, container-port lifting systems and automated warehouse systems. Otis' field, said the report, was the "short-distance movement of people and materials."

With momentum, the acquisition fever had gained a sort of logic. Otis' defense business had withered away. With the purchase of a controlling stake in Transportation Technologies Inc. of Denver, Otis' direction was channeled toward a vision of an electronic future. TTI was only two years old, a division of an architectural/engineering firm, and its leading-edge developmental projects relied heavily on Department of

Transportation funding. Under Otis, TTI actively sought new ways of moving people through congested cities and foresaw production of a wide range of short-haul transport, from electric buses and small vehicles to moving guideways, all networked into a system of "building-to-building service in dense downtown business areas." There was also to be a linear motor shuttle riding on a cushion of air—a prototype was installed at Duke University—and much excitement attached to the possibilities of unmanned hospital vehicles, which would glide all manner of needed materials through busy hospital corridors and whose every movement was to be shepherded by Otis' futuristic products, whether up and down, or back and forth, seamless and smooth and, like the touch panel, magical. They would deftly position Otis in a market that had no well-established players and that turned out, of course, to be not much of a market at all.

If expansion along new lines was a response to Otis' relative decline in elevator manufacturing, it seemed to contribute to it as well. What made both trends possible was Otis' archaic management structure, a structure that in the mid-1960s, when Otis was a $450 million corporation with some 38,000 employees around the world, had not much changed since the 1930s. At its apex stood the president, Leroy Petersen or a man like him, aloof and commanding, his powers indivisible, his decisions beyond challenge, with a natural tendency to treat the company as though it belonged to him, or perhaps like Fayette Dunn (president in 1964–67), the ultimate "safe pair of hands," who was trained in that science to which business pays court, and from whom it buys security, the law.

Petersen had become president in 1944 and chairman in 1961. He retired in 1966. Like many an autocrat, he was feared but not loved. It was said that his integrity was unshakable, and though he reportedly believed in hard work, quality service and quality engineering, the citation of these virtues only suggests how little he knew or revealed of himself. For 17 years he remained too splendidly isolated to be known, at the heart of a highly centralized decision-making structure in which every operating decision, every functional question, every general management query that arose anywhere, at any level, in the Otis corporation had still to be referred upward through the classic pyramid of line and staff.

Sandwiched between the president and the rank and file, the field officers, factory managers and sales executives were a surprisingly thin layer of executive support. Their numbers had grown since the 1930s, but not as fast as Otis' activities. Like the president himself, they operated in a cloud of decision making. When minor queries had to be addressed in the same breath as major structural alterations, every executive had to be, at one and the same time, index and encyclopedia. Perhaps it was hard not to be confused, to mistake tactics for strategy and to blur the line between what only seemed urgent and what really mattered.

Petersen had never trained as an engineer, as most of his executives had, and those who followed would. His successor as president, Percy Douglas, was more qualified. An elevator man by birth and training, he had rebuilt Otis' foreign business after World War II, and he did not follow Petersen's lead into diversification. In three short years he made substantial investments to improve the company's core elevator facilities at home and abroad, opening what was to become the company's major North American manufacturing plant in Bloomington, Indiana, in 1963. He also consolidated reporting on Otis' international and U.S. operations for the first time, after Petersen's dogged refusal to entertain any suggestion that Otis was doing better, and had grown larger, overseas than at home.

But Douglas died unexpectedly in October 1964. He left instructions that Fayette Dunn, the corporate counsel, was to be given caretaker control of the company in the absence of a suitable successor—but it was still a measure of the autocratic character of Otis' management that nobody else, in Douglas' view, was yet ready for the job.

Dunn was a temporary appointment, as he famously explained at his first meeting of securities analysts, and had been on the company payroll only five years. After handling the Otis account at a Chicago law firm for a quarter-century, he had been chosen by Petersen to head a new in-house legal department and had formally entered the Otis structure in June 1960.

The temporary president lasted four years. He was not, as some veterans sourly pointed out, an elevator man. He had no engineering training. He had no sales experience. He had never run a company, let alone a corporate giant like Otis. His experience was almost suffocatingly hermetic: boardrooms, directors and the corridors of power. Otis executives received the news of his succession with bemusement or downright skepticism. But Dunn was just a temporary, after all. Only as the years passed and temporary became permanent did the mood evolve dangerously into one of resignation, as people stopped asking themselves what, exactly, was going on.

For the answer was that Otis was drifting into a rarefied miasma in which action lacked force, like the clumsy, weightless exertions of the men whose arrival on the moon was soon to be broadcast around the world. Diversification brought a retreat from reality, and with hindsight the drift is obvious. Competitors had levered themselves upward and were beginning to enter sectors of the market traditionally reserved for Otis machines: there was drift. Dreary appointments spoke of it, too, when the company vainly searched for people of caliber to replace those who were moving out at the top. For many years the company had been good at nurturing and recognizing talent within its ranks. Like an empire, Otis took fire from its borders and balanced the traditionalism and security of the center with the kind of maverick creativity that flourished on the boundaries. Again and again, the controlling center had sucked in talent from the edges at the right moment—like Cecil Jackson of Springfield, Illinois, who had invented the notion of maintenance contracts back in the days of World War I, or like Percy Douglas himself, son of old Henry, who had built up the company in Canada at the turn of the century. These were lessons that Otis would remember just in time to rescue the center from its systemic weaknesses.

Coinciding roughly with Dunn's lackluster tenure, the job of chief engineer went begging. If the chief executive was the captain, then the chief engineer was the stoker; on him depended the power train that supported the entire operation—all the more when the CEO was not himself an elevator man. Men of David Lindquist's day were retiring. Similarly, when William Bruns, who had headed Otis' R&D department since the 1930s, died of a heart attack, no successor of comparable stature could be found.

Just as the business atmosphere grew more challenging than at any time in 30 years, Otis' key jobs fell to temporaries. The engineers had been unionized toward the end of World War II, largely as a result of Otis' taking on so many previously unionized engineers and draftsmen from other companies to cope with the new work. In later years, as part of the quietist philosophy of management, many engineering managers emerged from among the officers of the union. Meanwhile, there was drift in the engineering department as people came and went, opening a gulf between managerial and engineering sides of the corporation through which Otis' position as the spearhead of elevator design and technology began to slide. Top flight technical graduates sniffed the wind and looked for work with firms closer to the cutting edge.

The boardroom was increasingly disconnected from Otis' core activity. Its members' understanding of the elevator business was weak, and perhaps there was a tendency among non-elevator men like Dunn to draw the company onto ground where they enjoyed a more level footing with the old elevator hands. There was the problem, too, of a welter of questions snowing them under, so that the easiest answer was always no—foreign operations suffered from this, their proposals to meet unfamiliar local competition all too easily turned down. The effect of Otis' diversification was to carry confusion right into the field of hands-on operation. Each new area of investment brought with it a whole new culture to be absorbed by the men in the field as well as the executives at the top. Top management spent far too much time sorting out the integration of small firms whose contribution to Otis' overall business was minuscule, while every elevator salesman in the field had to become an expert, say, on truck design, truck mechanics, truck repair. He needed to know what products were coming down the line, and why; he needed to deal with complaints and inquiries in addition to his elevator work, which was itself heating up as Westinghouse turned aggressive and the independents began to emerge as a major threat. And he wasn't getting help from above. The long-term result of diversification was not synergetic improvement across the board but divided attention, red tape and wasted time.

The confusion affected even the development and production of elevators. Maybe it affected them most of all. There was nothing inherently wrong about Otis' accepting the brief for the World Trade Center in New York in 1967, when even Westinghouse had decided not to chase the contract. What was wrong was Otis' reliance on these sorts of *grands projets* whose fulfillment, however brilliant, however profitable on the books, involved the company in an unseen loss. As Otis developed a system for the 110-story twin towers in lower Manhattan, eight years passed in which the company's best minds were addressing problems and devising solutions relating to a very specific set of circumstances. Much was learned along the way, and some of it trickled down into more popular elevator ranges; but it did little to improve Otis' capacity for technical innovation across the range of its products. On every front the firm's energies were directed at precisely those areas where the returns were likely to be smallest for the effort involved. Worst of all, for Otis, was its luck. The World Trade Center appeared to herald a return to the skyscraper frenzy of the 1920s and 1930s, but in fact it did the opposite. With the oil crisis just around the corner, the appearance of two monster office blocks in New York flooded the city with office space and nipped the boom in the bud. Much the same disenchantment occurred around the country.

But Otis' monolithic structure tended to reproduce inertia, and many apologists found a justification in events; they said that the U.S. market was mature and that Otis elevators needed to be no better than they were.

The same malaise bedeviled the subsidiary operations. While Otis' arrival on the scene tended to sap their entrepreneurial energy, it did nothing to lessen the risks of entrepreneurship itself. By 1974, when the diversified industries already contributed 14 percent of Otis' business turnover but were not profitable, Otis made its last lunge into futuristic technology with the purchase of the Electrobus Division of the Tork-Link Corporation. Almost immediately the Nixon administration— perhaps urged on by the automobile lobby—made savage cuts in R&D funding for alternative transit systems, the very funds on which Otis' experimental companies now depended. TTI, the company that was supposed to create an electric future for transport in congested cities, went up for sale. There were no takers, even though the company was hawked as far away as Japan, where the demand for rational transportation was very high.

The sudden ensuing oil crisis and consequent economic slump hastened cutbacks to Otis' diverse operations. This was an extension— perhaps seriously overdue—of a far wider program to cut costs, one that had been gathering steam ever since the mid-1960s, when the depth of Otis' competitive disadvantages had begun to become clear.

Some of the root causes of the company's troubles were now easy to identify. Otis' factories were simply too productive for their market, their machinery standing idle, buildings half-empty. Too many escalator and elevator components were produced in-house, after a tradition perhaps laid down by the company's inventive founder, although they could have been bought more cheaply on the open market. Profit margins were down, but wages were up, and rising.

If the causes seemed clear, however, their solution was problematic. A program of retrenchment brought with it rising tensions with the IUEC, the union that represented the majority of Otis factory workers. In 1967 discussions on the possibility of containing wage increases and liberalizing work rules broke down; and just when most unions were negotiating three-year master contracts, the IUEC mounted a strike that brought Otis operations outside New York to a standstill. Managers held firm for seven weeks as Otis factories remained closed. But when the IUEC called off its strike, it had given only a little ground on the problem of wage increases, and none at all on the traditional arrangement that still obliged Otis' U.S. factories to deliver elevator parts to the field unassembled.

By then the deficiencies in management structure were also getting attention. There were now more vice presidents to help channel the deluge of questions and demands that rode up and down the chain of command. Emmett Hines had been made senior vice president for Regional Operations, overseeing eight regional divisions. A new office had been established for Diversified Operations, to isolate executive responsibility for non-elevator business. In 1965, on Hines' retirement, Dunn had created an umbrella organization for Domestic Elevator Operations which would place overall responsibility for production and regional sales together under an experienced executive vice president, Roy Olson, who remedied a long-standing weakness in communications between production plants and field operations.

With Diversified Operations, Otis' management structure began to look more like the decentralized, divisional model that had already become quite common in U.S. corporations. Robert Bry was made head of the office in 1966, and he was able to take some basic strategic and policy decisions before they began to clutter up the offices of the corporate CEO. By the time Ralph Weller took over as CEO from Dunn in 1969,

New York was awash in vice presidencies, and Europe, Asia, Latin America and North America were under separate leadership. Eugene Hull, senior vice president for North American Operations, would soon become responsible for "profit improvement," which at the time meant looking for further opportunities for diversification.

And yet the decisions were still coming from New York, still dependent on the ability of the men at central to absorb and act on the vast flow of information that poured in. Under the circumstances it was hard to foster general management skills further down the line or quell the rising tide of complaints about red tape and wasted time.

Worst of all, the sense of drift was bearing bitter fruit at the level of elevator design and technology. The more it seemed that elevator operations were being starved of attention by forays into glamorous technologies, the more eagerly elevator engineers sought to create dazzling displays of technical wizardry like the World Trade Center and to sideline, in turn, the more mundane market for low-rise machines. Like a threatened aristocracy, they reacted by becoming all the more aristocratic. The accent on craft, on the "Otis Way," seemed to grow more pronounced just when competitors were reaping the fruits of standardization. John Inglis, an Australian engineer, saw that Otis' hydraulic technology was already years behind when Dover demonstrated its viability in low-rise buildings. He found Otis "obsessed" with safety design and very conservative in outlook. When the company did respond by producing a hydro of its own, it was, typically, overengineered. Not until Ralph Weller, stepping up to Otis' deficiencies in this boom area, pushed the engineers to come up with something competitive on price did they develop the successful HVP hydraulic in 1970. By 1975 the HVP was responsible for 30 percent of hydraulic bookings in North America.

The scale of Otis' slide nevertheless had become common knowledge when, in 1974, an internal report was commissioned to examine production costs. Otis was floundering under cost disadvantages across the board: 15 percent in gearless elevators, 12 percent in geared, 7 percent in hydraulics, 8 percent in escalators. As market leader, Otis should have been the high-volume, low-cost producer. And now there were even challenges to its lead. By 1974 both Westinghouse and U.S. Elevator had introduced solid-state motor controls, solving problems that Otis was still trying to address, and confirming in the minds of customers and company engineers alike that Otis was no longer the pioneer in this most vital sector of the elevator industry.

For 30 years Otis had reaped its fortune on the wing, for good and ill. Its products had improved incrementally. Its structure had evolved very slightly. Its lead had eroded only gradually. But all of a sudden, competitors across the market seemed to be offering elevators at least as good as anything Otis could produce. They were not only often cheaper; in Japan, at least, they were actually better. Otis was still a billion-dollar enterprise, with half the U.S. market for elevators and a quarter of the rest of the world's, and slowly improving its profits, but it needed to be yanked out of its spiral of genteel decline and lost direction. Toward that end, Otis would find Hubert Faure. The corporate raider Harry Gray, on the other hand, would discover Otis.

Chapter 17

Postwar Europe

Percy Douglas was the son of William Baldwin's friend and adviser Henry Douglas, who had established Otis' first foreign venture in Canada back in 1902. Baldwin had been staying at the Douglas house on the night the boy was born in the house, and Henry greeted his chief at breakfast with the words, "You have a new member of the Otis Company." ("I know," Baldwin replied phlegmatically. "I heard.")

Henry Douglas was no longer working for the company when Percy joined Otis in New York in 1924, with an engineering degree from McGill University in Montreal. Married to a socialite and heir to one of the founders of Phelps Dodge, he had worked for 12 years in residential construction. His wife, Katherine, soon realized that Otis was going to be his life and generously agreed to move to New York. She watched him read his paperwork in bed. She allowed him to bring business contacts home for drinks or dinner at a moment's notice; and rather than be apart from him in the early days of their marriage, she would tag along when he answered night calls, sitting in countless hotel lobbies while her husband tested elevators.

Douglas joined the International Division not long after it had been established, for his diplomatic skills, his range of high-level contacts and his capacity for hard work made him a natural for the International scene. By 1936 he–and Katherine–were paying visits to Europe and

Brazil. He did not always travel with his wife. He had a small overnight bag already packed with a spare pair of flannel slacks, a sportshirt and light shoes, and with this he was ready to go anywhere. But it was with Katherine that he visited Germany in 1939. He came back oppressed by the atmosphere.

Perhaps that was just as well. His rival for the top office after the war, Charles Grandgerard, never quite recovered from identifying too closely with Japan during the military build-up to war in the late 1930s. He spent the war in another important overseas post, Brazil, but by the time he returned to Japan in 1947 he had lost the initiative. Douglas had spent the war on loan to Nelson Rockefeller's Agency for Inter-American Affairs as assistant coordinator to stiffen support for the war effort among America's southern allies. While his wife believed he was hunting for spies up and down the South American coast, he was really acting as a sort of undersecretary of state in the region, handling a range of delicate diplomatic missions. Late in 1944, with the end of the war in sight, he returned to Otis in New York as general manager of the International Division; following Fred Town's retirement at the end of 1945, Douglas was appointed vice president in charge of International Operations (two years later, in 1947, he was made a director, and it was he who sent Grandgerard back to Japan).

Percy Douglas and International hit the ground running at the war's end—on General MacArthur's invitation, two Otis engineers were with the military force that occupied Japan. Douglas himself made a whistlestop tour of liberated Europe soon after VE Day.

At that time international operations were still at a standstill, and the Allied victory over Germany and Japan had altered all bets on the future. Britain, whose own market for elevators and escalators had equaled only one-tenth of the U.S. market between the wars, nevertheless had controlled Otis' operations in Southern Africa, New Zealand, Australia and India, as well as smaller client states around Africa and the Pacific. Japan had been a large market, the largest in Asia, but its rate of growth had been slow. Both Argentina and Brazil had shown signs of healthy growth in the 1930s, and their market had seemed to be forming on exemplary American lines. Continental Europe had shown promise, too—Germany rather more than France, France rather more than Spain, and Italy, as ever, something of a special case. By the late 1930s, Otis' overseas empire had been contributing some 10 percent to Otis' bottom line.

By 1946, however, the lessons of the past no longer served as a guide to what Douglas might expect from the various countries where Otis had operated. South America had escaped the war unscathed, though the coming dollar shortage would depress the markets there. Production in Britain and Australia had been diverted to purely military needs, although companies in both countries could retool fairly quickly. South Africa looked like a place where one could do business—the only country in the world, outside America, with money to spend. French Otis was a basket case. China, wasted by the Japanese invasions and racked by civil war, no longer offered much promise.

In Germany and Japan there was nothing to revive at all—no factory, no payroll, no market. As late as 1947 the Allies in Europe were still considering whether to turn Germany once and for all into a country that could never fight again, confiscating what remained of its industrial infrastructure and returning its population to a peasantry. "Developments during the past year with respect to our interests in these two countries have not been such as to permit any forecast as to when, if ever, it will be commercially feasible to reestablish business operations," the annual report told stockholders in 1947.

Even where something—factories, skilled people, service contracts—could be reclaimed, the circumstances provided few guideposts as to what would happen next. "The overall results," Douglas explained in 1947, "were gratifying," but would continental Europe, for example, grow again? General MacArthur personally liked elevators, but how would Japan ever rise? Just to compare International's 1947 earnings of half a million dollars* with those of 1927 was to make clear that the world outside America had been set back 20 years at least. It was a much poorer world than it had been before the war.

It was hard to slide the matrices one above the other, the predictors and the indicators, to arrive at an overview of prospects. Percy Douglas had to move into uncharted waters, sounding his channel in

---

* The first time, interestingly, that stockbrokers received precise information about Otis' foreign earnings.

every country in which Otis did business. "It should be understood that the general situation is fraught with so many uncertainties that the results for any given period are quite unpredictable. Shortage of dollar exchange, trade barriers, pending devaluation of local currencies, growth of nationalism, government licensing of imports and exports, political and economic instability, shifting international alignments and numerous other factors may temporarily upset all previous plans and expectations. Under the circumstances," Douglas assured the stockholders, "it will be our policy to proceed with even more than ordinary caution."

Why did Otis go back into the world market, working so hard for so little, when it would have been simpler to draw up the bridge and concentrate on supplying the domestic boom? Partly, of course, because the world's largest elevator company had the world's largest number of elevators and escalators installed around the world—69,149—and could hardly walk away from them. Partly because it had investments to protect, expertise to tap, markets to explore. If recovery did come, then Otis ought to be in at the beginning, particularly when the capital outlay required—in devalued currencies—was so small. Profit, in the short term, would be hard to take, at least in the clear-cut way a business like Otis might reasonably expect. Yet Percy Douglas was sure that the money would eventually reach New York, and that while business cycles around the world did not necessarily coincide, Otis' productivity would be enhanced in lean domestic years by foreign sales. Sooner or later European countries would have to rebuild, and there lay a golden opportunity for Otis.

The reason Otis re-entered the world market was at least partly cultural. Otis returned overseas because Otis was an American company, and after 1945 the world looked to America. The "Free World"—a term gradually coming into vogue as Stalin revealed his intentions toward eastern Europe—badly needed companies like Otis. Successful free enterprise could weave a protective screen around all those countries that had not yet fallen under Soviet hegemony. After an uncertain start, America was beginning to see itself as the arbiter of the Free World's fate and to understand that American commitment—military, financial, moral—was the price it had to pay to fulfill its responsibilities as one of the world's superpowers. This perception created the moral climate that allowed Secretary of State George C. Marshall's massive foreign aid package to get through Congress, and out to Europe, in 1947; but it would be up to private enterprise to invest and deploy the money. Douglas reflected this view when he commented on the Marshall Plan in his 1947 Report:

> *The Marshall Plan may temporarily relieve the dollar shortage abroad but no permanent correction can be accomplished so long as the USA remains a creditor nation and continues to pile up favorable trade balances year after year. Dollars can only be obtained by foreign countries through our purchase of their goods or services or through our investing funds in their countries. Until we buy or invest abroad no permanent relief can be expected. It is only to be hoped that the Marshall Plan will allot only the minimum relief requirements of the foreign countries participating and that there will be no detraction from the necessity and incentive for these countries to redouble their own efforts to achieve a steadily increasing standard of living for their people.*

For Europeans, 1947 was a memorably horrible year. The end of the first full year of peace brought not rest but a bitterly cold, long winter. Later harvests were poor; on the continent people struggled to survive. In Britain the new Labor government, working on ambitious plans to nationalize key industries and found a welfare state, maintained a system of rationing that was actually more grudging than it had been in wartime. In spite of this, Britain's industrial base, though in disarray, had survived, which was more than could be said for much of France and the whole of Germany.

In Germany, Otis' business had been largely blown away: as late as 1952 the company was vainly seeking to recover whatever was left in the French-occupied zone, and Otis' ultimate re-entry into the German market was made in the form of an alliance with a local producer, Karl Flohr. Elsewhere, existing Otis operations cried out for help.

The obstacles were many and varied. In a dollar-hungry world, governments were reluctant to allow profits to leave. In Brazil, where several Far Eastern executives had spent the war, the government limited remittances to 8 percent of registered capital and insisted that a year's profits could only be fully distributed over five years. Currencies other than

Brazil's were difficult to exchange into dollars. Everywhere governments were raising taxes to pay for reconstruction–levies on capital, levies on distributed profits–"everywhere business corporations are looked upon as a source of almost unlimited revenue,"[9] Douglas complained. Labor relations were difficult, for men who had fought a war wanted higher wages in return, and many countries were dogged by inflation.

Notwithstanding the "distress" of the immediate postwar period, the competitive situation proved surprisingly robust. Atlas remained vigorous in South America, and in Europe various companies had benefited from neutrality to establish themselves as European players during and immediately after the war: the Swiss Schindler, Sweden's ASEA, Kone in Finland. One of Douglas' first recommendations was that Otis should do as it had done 20 years earlier in Italy and establish factories in each of these countries to spoil their home markets. This could be undertaken, after all, with a certain high moral relish.

Every year Douglas toured the world to assess the company's global strengths and prospects. A workaholic, the very model of a high-flying executive jet-setter, Douglas must be credited with the creation of the new, postwar Otis abroad. It was his energy, his inveterate traveling, his plans and analyses that made the company take note of foreign affairs. It was his cool appreciation of the scale of difficulty–and of Otis' ability to surmount it–that persuaded his colleagues to join in. "The wider our coverage becomes and the more flexibility we can achieve in our source of supply, the greater will be the stability of our foreign operations," he wrote. Douglas, in effect, sucked Otis into his slipstream, much to Otis' eventual good fortune.

Chapter 18

Percy Douglas Tours the World

"**A**BOUT THE ONLY PLACE IN THE COMPANY where you can safely buy the boss a one-way ticket...is in the International Division in New York," the *Otis Bulletin* reported in February 1949. "They did that recently to Mr. P. L. Douglas. On the morning of September 23, 1948, he started eastward on 26th Street. For 88 days and 34,822 miles he traveled more or less in the same direction. By that time he had gone all the way around the world and back to New York again—somewhat sat-through and a little overdue on sleep!"

Back in the 1930s the telephone, as well as the infant industry of commercial flying, had made it possible for Otis to manage its foreign affairs from New York more closely than ever before. By the late 1940s that situation had been revolutionized. A plain airmail letter sent from Shanghai in 1948 could be expected in New York four days later. PanAm began the first round-the-world scheduled flights in June 1947. International travel, especially after the introduction of jet commercial aircraft in 1958, was swifter, cheaper and far pleasanter than before the war.

For Americans in particular, travel was easier. Not only were some of the great airlines American, but American Express had become an almost unofficial consular service, while the dollar, of course, was the international currency par excellence. Other countries' efforts to maintain

parity were doomed to failure, and the French triggered a series of deval-
uations that increased American spending power around the globe.

Executive travel had come of age. America had led the way in providing its roving salesmen with reliable accommodation in hotels, and
what worked in America was by the late 1940s being cautiously extended
to other countries to cater to the needs of visiting businessmen. Howard
Johnson, Hilton, Sheraton—all the major U.S. chains, with their style,
their elevators, their telephones in every room and their private bath-
rooms—were expanding into Europe and South America, where they
found no dearth of local imitators. The new breed of hotelier made
sure that guests could be attended to in the English language and that
expense sheets could be legibly supported. By 1956, when the *Otis Bulletin*
inquired solicitously of Van Schoonhoven, "How did accommodations
throughout the world compare...?" Van Schoonhoven was able to say
that, on the whole, they were much the same as in the United States, but
"usually without room-service," adding, "I was fortunate in having air-
conditioning in nearly all the rooms where I stayed."*

Many Americans who had served in the war remained overseas to
keep the peace, so that the idea of an American presence was fairly
well established almost everywhere. Being rich, these Americans were
open to rip-offs, but they were sure of prompt attention, too.
Moreover, they were more aware of the world outside America than
ever before. Cairo, London, Paris and Tokyo were more than names;
they were recognizable places.

The new mobility, however, had its drawbacks. "TRAVELING MAY
SOUND FUN TO YOU," the *Otis Bulletin* reminded its readers in a headline
in March 1952, "BUT IT'S HARD WORK FOR THE COMPANY'S OFFICIAL
TIMETABLE EXPERT."

"The clock never stands still in the headquarters of a world-wide
business organization like Otis," the report notes. "Are you going to meet
the 3.00 pm plane from London? Will you get back from Idlewild in time
to meet the 'Independence'? And, oh yes, Antonio Baca, Service Manager
from Mexico City, just got in from Atlanta and wants to be in Cuba for

---

* Fortunate indeed; most public buildings in New York had air conditioning of a kind as early
as 1945, but that was New York, not Karachi.

an inspection trip by tomorrow morning. Do you think we ought to try to get him aboard the 2.00 pm plane connected with Cubana to Havana?"

Running Otis' travel department was Murt Cavanagh's job.* "Take a look at this little junket," he asks, reaching into a fat file of past tasks. "This one was taken by one of the general Service Department men. The name's not here, but it might have been Cecil Jackson, our retired Maintenance Promotion Specialist, possibly Ray Kline, who succeeded him.... Departure from New York City. First stop, Buffalo, then Cleveland, Detroit, Chicago, Kansas City, St. Louis, Oklahoma City, Dallas, Fort Worth, San Antonio, Houston, New Orleans, Memphis, Birmingham, Atlanta, Washington, and back to New York. And how long to do all this? Twenty-nine days! That means nearly a month straight of working eight to ten hours a day, sleeping en route or in places you're not used to, and everything else you can think of that might wear you out...."

Foreign travel had peculiar exhaustions. Murt had been working for Otis since 1929, so he indubitably organized the trip that Douglas took around the world in 1948, which was written up in the February–March 1949 issue of the *Otis Bulletin*. Douglas set out to cross the Atlantic aboard the *Queen Elizabeth*. Thanks to bad weather, the ocean liner docked at Southampton at 10 p.m. almost a day later than scheduled. Fortunately for Douglas, "Mr. W. A. Frater, managing director of Waygood-Otis, was on the pier." Apparently Frater had waited for him all day, having journeyed down from London to meet him. He spirited his visitor off the ship, and "two hours later he and Percy Douglas were in London." ("Murt usually advises shipboard passengers to leave their luggage in their quarters while docking," a later *Bulletin* confided. "That way, it can be located easily and picked up in one fell swoop....")

Douglas crossed from England to France by ferry, and from France to Italy by rail. All these journeys were strictly local experiences. "To get to the dining car for breakfast," he wrote en route to Milan, "is an athletic venture. As soon as one leaves the Pullmans and tries to get through

---

* The hardest part, he said, was organizing shipments. "People can always think for themselves in tight situations. An elevator machine is a little different—you've got to lead it by the hand every mile of the way. It calls for experience and fast thinking."

the second- and third-class coaches...it is like trying to push through a New York subway train at rush hour, except that the subway authorities discourage passengers from bringing chickens and other farm animals into the train."

In England and France, Douglas' brief was relatively simple. Waygood-Otis' London headquarters, after all, remained Otis' largest operation outside the United States and was worth four days of Douglas' time: "Department heads...prepared everything in advance, and because I was a visitor they gave my limited time first consideration." In Britain the task of reconstruction meant that every emphasis was laid on export; domestic demand was still limited—by government fiat—to "replacement or repairs in war-damaged buildings," and involved much wrangling with the authorities to secure supplies of rationed materials. "It was one thing to get an order for a lift," Harry Pettinger recalled, "but it was an entirely different matter to get a license for the material—steel, timber and things of this kind—from the government, before you could go ahead with it." The result was "wheeling and dealing with government officials to get a license for customers to do the actual work."

At least Waygood-Otis suffered little serious competition as the post-war recovery took off. Whole cities needed to be rebuilt after bombing damage—Plymouth, Coventry, much of London, Portsmouth, Southampton—and demand soared for elevators in the new office blocks and department stores. At the same time, the opportunity was seized to begin the "slum clearances" of low, unsanitary, "back-to-back" terraced houses. Waygood focused on the commercial market, where demand for its high-quality products ensured a premium, and eventually the company put up a second factory in Liverpool to escape from the rigid planning constraints that hemmed in the Falmouth Road plant in London.

The British company was still functioning along imperial lines in 1948, although Waygood-Otis (South Africa) Ltd. was reregistered as a South African company in 1947.

In France, Douglas had scheduled another four days, basically to hear grievances. He knew France well: in June 1945, a month after the war's end in Europe, he had visited Paris. "After a period of five years of oppression and suffering both mental and physical," he wrote, "it was not surprising to find France in a state of social unrest. However, it was a shock to find the almost complete breakdown in spirit or morale that seemed to be everywhere.... There seemed to be an absence of hope for the future; everyone blamed their predicament on other nations, and expressions of censure against the United States and Britain were common. All in all it was a sorry sight."[10]

Sorry, too, was the plight of Otis-Pifre, branded as a collaborator and threatened with the confiscation of its profits and a 300 percent fine. It took Otis a year to regain legal control of the company, when Seymour Jacquet was reinstalled as company president. Yet the French seemed determined not to succumb to the American love affair with the elevator, tall buildings or big business. They would, in a pinch, agree to squeeze a very small, low-cost machine into certain apartment buildings: 90 percent of all elevators in France between the wars fitted this description. The remaining 10 percent, though, were seldom bought from Otis-Pifre, which faced the same cultural discrimination in France as it did in Japan. The German occupation of the country, as we have seen, hardly helped matters. In 1947, Douglas reported, Otis-Pifre was the only elevator company in France unable to provide modern equipment. It needed investment of $300,000 merely to regain its position in the market.

Government rent controls were maintaining the historic cheapness of French housing, all of which militated against the introduction of frills like elevators. Even before the war the average French citizen had spent a mere 8 percent of his income on housing, compared with a European norm of 20 percent, and by 1945 the sum had dropped to an incredible 2 percent. Some 700 new elevators were sold in the whole of France in 1946. Meanwhile, workers were still smarting from the imposition of wage controls: strikes broke out everywhere, making steady work almost impossible.

But Douglas had begun to invest heavily, especially in worker training, and by 1948 the situation at Otis-Pifre had improved. By 1949, Otis-Pifre would be ahead of its national rivals, having improved its output threefold while employing only twice as many workers. It was just in time. Confidence had at last returned to the French economy, and apartment buildings built with elevators in mind began to appear at the edges of French cities. (In 1951 the company renamed itself Otis Ascenseurs.)

In Italy, where meetings in Milan "lasted until daylight on the following morning," Douglas carried out what he gamely called "a tough but interesting assignment." He firmly believed that Italy was the biggest potential market outside the United States, but the rapid fusion of Otis, Stigler and Sabiem immediately after the war had proved an operational disaster.

Stigler and Sabiem, as noted in Chapter 14, were both controlled by an industrial combine called Meridionali. Helplessly burdened with debt, Meridionali resisted calls for further investment while allowing Sabiem to maintain virtual independence from Stigler-Otis. The result was that Stigler-Otis' expansion was limited; competitors were lured into the market, and Otis was stymied. Otis' troubles in Italy were not really solved until 1955, when Meridionali relinquished its hold on Stigler, having already withdrawn Sabiem from the merger. By then, Stigler-Otis' market share had dwindled from 65 percent in 1949 to 25 percent.

"To break the tension of the meetings, many of us spent one evening at the famous La Scala Opera House, where we witnessed the premiere performance of 'L'Amour des Tres Res....' Charge it to the soothing and enchanting music if you will, but in any event the following morning saw a long list of important decisions approved unanimously."

Douglas went from Milan to Rome by train, an edifying experience, he wrote to the *Bulletin*. "When the Germans left Italy they dynamited all the tunnels and bridges on one of the finest electrified railways in Europe. The Allied armies made emergency repairs, but much of the rebuilding was left to the Italians. Much to their credit, the job is practically completed." In Rome, Douglas met Augustus Stigler, grandson of the Stigler who founded the company, and manager of the Otis-Stigler office there. "Sightseeing" he reported, "consisted of a quick look at the spot in the U.S. Embassy where four new Collective Control elevators soon will be installed." So much for the lure of the Eternal City.

In Cairo, which he reached via Athens, the Egyptian customs officials who went through his belongings made it "evident," he said, "that anyone having anything he was not supposed to have was not going to have it very long." As the *Bulletin* revealed, Douglas traveled with nothing like the casualness of the modern traveler, whose presence "on business" is usually enough to waft him painlessly onto the next plane out. "Mr. Douglas is a Director of Otis Elevator Company and Vice President in Charge of International Operations," the *Bulletin* pointed out, "but that doesn't mean he travels on his job as a Very Important Person. The Consulates of fourteen different countries had to visa his passport for this particular trip, and to most of them he was the usual Very Suspicious Character. The doctors took their customary glee in inoculating him for Tetanous (*sic*), Typhoid, Typhus, Smallpox, Yellow Fever and Cholera. He required all of the official papers a world traveler needs these days, including a Certificate of Good Behaviour. 'Mr. Douglas,' wrote the chief of police carefully, 'does not have a criminal record. As far as I know.'"

In Cairo, Douglas met W. Steel, who had flown up from Cape Town to discuss South Africa and Europe. South Africa was a particular bright spot—a mature economy, promise of growth, and a very sophisticated market, in the one country in the British Empire which suffered no dollar shortage. Westinghouse, Otis' major rival, had already attempted to enter the gearless elevator market there, through a licensee, and Otis' involvement in South Africa was to produce excellent profits for another decade, not least thanks to a lenient tax regime. Prospects in Cairo itself—"a tremendous city with many modern office blocks and apartment houses," Douglas observed—seemed good, although the city was subject to enemy air raids, which Douglas witnessed. His flight to Bombay (with a stop in Saudi Arabia) was recalled once by the military before finally arriving in India at 4:30 a.m.

Douglas made friends—and powerful contacts—easily. He reserved much of such scorn as he had for his erstwhile rival Grandgerard, whom he had appointed, via Petersen, to run Asia. "Mr. Grandgerard (Far Eastern Manager, New York) was at the airport with an automobile that promptly ran out of gasoline," he reported. "It isn't an easy thing to get gas in India at 5 am, but through the courtesy of the TWA manager we soon were underway again only to have the car's cooling system break down. It took two hours, and uncounted buckets of water furnished by friendly Indians, to cover the twelve miles to the Taj Mahal Hotel. Then a bath and breakfast and back on schedule again."

This, in the *Otis Bulletin,* was perhaps rather below the belt. As Far East Manager, Grandgerard was hardly responsible for the condition of the car. Moreover, India was not an efficient country in the best of times, and in 1948 it had just suffered the lethal agonies of partition. Douglas could appreciate the immense difficulties the country faced as the first major nation to emerge from colonial rule since 1776: "The Indian," he wrote, "is beginning to realize that his new independence means that he must now solve problems that previously were the responsibility of others.... The Indians are working hard to improve themselves," he added later.

From Bombay to Delhi to Calcutta, Douglas traveled, noted improvements and passed on. His plane arrived in Shanghai at 2:45 a.m. Once again he was met by Otis men, including Murloh Woo. Shanghai had been one of the growth spots for Otis business before the war, the financial capital of the Far East, the famous Bund or waterfront lined with the banks and clubs of the city's European governors; but Douglas picked up a mood of disenchantment. "Today," he wrote, with massive understatement in hindsight, "the prospects of new business in China are not good, but there remains a considerable amount of installation work to be completed...." More significant, really, was the fact that "the financial situation in China was reaching a critical point for the second time in less than three months." Nearly every store had closed its doors and refused to sell any more goods until the government would declare a realistic value for gold yuan in terms of U.S. dollars. It was the same old story: the people had lost confidence in the value of their currency. So had Douglas. "Prior to the war, this was a very active elevator market, but now it is a city of depressed people who wait only to see what will happen to them."

Douglas flew to Hong Kong, where plenty of apartment and office buildings were going up with Collective and Signal Control elevators, then on to Manila, where he found extensive war damage but the Otis office busy with installations. Along with independence, the Philippines had been given a $500 million line of credit to draw on, most of which had already been used up.

After an eight-hour flight, with a refueling stop in Hong Kong, Douglas reached Bangkok. Thailand was a long shot for Otis—only nine elevators in the whole country, and some were out of order. But "a fine new hotel" was waiting for its Otis elevator to arrive, which would be "the first post-war lift in Siam." Having shown the flag, Douglas flew KLM to Singapore, where the latest tall building was the 14-story Bank of China, equipped with Gearless Signal Control. Here Douglas' schedule came hopelessly unstuck when a delay at the airport turned into a four-day wait before the long flight to Sydney, via Darwin.

This was Douglas' first trip Down Under, and he found Australia in the grip of rapid development. Rather as the Civil War in the United States had spurred the development of industry there, so the Second World War had encouraged the Australians to become largely self-sufficient. In Melbourne, Sydney and Adelaide, Douglas visited 20-story buildings equipped with the most modern escalators and elevators—all except a small amount of specialist equipment produced at the Waygood-Otis plant. Newly installed escalators were drawing capacity crowds in Melbourne. Time was short as he took off on a flying boat across the Tasmanian Sea to visit Auckland, New Zealand.

On December 17 he began the homeward journey on Pan Am—9,200 miles to go, with five stops (Java, Canton Island, Honolulu, San Francisco, New York). The journey took four days, the *Otis Bulletin* reported, "It would be nice to say he had gone 35,000 miles around the world on a tight schedule planned months in advance, and then completed the job exactly on time. But that would not be exactly true. He was twenty minutes ahead of time."

And so, in 1948, Douglas bypassed Germany and overflew Japan. He was probably wise to hand the poisoned chalice of Japan over to Grandgerard, who was already struggling with the teeming subcontinent of India as it broke apart. Grandgerard had returned to Japan for the first time in 1947 and found it in chaos.

Chapter 19

The American Dream

ONCE IN CHARGE OF INTERNATIONAL, Douglas set about bringing Otis' scattered overseas operations into some kind of order. By planning and coordinating the company's overseas efforts, he believed Otis could reassert its reputation for producing quality elevators, making Otis' standards in the United States standard for the world, too.

This meant preserving the highly centralized structure that allowed New York to respond quickly, prescribe with confidence and keep tabs on foreign operations. In New York, moreover, Douglas could win the capital funds from headquarters to invest in production facilities and worker training abroad. Naturally Otis in the United States provided the norm, the model, against which foreign operations were judged.

Very strong links were forged between the various departments of International's head office in New York and its corresponding departments in foreign subsidiaries—the so-called dotted line. Accountants in New York spoke to accountants around the world and ensured that procedures were standardized. United States service technicians provided models of conformity to service operatives. New York production managers, sales executives, designers, draftsmen—all were engaged in communicating directly with their foreign counterparts to achieve "improvement over the standards" of each foreign region. Douglas and his staff controlled the gate through which the information flowed, though other managers in the United States forged contacts and some-times pressed ideas abroad without their knowledge.

Douglas was trying to do for International operations what Baldwin had done for the corporation in America 50 years earlier, to weld all the ramshackle survivors of the war into a single, accountable and responsive unit. This second round of restructuring reverberated with echoes of the first. In Baldwin's day *The Indicator* had inculcated a kind of bravery-under-fire ethos, in which the challenges were tough but the rewards for men who met them were guaranteed. Reinforced by the new manage-ment sciences, Baldwin's ideal had been to weld the company into a single battalion so well organized, motivated and drilled it would respond automatically to orders from above.

The warrior image, however, was less persuasive for a generation that had experienced the real thing. So Douglas, with Petersen, drew on a more contemporary stock of imagery to flesh out their family ideal of the company—an ideal with obvious relevance as it sought to reanimate and extend its position in more than 30 different countries after the war. Where *The Indicator* had trumpeted achievements and technological data, with rousing exhortations to its people, the *Otis Bulletin** put people first.

No employee was too humble to be spotlighted for a cover photo. The caption compilers never forgot a name. Otis employees' lives were explored in often fascinating detail. Whereas *The Indicator*'s authors had labored under an elitist fear that the workers would slack off if left alone, the *Bulletin* exuded a calm confidence that everyone would do his or her duty. That much was a legacy of the universal mobilization of 1939–45. If the new focus had a fault, it was that, in cheering the work that Otis did rather than exhorting it to do more, it risked the charge of complacency.

But the Europeans were excited by what Douglas' organization had to offer. America was the cynosure of easy glamour and techno-chic. The war had been won, after all, by U.S. hardware, and the world had grown used to handling desirable American goods, from chewing gum and "nylons" to Sherman tanks and submachine guns. Otis people abroad basked in Otis' reputation for building the glossy beasts of

---

* It actually started up in the Depression, fell silent during the war and returned to print in April 1947.

American elevatoring–the big gearless machines, the swift geared electrics–Otis was famous for.

Erik Warners, working at Otis' Netherlands company, remembers how European elevator men were swept up "in the glamour of high-rise buildings" in the early 1950s, when American styling and American design seemed to many people to be the goal of all their aspirations. Those who actually traveled to America went in active anticipation of a country overflowing with wealth, glamour and exuberant self-confidence. Many Europeans expected recovery to come with a new American accent, and for the European metropolis emerging from the rubble of World War II to be higher, more modern, more *American* than before.

It is hardly surprising that New York found itself dictating to its satraps when they appeared so eager to listen. In 1952, in a report written for the *Bulletin*, a German trade union representative brought to the United States on a cultural exchange was struck by:

> *the freedom and lack of regimentation on the job and at home, and the openmindedness and optimism.... Life in the streets is pleasant and friendly. The tremendous traffic...has created an exemplary traffic discipline. One does not hear a voice shout from a car, "Look out, you jerk!..." Skilled craftsmen have their own automobiles and in other respects live like persons in the higher income brackets.... And there is something else which is unknown in Germany: unions and management are not unalterably opposed, but work together in complete understanding; unions do not desire to harm the employer, but rather do everything to improve production....* *

European enthusiasm for things American was good news for Douglas and Otis, who looked forward to peddling in Europe the kind of elevator systems popular in the United States, where International policy was formed. Yet the pleasure foreign nationals took in working for so

---

* This lavish praise, the author added, was not based on superficial impressions but on those "imprinted by our stay, by training courses in Washington, and by everything we heard and saw." The author even became "the first German national to give blood...for American fighting men in Korea." Interestingly, the kind of praise he heaped on the United States in 1952 would have fitted Germany 20 years later, raising the interesting possibility that Germans modeled themselves on the American Dream.

solid and well-supported a company, and the success of its highly centralized structure in the first decade after the war, owed much to Douglas' leadership of the International Division. In a world short on confidence and stability, Douglas' staff provided both. Whether one was chasing markets in the Netherlands, trying to increase exports from the British Isles, or riding the boom for high-rise building in South Africa, New York was steady and ready with advice, blueprints, business assistance–and cash. Relations were close. The International Division's records show dozens of foreign managers flying in and out of Idlewild Airport every year. In 1955, for instance, 29 foreign managers came to New York from every outpost of the Otis empire–construction managers from Uruguay and England, the works manager from Brazil, no fewer than five executives from Germany, others from France, Argentina, Colombia, Cuba, Egypt, Hong Kong, India, Italy, Japan, Mexico, the Philippines, Puerto Rico, Singapore, South Africa and Venezuela.

Douglas and his staff–a team of 11 in 1955–went trouble-shooting all around the world, "by railway, inclined railway, motor launch, ferry boat, sampan, rickshaw and trishaw," as Van Schoonhoven explained in 1956, and the list of places they visited reads like a full-blown gazetteer of the Free World. They went to the Dominican Republic and the Belgian Congo. They saw Nairobi and Guam. They piled into India and Italy, Holland and Germany, England, France and Belgium. Often they went more than once. Often several of them went together. There wasn't a continent on the globe in which New York men didn't show their faces and forge relationships with the people "on the ground."

The friendships they made counted heavily in making the whole system work. They were first-rate managers, personally selected by Douglas, whose spirit of frank confidence inspired a whole generation of foreign managers. Douglas in particular was held in very high regard by everyone who dealt with him. He was a statesman. He was a born diplomat. He radiated confidence and inspired trust, so that people who knew him testify unanimously to his grace and charm, invariably choosing to describe him as a gentleman.

Hubert Faure, a young Frenchman job-hunting in New York in 1947, experienced Douglas' charm and was thoroughly disarmed. For Faure was the very model of a gentleman himself.

Hubert Faure was born to a well-to-do family in 1919. His mother was an aristocrat; his father, who did not need to work for a living, pursued literary ambitions. The family wealth was founded on African zinc. Faure attended a Jesuit school and was admitted to the Ecole des Sciences Politiques, a training ground for France's governing elite. The German occupation interrupted his studies, and after the war he joined the French foreign service, spending two years as an attaché at the embassy in Bogota. On his return to France, his father, with unconscious irony, suggested that he look for a proper job.

Faure began with a small manufacturer of heavy coil springs in France, where he learned to manage cost accounts, but after two years he accompanied his American wife to New York. There he spent months in the New York Public Library, "trying to complete my education," as he said, "without a formal discipline," perfecting his English and enjoying society. He met Percy Douglas at Douglas' house on Park Avenue and was promptly offered a job. He had already been considering U.S. multinationals—perhaps IBM, perhaps International Harvester. He had had several interviews. A week after their meeting he called Douglas. Slightly to Faure's surprise, Douglas came on the phone immediately—it was hardly what Faure expected from a hard-boiled U.S. businessman. And Douglas came straight to the point: "I'm so happy to hear from you," he said. "I was thinking about you." Faure took up Douglas' offer of a job without even getting back to IBM.

Otis' products, as Faure would be the first to point out, belonged to the America of dreams. The first non-attendant elevators had already reached the marketplace: in New York, Faure's trips to IBM and International Harvester alone would have introduced him to buildings that were breathtakingly efficient and high-tech by the standards of the day. The acid test of a good elevator is that one hardly notices it (fast, silent, an integral part of the building that contains it), and Faure had scarcely noticed the elevators he had encountered in his months in New York. They rose; they leveled; their doors slid effortlessly to and fro; and they looked immaculate.

All the more extraordinary, then, to step behind the scenes to see how these polite expressions of American technological grace were produced. Hubert Faure was placed—entirely by accident, as he has since maintained—into a trainee program at Yonkers and plunged immediately into a Dickensian caricature of factory life. Raw materials were heaped one upon another, fed haphazardly into the mill, moved along without timing or reason, heaped up here, called for there. In one department the men stood idle while next door they might be working in desperate haste. Production, at the end of it all, seemed as much a matter of faith as planning. Weirdest of all, perhaps, was to see the precious parts so painfully brought together as complete elevators torn apart and packed into hundreds of boxes, to be separated, stacked, perhaps to be lost, forgotten. Faure asked questions, and someone was always on hand to reassure him. Someone knew, or claimed to know, that everything was going to turn out right.

"I was there with people who had worked as foremen in factories," he recalls, "people who had studied some engineering, or manufacturing techniques, for years. I was absolutely the only one without any technical background at all." Perhaps ignorance made him look harder to understand the processes involved. He remained baffled. "I didn't understand how it worked—how the raw materials came in and the way they came out." But if factory methods seemed 19th-century, when he was at last sent out on-site the whole installation process took him further back still, to the medieval age.

For several months—to his utter astonishment—he was paid to watch men installing elevators in the new United Nations Secretariat building in New York. Union rules prevented his lending a hand as he crammed into an elevator shaft with his tutors, the installation men, marveling at the unruffled calm in which they worked, the breadth of experience they brought to the job. American hard-hatters working at a hundred different tasks in the confines of a shaft seemed to him like the master craftsmen who had built the great cathedrals of Europe.

The work practices were so arcane as to resemble the guild restrictions of another age. He was allowed to look but not work, so that "most of the day was spent not really working very hard but doing things, doing work." Parts would arrive helter-skelter, shipped whenever it suited the factory, then be torn from their boxes and scattered around the site until they were needed. Faure was impressed by the "formidable competence of the American hard hatters, that could sort out all these hundreds of pieces.... They had some vague diagrams and plans...and at the end of six, eight months, twelve months, eighteen months, we would end up with a lift that worked perfectly well."[11]

Faure came to the conclusion that the company was absurdly bound by its traditions of production, employment and organization. The startling inefficiency of the enterprise was addressed in piecemeal fashion, for no one really wanted to take stock and shake the whole operation down, from the factory to the elevator shaft. Faure's perception of Otis' operating methods was further sharpened by his relative ignorance of engineering–ignorance at the level of detail, that is. The only tool Faure brought to the study of Otis' field and factory methods was his reasoning ability. He questioned the way materials moved in the plant, the way they moved out of it, the way jobs were assigned, the way completion was finalized. Otis people had already devised a rule of thumb: they said that a job was done when the weight of the car installed was matched by the weight of the paperwork that went with it. Years later Faure went gunning for paperless installations.

It seems hardly surprising that Douglas eventually sent Faure back to ask questions in France, ending what had been, by Otis' standards, an unusual experiment in culture-crossing. Certainly, as International's reports showed, foreign managers had visited New York, toured the plants and been briefed at headquarters; but it was rare for any of them to examine Otis' methods at the cutting edge. The questions they might have formulated never sprang to mind, and it is doubtful whether they would have considered it entirely polite to voice them if they had. They belonged to the system.

Faure, on the other hand, was foreign, lowly and perfectly ignorant. He was also, by Otis' recruitment standards, something of a freak–a generalist who, faced with something that interested him and which he did not understand, thought it natural to ask questions.

The idea that Otis might adopt, within a decade, a strategy in Europe different from the one it pursued in America, Canada, Australia, South America, Japan and southern Africa would have seemed unlikely in the early 1950s, when Douglas' policies were bent toward realizing a single benchmark of quality–a benchmark stamped in America and, more precisely, at International Division headquarters in New York.

True, as prospects in Europe brightened, a certain small degree of local variation was not actively discouraged by the parent company. Compared with the more rigid stance adopted by Otis engineers between the wars, who allowed only the dimensions of the cab to diverge from U.S. norms, Douglas and his staff let local prejudices and traditions be taken into account, though usually reflected more in organization than in product. Douglas could be reluctantly persuaded to license the manufacture of certain machines on the understanding that these would be shelved once the local economy had completed the process of healing and redevelopment.

As industrial growth took off in Europe and farming became increasingly mechanized, people were moving from the country to town—a repetition of the mass migration to the cities that America had experienced 60 years earlier. Between 1948 and 1964, for example, the proportion of continental Europe's population living in the countryside dropped from 25 percent to just 7 percent. In many countries, but especially Germany, there was an urgent need to replenish the housing stock. Capital was scarce, and the authorities took over the provision of "social housing" as a matter of priority.

Utility, not beauty, was the top priority: Guy de Viaris described the unitary housing models introduced in France as "those very gray looking, sad looking buildings in long bars...with all sorts of crude, prefabrication processes,"[12] but they were warm and cheap, and once the buildings had topped four stories they created an overnight demand for suitable elevators. Faced with this burgeoning market, elevator companies worked in close collaboration with the housing authorities to provide cheap, standardized machines that architects and builders could slot into their designs. In West Germany in the 17 years from 1948 to 1965, some 8 million homes were constructed. Flohr-Otis introduced its Standard Wohnung Aufzug (SWA) in 1954. It was nothing like the American dream; it had one speed, was cheap and reliable and was built out of wood and formica. Contractors could take it in gray or blue. It grew a little more sophisticated over the years—it developed a two-speed AC motor and came to be made in sheet metal—and it had sold in its thousands by the early 1960s. Douglas was probably strong-armed into letting this product out by the conditions under which Otis had re-entered the nascent German market, as an ally of an old competitor and neighbor, Karl Flohr.

A similar leeway had to be given to the Italians, although not entirely for the same reasons. Eighty years after Italian reunification, Italy still resembled in some respects a coalition of independent nations, deeply divided by social differences, political allegiances, dialect, culture and history. Each of these small statelets viewed the others with profound mistrust, and the central authorities with zealous contempt. A Tuscan was as much a foreigner in Rome as Douglas himself, and when it came to providing, say, service to elevator installations, the job had to be done by a local man if anyone was to have faith in the work done. On the economic side, this particularism made the Italian economy astonishingly robust: it was on GNP figures for Italy as a whole that Douglas based his rather startling deduction that Italy would soon be the biggest card in the Otis pack after the United States and Britain. Certainly Italy rebounded quickly after the war. But with myriad small-sized, locally based factories and an unrivaled supply of competent engineers, Italians wanted small elevators for small businesses; they wanted them made of aluminum; and they wanted them installed and serviced by a local team. Italy's AT machine was unveiled in 1956.

In Italy and Germany, Otis bowed to the pressures of circumstance, deigning to enter the low-rise market in which it had traditionally little confidence and next to no interest, but the company had brighter hopes for France. Business had begun picking up there from the early 1950s. In recognition of Otis' all-powerful grip on Otis-Pifre, the company, as previously mentioned, was renamed Ascenseurs Otis in 1951, and looked forward to furnishing hotels, hospitals, factories and government buildings with big elevators hand-built at its factory at Bezons. Thanks to one young man's superior patience, however, France turned out to be the joker in the pack.

Otis grew worldwide as post-war industrial expansion created
a more robust global economy.
See Appendix.

Chapter 20

Breaking the Mold

ASCENSEURS OTIS WAS THE CHILD of corporate headquarters. Since Douglas' visits in 1947 and 1948, the technicalities of its wartime debts and ownership had been sorted out and its systems rebuilt to conform to U.S. policy. By 1951, Otis' sales in France had risen comfortably, reaping the benefits of intensive investment and modernization, and in Paris itself there was an air of confidence that had been noticeably absent six years earlier. Under its chairman, M. Aspar, Ascenseurs Otis was a small but solid player in a market that remained slow, producing a variety of those impressive, highly crafted elevators at its plant in Bezons that made Otis' reputation and defined its market niche.

Otis' market in France was further defined—and confined—by the members of the elevator syndicate, a body originally established by the Vichy government during the war, which every month, by law, still met to allocate market share. The syndicate was pleased with the overall progress of the industry and viewed prospects for the future with equanimity. Sometimes Otis overstepped its allocation, whereupon it was duly rebuked with a small fine.

At Douglas' instigation, Faure went to Paris to see M. Aspar, who dodged for a while, reluctantly gave Faure an empty desk and "the smallest amount [in salary] that he could find that was legal," and after several months sent him over to fill in at the sales office. It was a windowless garage with a telephone and four staff members. The telephone was for taking orders. The job consisted of waiting for the telephone to ring and, when it did, filling in the forms.[13]

At last Faure could stop asking questions and start working. He began in 1954, very simply selling elevators. In defiance of tradition, he left the windowless office and visited potential clients. France's building boom was hitting its stride, and everybody wanted a lift. All it took was a little organization—"taking the names of the architects, visiting systematically the architects, the developers"[14]—and the orders began to mount up. Within the year, Faure was in charge of the Paris sales department.

Europeans might be enthusiastic about things American, including the possibility of high-rise buildings, but skyscrapers cost money. Even in America, tall buildings put up in the 1950s were strikingly utilitarian compared with the bold, elaborate productions of the past—architectural historians have struggled to give a name to the numerous cost-conscious stumps of real estate that sprang up between the decline of Art Deco and the rise of International style. And while this was true for America, in Europe the financial constraints were even tighter, and the need for economy more urgent. Land prices were rising while capital remained scarce.

The elevators that Europeans wanted, therefore, were essentially low-cost, simple, slow-speed apartment elevators that served the rash of five- to 10-story blocks put up to house the new influx of rural migrants. Faure promised that Otis would deliver the type of elevator developers required with all the technological resources of Otis at their back and the assurance of Otis' good name and reputation. Nothing, after all, had shown him that Otis was not the best elevator maker in the world. What he questioned—the opportunity he recognized and seized—was the laxity of Otis' procedures.

Over time, the dotted lines to New York had been growing denser. Vigorous and effective action is inherently unsustainable. Somebody's revolutionary idea becomes the next man's comfortable piety, and Douglas' energetic response to Otis' problems overseas eventually wore grooves that were difficult to escape. When it came to an operation like the French Otis, where the entire company had effectively been rebuilt from the ground up by a cadre of executive officers stationed in New York, any operating decision, any change of specification, and any job that called for fresh design work had to be cleared with New York first. The process was slow. New York's control extended even to the choice of paint used to decorate executive offices, as Hubert Faure discovered in 1959 when, as the newly appointed sales director, he moved in next door to Aspar's office. It was, he recalls, the "most depressing color of green. One of the first things I said was, 'I want to have this office painted white.' For me it was symbolic."

Faure's insistence on pursuing the "tin box" market was culturally and strategically problematic for Otis. Germany had done it; Italy had done it; but for France—unexceptionable France—to do it, too, looked like turning an anomaly into a trend, and suggested the possibility that Otis centralist policies were breaking down.

From New York's point of view, the sooner European countries were weaned from their infantile enthusiasm for small elevators the sooner Otis could kick in there with its high-tech products and reap the profits. To feed the market's desire for tin boxes was inevitably to delay the flowering of Otis' investment—if not worse. Faure remembers picking up Petersen at Orly Airport and driving him back through Paris—then in a mood of expansion, with new trains, new cars, new buildings everywhere. When Faure showed Petersen new elevators, Petersen grumbled, "I don't want any of these. These are not Otis policy." Lest there be any doubt, he continued: "Otis policy is big machines, and the French don't understand that they need these big gearless machines and not only small elevators. And they better do it, otherwise the economy of France will go bankrupt."[15]

There were tactical objections, as well, to expanding down-market, although few people recognized them as clearly as Faure himself. For the factory men at Bezons, it implied a descent from the Olympian heights that they monopolized in France with their access to sophisticated American technology. The low-rise was a relatively crowded market, in which regional players already jostled with a host of robust but small, cost-competitive local manufacturers—nothing like Italy but nonetheless crowded. The elevator business in Europe at the time tended likewise to be separated into national markets because of different national building codes and different tariff barriers. Otis, meanwhile, succeeded on quality. To succeed in this new market, it would have to attend to costs. Cost *and* quality? It looked as if Otis might be asked to square the circle.

Bezons shuddered, but Faure was right in his analysis of what France–and ultimately Europe–wanted from an elevator. Demand for Otis' traditional machines would grow, but the bulk of Otis' work was in those very tin boxes, and Faure had no qualms about securing those orders and asking Bezons to fulfill them. It wasn't long before Otis' top brass sanctioned a modest expansion of the factory.

All the same, a bigger factory could not give Faure what he needed. Factory, sales, engineers–all were so rigidly compartmentalized that he could scarcely speak to the factory men, let alone discuss business with them. And Bezons felt pressed.

One of Faure's allies–at least a man who listened sympathetically to his arguments–was Bill Reid, a Canadian who took Douglas' place at the head of the International Division when Douglas became president of the company in 1961. Reid had run Otis in Canada as an exemplary organization–the Hamilton factory was forever being held up to U.S. factory managers as the goal they should strive toward, particularly in the area of worker safety, where its record was unsurpassed.*

Reid still shared some of headquarters' fears that Faure's strategy in France risked institutionalizing the company's commitment to the low-rise market, and he made Faure an extraordinary offer in the summer of 1959. Aspar was retiring. Faure, said Reid, should take his place. He would have responsibility for sales, installation and service, but the factory and engineering would be handled by a separate executive.

Faure could be captain on the bridge, in other words, and the wheel was his to command, but all communication to the engine room was cut. It was managerial never-never land, of course, an echo of the functional irrationality that had startled Faure in America 10 years earlier. Faure turned Reid down, and the fantastic plan collapsed like a house of cards. Reid did make a show of considering his next move, but he really had no choice but to agree to the terms set by one of the most

---

* That in itself was a testament to Reid's ability to change mentalities, for there was little doubt that accidents were caused as much by insouciance and machismo as by any danger inherent in the factory process. Following Reid's example, the *Otis Bulletin* began a campaign against "badges of courage"–injuries–sustained by people perpetuating a "tough guy" approach to their work. "The law of averages always seems to catch up with him sooner or later. That helps explain the growing shortage of 'tough guys' these days, that and the increasing number of 'sissies' who figure life is short enough as it is."

effective executives in the International Division. By August 1959, Faure was the chief operating officer of Ascenseurs Otis.

The surreal struggle over Aspar's successor was more than a hollow tussle over title. It was a battle over responsibilities that cut straight to the heart of Otis' future in Europe–and ultimately beyond.* Faure was not yet ready to challenge the bureaucracy he served–that would have to wait three more years–but he meant to ensure that the bureaucracy which served him served his vision of the business. Meanwhile he waited for the germ of an idea he had planted in the mind of a French competitor to bear fruit.

When Hubert Faure went to America in 1949, his dreams of efficiency had echoed Charles Otis', 80 years before. Charles tore through his factory in 1887, asking the questions nobody had asked since 1882, turning on stockholders and employees with exasperated abandon, riffling through figures and processes until he retired, baffled and angry, at the age of 52. Faure took a cooler approach and wasted no time tilting at windmills.

By now, 10 years later, Faure was crystallizing his ideas. On one occasion he prepared a paper on the proper relations between the center and the periphery–a discussion of line and staff responsibilities–in which he quoted, with a few pertinent changes of image, from an acknowledged expert in organizational sciences, Mao Tse Tung. Mao had responded to his military situation in the 1930s by creating a flexible command structure, one in which the central command retained overall strategic control but delegated responsibilities to semi-autonomous regional brigades. Paris was not Marseilles; France was not Germany. Faure wanted Otis to adopt–in the broadest possible sense– a guerrilla strategy.

Otis in America, like the United States itself on the international stage, had become a leviathan whose assumptions could be challenged only by outsiders who remained light on their feet. The trouble with Otis in the United States was that it insisted on grinding its executives in the

---

* Otis at that time was the largest manufacturer of elevators in the world. By the end of the 1960s it had affiliates in 46 countries and sales representatives in 69. Overseas sales made up almost half of the company's total of $536 million.

same mill. A nation with more than its fair share of flair, dynamism and eccentricity tended to organize and train its personnel along humdrum lines. Faure was in a good position to see that the classic Harvard Business School career trajectory perpetuated attitudes and assumptions—the same observation he had made early on in New York, among American hard-hatters—which precluded vision. Too much emphasis was placed on learning the processes, on how to manipulate the levers of business, and rather too little on examining how the levers worked, or why they were there. "I had recommended—with very little success—that instead of sending high flyers back to Harvard for advanced management courses, they should send them God only knows where on a mountain with their wife with an absolute obligation to read history, poetry, psychology, never anything to do with technology, computers, systems, anything...."[16]

Faure was punctilious, polite—the diplomatic service had taught him that—and ready to persevere. He knew that it was not the product that was at fault but the whole mechanism for delivering elevators to customers, from first approach to the signing of the service contract. Typically, three years would elapse between the initial proposal for a big, gearless elevator installation and the completed installation. He had a good idea where problems lay, but meanwhile he spent months asking his people to explain their jobs to him. "I always thought that when people explained something to me that I didn't understand, there was something wrong in their explanation, especially regarding systems or subjects in a specialized field that I didn't know anything about." He asked them to try again, using terms a 12-year-old child could understand. Often he would discover people engaged in processes that had been sanctioned, even set up, at headquarters, without any real effort to integrate their work into the local system; and sometimes he found operations underway that nobody locally knew anything about at all.

What prompted his confidence was not management doctrine, which Faure had never studied formally, but the precepts of an 18th-century Enlightenment rationalist, a mind in line with the suppositions of Diderot, Adam Smith and the framers of the Declaration of Independence. What he was already beginning to develop, as a result, was this curious inspiring confidence–the sort of confidence Charles Otis never managed to attain–that reasonable demands were irresistible.

One of Faure's first moves as head of Ascenseurs Otis was to ask the factory for figures to show what everything cost. The factory manager told him that it was none of his business. After much pressure had been brought to bear, he finally sent up the forms Faure wanted to see. The figures had been blacked out. As far as the manager was concerned, Faure would have to ask New York's permission to read them.

Meanwhile, on the other side of the world, Japan presented even more vexing problems for Otis. Japan had been gutted by the war. The atomic bombs that razed Hiroshima and Nagasaki were no more destructive in the aggregate than the conventional carpet bombing that had shattered and burned Tokyo. Hundreds of thousands of Japanese civilians had been killed, as had 2 million soldiers.

At the war's end, infrastructure had been nonexistent in the big cities. Almost all the elevators in the country had been scrapped at the height of the conflict, so desperate had the Japanese military been for metal. Gangs had attacked the machinery, knocked it to pieces and slung it down the hoistway, where piles of scrap awaited collection. At the end of the war, some of this had been melted down, some of it stacked in scrap yards, and some of it, buried under piles of rubble, still lay in ruined basements.

Nevertheless, elevators, strikingly enough, were at the heart of General MacArthur's program of reconstruction. "Buildings without elevators are worthless," he declared, and elevator men were almost immediately permitted to collect and recondition as much of their old equipment as could be found. The U.S. occupying forces actually set up an Otis man, Kermit Kraus, to run elevator work for the U.S. Army. Kraus had been a civilian prisoner of war of the Japanese, and a contemporary photo shows him stepping up to his new command with a certain look of reluctance. But while elevators were in serious disarray, the Toyo-Otis factory itself was a bombed-out wreck, and the very survival of the company was in question. Mitsui had unilaterally bought out the Otis shareholding in the company on the outbreak of war, depositing the money in the Bank of Japan, where Grandgerard, now back in Japan, found it in 1947. It was worthless, like everything else.

When Grandgerard examined the books, he found that a small factory bought during the war for 500,000 yen was now a hole in the ground worth 2,000 yen, or $10.

Grandgerard was not happy about the valuation, nor the way that the Allied Supreme Pacific Command (SCAP) organization proposed to tackle the issue of recovering Otis' 60 percent stake. The Mitsui management team put in place during the war was dismissed by SCAP, but in the meantime employees returned to the Kamata factory and started producing elevators from bits and pieces scrounged, saved or rediscovered in the rubble, frequently working under umbrellas to protect the machinery from rain that spilled through the broken roof, and using hand-held lights. Otis was still not properly in charge. Grandgerard counseled patience. Perhaps for that reason, Douglas grew bullish.

Douglas was no doubt influenced by the way Grandgerard's original deal in 1930 had turned out to give Mitsui total executive control. Perhaps Grandgerard had underestimated the tendency of Japanese business to look after itself, or perhaps he had overestimated the Japanese public's taste for things American. "It may have been necessary for us to tie up with a big enterprise like Mitsui at the early stage of organization...in the Japanese market," an internal memo reflecting Douglas' view explained. "The name of Toyo-Otis is now well established...as an independent company not being connected with any of the former Zaibatsu influence. So, it would do us more harm rather than benefit if we tried to tie up with any particular or specific financial or business influence in Japan."

All the signs suggested the opposite. Of all the options that presented themselves, Douglas insisted on the one most likely to alienate the Japanese: he insisted that Otis should buy out the Mitsui interest and run Toyo-Otis as a fully owned subsidiary. Just as in the Meiji period, the Japanese had been determined—with American prodding—to reconstruct their country and its economy; they now undertook their postwar reconstruction with the minimum of outside help. In the meantime, a penny spent abroad was a penny wasted. The leader of the newly restored Metalworkers' Union spelled it out firmly in a letter to New York: "Our customers in Japan will not favor, by national sentiment, your company if our full profit is known to go outside Japan." In the circumstances, the Toyo-Otis management had outlined a plan, approved by the union and various factions within SCAP, to turn at least a part of Mitsui's stock over to the employees. If this did not happen, the union warned, the employees' "attitude will plainly be changed."[17]

Toyo-Otis' directors believed this to be so self-evident that when Douglas remained adamant they instead committed the company to paying the employees a 6.5-million-yen lump sum by way of compensation. It isn't easy to see why Douglas chose his lonely furrow in Japan: in Germany, for example, he was happy to authorize a new joint-venture with Flohr, and partnerships had always been the Otis way into foreign markets. Douglas did not underestimate the importance of the Japanese market, but he remained convinced that the company needed careful babying from the head office if it were to grow, and that it would be wise to insulate it from the gyrations of East Asian politics. Perhaps he feared a Communist threat. Perhaps, with reason, he feared a resumption of the old Zaibatsu, arrangements whose tie-ins with the authorities had compromised Toyo-Otis in the 1930s. Perhaps he was simply exasperated by the Japanese. What he pointed out to the commission set up to adjudicate these matters was that Otis had lent its good name to the Toyo-Otis equation in the prewar years, as well as making investments that, thanks to Japanese militarism, it had never recouped.

The results were predictable. Otis took on Mitsui's shares itself, and when Douglas flew to Japan in April 1951 to finalize the deal, he was forced to disavow Toyo-Otis' promise to its employees. Everyone lost face, and the hitherto sublime relationship between Otis employees and management broke down almost immediately. A militant left-wing movement, enjoying the air after 20 years' repression, campaigned directly against the "imperialistic Americans" who owned Toyo-Otis.

Toyo-Otis became that most unusual thing, an American company operating at the heart of the Japanese industrial scene. It was a lonely place to be. To keep employees, Toyo-Otis had to review workers' wages semiannually. It actually had to pay them more (6 percent more) than workers in comparable industries. But perhaps no one at Otis could have predicted the economic miracle that would turn Japan into the richest country in the world in less than 30 years, nor the tactics that Japanese business would employ to sideline Otis on the way.

Unlikely as it might have seemed at the time, Japan was at the threshold of a second Meiji period. Like the first, this one followed on American intervention and demanded self-discipline and sacrifice. As soon as the American occupation government withdrew, in 1952, the Japanese government began to stitch together new economic combines, successors to the old, discredited Zaibatsu, to manage the return to economic self-sufficiency. Every encouragement was given to enterprises that succeeded in exporting goods, for Japan was still strapped for raw materials; in this atmosphere Otis, still insisting on repatriating its profits, suffered badly.

Otis' last chance to oversee the growth of its business in Japan vanished with the outbreak of the Korean War. The ensuing boom in Japan brought the company more work but also encouraged competition and hustled the economy along toward a maturity Otis executives were not prepared for. Some of Otis' most up-to-date American models were produced at the Kamata factory, including the 131HT. In 1954 the company felt confident enough in its reliability and spare-part inventories to lend its name to the Full Maintenance program; it was also generous enough to explain and demonstrate the entire system to Japanese competitors, in the belief that this would help establish the need for maintenance in the public's mind.

Winning in the increasingly competitive environment of Japanese construction, though, was seldom easy, and by 1957 Toyo-Otis' market share was slipping, although the company paid a 40 percent dividend. Its competitors had used the time to form "enterprise groups," *keiretsu,* whose elevator divisions benefited from economies of scale, purchasing power and marketing connections; by the 1960s only about 45 percent of all available work was open to competitive bidding, the other 55 percent being awarded "by appointment." Otis had always let it be known that it would look for a Japanese industrial partner once it had safely restored the company to profitability, and in 1957 the company formed an alliance with Toshiba, a widely spread industrial group without its own elevator division. A share swap was arranged, one that speaks volumes about the relative size and power of the two concerns. Toshiba took a 20 percent stake in Toyo-Otis; Otis took 0.03 percent of Toshiba.

Despite Toshiba, New York's hand fell heavily on Japan. Otis' reliance on high-cost, high-technology elevators still paid handsome dividends in Japan, and many major installations were made with Autotronic machines. Even government offices leaped at Otis' ability to eliminate elevator operators, and Otis maintenance contracts continued to grow on the back of healthy new sales in this area. Otis executives in America were pleased with the figures and with the type of work the company was doing in Japan. Despite prodding from the Japan Housing Corporation and from Toshiba, Toyo-Otis proceeded very slowly with the development of a small, standardized elevator suitable for mass production.

One problem was plant capacity. Made to produce 150 units a year, the Kamata factory was too small for the amount of work it managed— 158 units in 1958, 302 units in 1961. That was the year in which Toyo-Otis got permission, which it had been asking for repeatedly, to expand; and the reluctance of the International Division to increase its investment reflects a failure to recognize the danger of competition in Japan. But perhaps even more significant for Otis' long-term goals was the inability of the company to establish the web of harmonious relationships so important to the conduct of business in the country. Japan's history had proven the power of motivation, and the most successful Japanese companies depended on a contract with employees that would have been unthinkable in America or Europe. The best-known provision was jobs-for-life, by which employers guaranteed not to lay off workers. Otis, like Grandgerard in the early 1930s, still seemed not to understand the "Japanese Way."

In the 1960s Japan was still only one of a number of countries in which Otis had interests, and not necessarily either the most congenial or the most promising. The Japanese Way looked like a confusing mixture of the cozy and the cutthroat, decency and deceit. For strategic reasons, the United States permitted Japan to flout trade rules and grow rich. For historical reasons, the United States paid for Japan's defense and absolved it from contributing to the costs of policing the region. From a global perspective, Japan seemed more like an awkward problem, and then possibly a bubble, than a major opportunity. "Made in Japan" had been a byword for cheap in Western markets; it was only gradually that it came to denote reliability, of an ugly sort, and finally, of course, reliability and style.

The way the spheres of business, government and society interlocked made Japanese employment policies desirable domestically, but they made little sense to a company like Otis operating in dozens of markets across the world. It was both Otis' misfortune and good luck to be in the Japanese market as a producer at all. From 1950 the Japanese government had routinely refused to authorize joint ventures, so that Otis' position was that of a lucky man on the last boat in. Once in, though, the company had to fight for dwindling market share against very determined and well-adjusted competitors. Mitsubishi, for example, which produced Westinghouse elevators under license, and Hitachi, which had established its own elevator division, were able to organize both production and sales according to the Japanese Way, without further ramifications, whereas any concession made by Otis in Japan was sure to be scrutinized by union leaders in the rest of the world. Union busting in the United States and, to a certain extent, in Europe would be the vital corollary to introducing more "Japanese" processes to Otis' global operations; but Otis could only wait for political events for that.

Ascenseurs Otis, small but growing, already earned far more than Toyo-Otis in Japan; in 1963, with $15.7 million worth of new equipment sales, $22.4 million in total revenues and $692,000 in earnings. Waygood's revenues were bolstered by its profits from high-rise installations, a market still undeveloped on the Continent; Ascenseurs Otis had still managed to triple its revenues in eight years while taking on only 30 percent more employees.

It was a petty market all the same, and Otis' share of it did not reflect the company's predominance in elevator manufacture in America. The small elevator market was price-sensitive and potentially open to small firms such as BDR, which made elevators, steel beams and steel furniture. In 1961, Faure met its owner, Pierre Roussel, and with mounting enthusiasm—and a dash of inspiration—sketched out to him a vision of the future of the elevator industry in Europe.

Currently, Faure pointed out, the European elevator industry was helplessly atomized. In France, above all, elevators were being provided by myriad small companies, many of them traditional family concerns. As the pace of business heated up, there would have to be a period of consolidation, Faure pointed out, a concentration of the elevator industry. It would happen in France. It would, he felt sure, happen across Europe, too. Whether the national borders and tariffs fell or not, Faure was determined to manage the process of concentration and create a French-based company large enough to deal on the European level.

This was visionary in the early 1960s. The only continental trading bloc in the world–the United States–had taken centuries to come into being, and Otis belonged to it. But New York needed much prodding to accept even the earliest premise, that Ascenseurs Otis should grow by acquisition. Faure bolstered his argument by persuading Roussel to merge with Schlieren in 1960; in 1962, Roussel added Edoux-Semain, heir to the entrepreneur who had first introduced hydraulic lifts and who had made a respectable showing at the Eiffel Tower 100 years earlier. The new company was called Ascinter, and its 25 percent market share in France belied its capacity as the largest manufacturer of small, slow-speed elevators in Europe.

In Europe! There was a meaningless abstraction, a collation of a dozen or two countries, divided by history, politics, language and religion, divided by seas and mountains, divided by race and economic perceptions, a bickering and unwilling community of nations inhabiting, very roughly speaking, the Christianized tip of the vast Eurasian continent.

But Europe was real, too, a coherent idea exploited down the centuries by ambitious strongmen–Charlemagne, Napoleon, even Hitler had planned at a European level. It was in response to Hitler, after all, that a generation of politicians since World War II had spoken actively of a European community. From America's point of view, Europe meant something: a succession of art galleries, or just trouble. The British, those offshore islanders, treated Europe as a standing threat.

By the end of World War II, however, it was clear to many people that the threat had a specific locus: Germany, which was blamed for having begun two of the worst wars the world had ever experienced.

Everyone was aware of the problem, not least postwar Germany itself. For West Germans, the postwar division of their country—not just into two polities but between the two systems of government and belief that dominated the entire globe—served as a daily reminder of the perils of an aggressive, isolated Germany.* Germany entered the French-inspired Coal and Steel Union in 1951, a union that led in 1957 to the Treaty of Rome, which effectively established a presumption of community among the six signatories, France, Germany, Italy and the new Benelux Countries. The new European Economic Community aimed to remove internal tariffs, harmonize transport, agriculture and taxes, and encourage capital and labor mobility.

There could be no doubt that all these countries were economic powers of the first rank. The Old World, even after two world wars, had re-gathered its energies and skills and set out once again to exploit them. Its scientists, engineers, machinists, even its laborers had restored the status quo, and the 1960s were going to be Europe's decade. After years of living in the shadow of dictatorships and war, Europe in the 1960s acquired all the toasters and automobiles, the TV sets and the washing machines, that America had boasted in the 1920s—40 years late, perhaps, but right up to date. By 1964, Europe's industrial output was two and a half times that of 1938. The population boomed while unemployment—the great specter of interwar Europe—was so much a thing of the past that West Germany employed over 1 million foreign workers in 1964. Skilled labor was especially in demand. As the International Division report for 1964 explained:

> *The steady expansion of industry in Western Europe and the British Isles continues to place a strain upon whatever labor pool exists. The major source of labor, comprising the presently unemployed and the new generation now approaching working age, cannot supply the increasing number of workers for whom employers are competing. The release of workers from low productivity occupations and agriculture now being mechanised will add to the supply of industrial manpower, but the generally tight labor situation is expected to continue....*[18]

---

* "We love Germany so much," a French wag remarked, "that we are glad there are two of them."

The arrival of an affluent society in Europe brought with it teenage rebellions, tabloids, democracy and crises of identity. By the early 1960s countries like West Germany, France, Britain and Italy had "caught up" with the United States, even in their demand for tall buildings. What European nations shared was deemed, for political and economic reasons, more important than what divided them.

While Ascinter proceeded to build a modern factory at Gien to make standardized machines, doors and car enclosures with potential for mass production, Faure ensured that Pierre Roussel would not enjoy his newfound eminence for long. When Bezons turned down a contract that called for 100 small elevators to be installed at a large building project in northern France, Faure did not despair. As the factory men observed, it was not really an Otis job at all: contracts of this sort invariably went elsewhere on price. Breaking the rule that forbade him to leave France, even on holiday, without authorization from New York, Faure turned to his counterpart in Italy, Herman Krantz. To the horror of the French embassy in Rome, Faure reached an informal agreement that Stigler-Otis would sell him low-cost, small elevators that could be shipped to France and reassembled there, very cheaply despite the customs dues.

Otis won the contract. The imported elevators were reassembled in a temporary shed erected on site and slotted into the shafts. Pierre Roussel at Ascinter, who had been talking to Westinghouse, paid heed to Faure's renewal of an offer to merge.

International Division's intransigence almost scuttled the deal the moment it was unveiled—its details prepared in utter secrecy, along with astonishingly accurate forecasts, ready for the spring of 1964. When Faure sought permission to go ahead, Douglas told him to forget it. No one at headquarters was able to see how conditions in Europe had changed since the 1950s—how the tempo had increased, how ideas were being generated, how a new self-confidence born of economic recovery was changing the balance of power.

Faure was not the only overseas manager growing restless under New York's sway. All over Europe the growth of the national market for elevators was prompting Otis' elevator people to question the severity of New York planning. Construction was accelerating at a dizzying rate,

pushing interwar architectural and sociological theories into the mainstream. At the government level the idea of a classless society took root,
one in which everyone had employment and in which planners and technicians could effectuate the highest ideals through comprehensive
education and well-designed housing projects. At the consumer level,
people with money in their pockets looked for places to spend it.
Department stores spread. Office buildings erupted to accommodate the
flood of white-collar workers.

Erik Warners, running Otis in Holland, had learned as early as 1957
that a German escalator firm was preassembling escalators, bringing
them into department stores in one piece, and getting out in four or five
days.* "This was a big advantage for the department store owner. I saw
that and I said: 'I'm going to preassemble an escalator for the department
store of Vroom and Dreesman here in Holland.'"†

Warners at that time was getting his escalator parts from Flohr-Otis
in Germany, but to preassemble he needed to make the steel truss that
the machine ran on in Holland, for transport reasons.

As he later recalled:

> *Otto Erik von Klosterlein, Managing Director of Flohr Otis and a
> very good friend of mine—he taught me all about operas and operettas
> when I was in Berlin—said: "Well, Erik, if you want to make your
> own steel structure, ask New York whether you can have the escala-
> tor drawings for the truss." Van Schoonhoven sent me the drawings,
> but [they were] designed for American steel sections which are quite
> different from European steel sections. Although I knew I could get the
> proper drawings from Otto Erik, Van said: "No. If you insist on
> doing that, you can have the drawings for the truss." I said: "Yes,
> but I can't use your drawings because the strengths, the sections, the
> whole lot is not fit to the parts which come from Germany. Please give
> me the drawings from Germany."*

---

* The extent of field operations in elevators was reflected in a study of the composition
  of Deutsche Alzugs. A.G.'s employment in Europe up to 1969. Of a total work force of
  13,000, 6,000 were manual workers in the field while 3,700 were factory workers.
† As Warners wryly noted, it was a far cry from the days when Otis' Dutch director
  visited prospective clients in his top hat and decided by a glance whether they were
  suitable Otis customers!

The most remarkable thing in my life with Otis: Van Schoonhoven sent me a wooden ruler, with centimeters on one side and inches on the other.... I presented this piece of equipment in my staff meeting and said: "The latest joke from the United States is that we do not get the drawings but we get the ruler." I will never forget that moment which indicated how completely unknown the local situation was to the Americans.[19]

Significantly, preassembly was completely forbidden in the United States because it got the company into union trouble. By exporting that attitude, Warners suggests, Otis lost the escalator market in Europe between 1955 and 1970.

By the spring of 1964, Faure needed an answer on the Ascinter merger right away. And he needed the right answer. He was disappointed on the first count, but when at last Douglas came over in November, he inspected the plants, read the projections and told Faure: "You're on your own." For six months Faure had with difficulty kept Roussel waiting, although others prowled around Roussel, who began to wonder what it would be like to work with a company that took so long to reach decisions.

The merger called for advanced diplomacy between the two camps that formed in the company, as well as technical ingenuity to ensure that rival systems married. In principle, so Guy de Viaris thought, the work of combining forces was completed in about six months; Faure suspected four years.

But at every level that mattered the merger was a great success—the first of 31 different mergers and acquisitions that by 1970 were to give European executives unrivaled experience in dealing with the unexpected. To begin with, Faure worked from the understanding that while he had bought valuable cash assets and full order books, there was a psychological ingredient in the purchase, too. Pride was touched. Anxieties were aroused. People's emotions were engaged, and Faure was determined to manage the emotional fallout, too.

His solution was to install Roussel as chairman of the newly merged company while he took the job of his subordinate CEO, after the maxim, Never fight for what you already have. Otis people in the new organization, after all, needed no symbols of victory; Ascinter people, on the other hand, needed to see their old boss, and themselves by extension, welcomed and trusted in the team—and Roussel's position at the head of the company did effectively protect them. The company was known as Ascinter-Otis, in deference to French sensibilities, a decision that cost nothing. Faure, controlling Otis' 60 percent stake in the company, effectively made decisions. It was Mrs. Krantz, however, wife of the man who had helped Faure bust the dams separating one Otis country from another, who spotted the real beauty of the new arrangement. "Now you have a 40 percent minority in your company," she told him. "You can do exactly what you want, because any time you want to do something, you can say 'That's what the minority wants,' and everyone will be so scared of a lawsuit that you'll get exactly what you want from now on."[20]

Ascinter brought Otis exactly what it needed to become the dominant force in French elevatoring and the biggest Otis company outside North America. Two 25 percent shares in the market became, when joined, about 40 percent, and perhaps most crucially, Otis got Ascinter's new state-of-the-art production facility at Gien—a far cry from the Yonkers factory that Faure had seen on his first trip to America. With Gien came some impressive engineers as well as a service base that matched Otis' for size, and Ascinter's splendid new headquarters.* At last the European industry had a major player in the field, big enough to set the pace and push through the next phase of development.

The timing of the expansion was perfect. All the countries of western Europe had been building apartment blocks, just as all of them had experienced a postwar baby boom, but France had built rather more slowly than necessary. Between 1953 and 1960, for instance, the French had constructed fewer than 2 million new homes, compared with almost 4 million in West Germany and 2.5 million in Britain, where the need was less acute. In 1960, in fact, France had only just replaced the housing units destroyed in World War II.

In the meantime, France's population growth rate had been the highest in Europe. In addition, in the early 1960s, 1 million French

---

* Otis' headquarters building, by contrast, was not air-conditioned. When, for operational reasons, various people in the two office buildings were moved from one to the other, each group complained about the ventilation.

Algerians would arrive in the country. France was set to indulge in a frenzy of building.

Faure had been told by Douglas to go ahead, and warned that from then on he would be on his own. Fayette Dunn, subsequently, had the sense to stick to the agreement, and Faure effectively secured a three-year moratorium on visits from any New York personnel, save legal and financial experts, in which to create the necessary corollary to major production of small elevators: an Otis company integrated at a European level.

The direction Otis took in Europe in the last half of the 1960s obeyed the imperious logic of longer production runs and standardization. If Otis were to construct small lifts well at a low cost, it would have to benefit from economies of scale. Gradually, by specializing work into various existing factories, Otis could lengthen production runs and reduce costs; each factory would then gather the necessary parts and produce, in-house, a fully equipped elevator system. The foundation of the plan was the model elevator—a family of cabs and machines produced to standard dimensions.

Yet first, ironically, Faure had to bolster particularism in the industry: he had to create a vigorous company, or family of companies, at the national level. He had already showed what could be done when he set the French engineers to work on the cab doors for a cheap "tin box" elevator. The French had favored doors that opened on a hinge, and such were certainly cheap, if dangerous and unsatisfactory. Conventional wisdom had held that the introduction of sliding doors—a complex mechanism—would boost costs by about 40 percent. The challenge that Faure set his designers and engineers thus had been to come up with a sliding door cheap enough to prove acceptable, yet so self-evidently superior to the run-of-the-mill product that it would simply knock it out of the market. This is exactly what happened with the Orly door, a cheapish sliding door named after the new Paris airport. Otis' competitors were forced to follow suit, and the image of the entire French elevator industry was revolutionized overnight.

Architects loved the Orly door; they were far less keen on modelization and had to be encouraged by revisions to the elevator codes supported by Otis and the authorities. Buyers, though, registered their satisfaction immediately.

Following upon modelization was the aforementioned concept of preassembly—putting an end to the antiquated practice of assembling elevators in the field. "Field" has a nice open ring to it, but in reality it meant working in the cramped confines of the lift shaft. "The car of the elevator," de Viaris pointed out, "uses a lot of components—the safety, the door, the door operator, all of the signals, the buttons, a lot of wiring. In the building—with the wainscoting dark—the poor mechanic had to put all the wiring in piece by piece. The obvious answer was to manufacture the assembly complete in a shop...."[21]

Faure worked through the process with tireless logic. Mass production was the way to keep costs low. Mass production could only be achieved by sticking to a relatively small number of "lines." The U.S. car industry had demonstrated early in the century that a few models were sufficient to satisfy a large number of needs, and by the 1960s even aircraft were being modelized and mass produced. Elevators, as Faure pointed out, were produced in volumes that lay between automobiles and aircraft.

Until then Otis' components had been standardized, but not the product: 183 billion different permutations were theoretically possible. Tailor-made elevators generated paperwork and bureaucracy, and made manufacturing and field work expensive. The number of parts required for tailor-made elevators was compounded by the array needed because of maintenance requirements. In addition to parts for its own units, Otis typically provided parts for elevators produced by companies it had acquired over the years. If the number of components could be reduced, if Otis offered, say, two types of cars, three types of door openings, two types of fixtures, and fixed for each category of lift, heights, weights and depths, then the number of models could be reduced to, say, 10 and cover 90 percent of the total needs of the market for passenger elevators in new buildings. The only remaining variable would be the lift required.

Closely linked to modelization was the issue of preassembly. "Our Industry," Faure wrote, "differs from others by the fact that we cannot deliver a working unit out of our factories. We have to *install* it in a building." It followed that the operations related to fabrication and assembly should be done in factories, and those related to installation done outside, on the job site.

As in modelization, so also in fabrication, the elevator industry followed Otis' lead: all the fabrication but only part of the assembly work is done in the factories; the rest of the assembly work as well as the installation are done on the job site.

Logical, rational, Faure's thinking simply demolished traditional assumptions. Further extensions of Cartesian logic proved beyond any reasonable doubt that assembly in the factory was cheaper, easier and more foolproof than assembly in the field. Practical experiments demonstrated the validity of the new system.

Modelization and preassembly allowed the company to focus very narrowly on cost reduction: with growing specialized knowledge, entire processes could be examined at the factory, and even small improvements brought enormous gains over the long term. Simply switching to the new system brought radical improvements to cost and quality—the APL4, France's first preassembled model elevator, lowered prices by 25 percent. A second wave of cost-cutting would be required in the 1980s, when modelization and preassembly were the industry norm.

Faure was later to say that it took 10 years to change the mentality of a company like Otis—exactly the time it had taken Baldwin, 60 years earlier, to weld some of the leading U.S. elevator companies into a single corporation. "The main difficulty is our own people," he wrote in 1966. "They develop first a skeptical attitude, then a strong resistance and finally come out with the most imaginative and fallacious arguments."[22]

Salespeople claimed that customers would not accept the imposition of standard models. Field people muttered about the difficulty or the price of shipping completed cars. Production people shuddered at the amount of new work they had to take on—traditions, after all, were ingrained in Europe as in the United States. Because field work escaped overhead costs, they argued, it was cheaper to put elevators together outside the factory. Faure evidently had little time for such looking-glass logic. Finally, he noted, "Everybody will say: 'The Code does not permit it.'" As he dryly observed: "This is rarely true if we read the Code."

As de Viaris recalled, architects did, in fact, complain at first. Otis' answer was to do all it could to help with code formulation, by which modelization and preassembly were effectively forced onto a reluctant profession. Indeed, Otis' work on elevator codes grew more important as European integration proceeded. Here was a chance to influence the Common Market regulations and to make transnational production a possibility. Invariably, this brought Otis into conflict with smaller, national elevator companies, and in countries such as Italy with local elevator men, the so-called artisans. But Faure was already widening his horizons with a plan to draw the whole of Europe into a single holding company, with a view to combining ultimately into one operational entity. Events in Europe were now unfolding at a dizzying rate.

The model strategy paid off: As sales expanded, economies
of scale helped reduce cost per unit.
See Appendix.

Chapter 21

Breakaway

I N 1966, OTIS RECEIVED A NASTY SHOCK. Japan had always been an excellent escalator market—its demand for escalators, in fact, outstripped that for elevators, partly, as noted, because high-rise buildings were regarded with some suspicion in a country so prone to earthquakes and with such recent memories of fire. Until 1964, indeed, building regulations restricted building heights to 328 feet, or the height a fireman's hose could squirt water. Partly, too, the preference for escalators existed because the islands were so crowded that escalators appeared a natural corollary to mass transit systems. Toyo had in fact been responsible for the largest escalator job in the world—19 escalators installed at the Mitsukoshi Department Store in Shinjuku—but it was significant that while these see-through Escalaire machines had to be imported from Australia, a Japanese competitor had already begun manufacturing a similar product. A subsequent shake-up in Otis' worldwide operations meant that escalators were to be produced in the Flohr factory in Germany. Toshiba was not pleased.

Perhaps Toshiba totted up the list of Otis' adaptations to Japanese norms and simply decided they were not enough. Company headquarters had been moved to Tokyo in 1960—there face-to-face negotiations between executives and clients could take place more easily, and high-level talks are a part of the Japanese Way. The factory had been expanded to provide output of 400 units a year. Management had been retitled to conform to Japanese and American practice, instead of the European styles that had prevailed hitherto. But it looked suspiciously like window dressing. Toshiba's polite request for a small, cheap elevator range had met a cold response from New York.

Toshiba tended to judge its performance against the other members of the triumvirate, Mitsubishi and Hitachi, whose elevator departments were burgeoning. The extraordinary result was that Toshiba itself installed an escalator at the Kamata Station Building in 1966—an unpleasant surprise to spring at the very door of Otis' operations in Japan. Douglas, who had warned of the dangers of a Japanese alliance, was no longer in charge: he had died in 1964. His successor, Fayette Dunn, held a meeting with Toshiba in Japan, but no agreement emerged from the discussions. This was a blow, for that very year, after many false starts, Toyo-Otis had begun production of the Ready Made, the first standardized elevator for the Japanese market. A year later, Toshiba hired away many of Toyo-Otis' employees and began to manufacture its own elevators. Within a few years it had become the fourth-largest producer in Japan.

If Otis' Japanese operations were bedeviled by economic nationalism, the swing in Europe was in the other direction. In 1964, Hubert Faure had engineered proconsular powers for himself by securing the promise from New York's production staff and salespeople not to visit for three years. With Ascinter's modern factory at Gien, he was able to move directly into providing a standardized model elevator to the French market. Importantly, he was now in control of Otis' largest subsidiary and potentially at the apex of a European-wide Otis organization. That much was recognized in December 1965, when Fayette Dunn's new South African head of International Division, J. Alexander Black, set up a European Region organization to support Faure's attempts to implement a broad strategy for Europe.

By 1965 the urbanization of Europe had become so commonplace that the International Division's annual report puritanically eschewed "the customary repetition of 'all-time highs'" caused by "the population explosion with consequent almost universally intensive urban programs." For all that, the company's achievements in manufacturing "small, essentially standard units" for the new apartment houses were well worth recognizing. "Otis sold approximately 3,800 small, essentially standard units during 1965, as compared to only 1,400 comparable units sold in 1959. Practically all of this increase represents sales that Otis would otherwise have lost to competition and, as is worth noting, there is no indication that this volume of new low-cost units is reducing the Company's market for the larger so-called traditional equipment."

Fayette Dunn had his failings, but hidebound traditionalism wasn't one of them. He did not attempt to cast Otis in his own image. He was prepared to recognize talent and to delegate. He made a virtue of a weak management style: he gave Faure free rein in Europe, and checked only the bottom line.

Faure's first three years of independence from New York brought significant advances to the way Otis operated on the Continent. It was still too early to conceive of a pan-European elevator model, but significant economies of scale were already being realized by putting out work to specific factories. (Waygood-Otis, in line with British reservations over the European unification ideology, remained firmly set in its pattern of reporting directly to New York.) Rationalization was far from perfect in 1967, but already the small factory in Naples had been closed and sold, and plans to close others in Amsterdam and Brussels were in the pipeline. Much attention was being given to marketing the proposed "European Models"–devising new methods of market analysis and strengthening cooperation between marketing and engineering departments. The ultimate form that specialization took was of a number of "contract" factories producing specified components for the whole of Europe and a larger number of local "stock" factories where standard components were assembled to meet local demands, codes and tastes.

The growth of factory specialization spurred Faure toward expansion of the factory base. Otis had swiftly moved into other European countries through mergers and acquisitions–Fortis in Portugal, Freissler in Austria, Gendre in Switzerland, Voorwartts in Holland, Nielson in Scandinavia and, perhaps most significantly, Schneider in Spain.

Percy Douglas, looking for an entry into the Spanish market, had originally penciled the name Jacob Schneider–a family-owned company of Swiss origin that made elevators in Madrid. He had followed up with years of fruitless negotiations; the owners were not anxious to sell.

Then in May 1966, Faure received a phone call from a banker who owned a small stake in the company. Faure, to the banker's astonishment, arranged to meet him in 25 minutes, and a few days later he became the first person from Otis to visit the Schneider factory outside Madrid—a very old-fashioned concern, with a dominant position in the time-locked Spanish market. Negotiations, however, were agonizingly difficult. After two days' intensive talks with the family in Zurich, the meeting broke up late on a Friday night in deadlock, with the other side set to leave for Spain at 10 the next morning. At 3 a.m., Faure woke up with a solution, roused everybody else, and resumed talks at 4:30 in the morning to reach agreement by 9 o'clock.

On Monday morning, picking over the terms of the deal, the Spanish management resigned en bloc: they had allowed themselves to lose majority control to Otis and meant to make the company unworkable. Faure, unflapped, took over as general manager and chief executive of Jacobo Schneider SA, running Ascinter-Otis Monday to Thursday, and Schneider Thursday to Saturday (old-fashioned Saturday working came to his rescue then). Not until March 1967 did Faure appoint Leonard Mooney, a Canadian working in Italy, as managing director, by which time the company was making its purchase price every year. It was a very profitable acquisition, and it very soon proved to be also a unique strategic addition to Otis' European operations.

In 1972, Otis merged its Spanish operations with Zardoya, a young company of equal size and considerable sophistication—it had grown fast by pursuing Otis into modelization. Business continued to grow through the 1973 oil crisis, which affected most Western economies. (Franco's Spain was insulated, to a certain extent, from the gyrations of the global economy.) Compared with its other countries', Otis' management in Spain remained very stable over the years—after Mooney, Fransisco Ramos ran the company until 1982, followed by Mario Abajo.

The modelization program swept through Otis Europe on the back of Faure's concept of specialization "like waves of water," Warners recalls. In Italy the company even put on a road show—models and machines were trucked around the country to display the concepts to prominent architects. In Spain modelization cut installation times by three quarters. In France it slashed costs by 25 percent. A delicate system of barter had to be developed to ensure that no one suffered as work was shared out among the factories. (The Italians, thanks to the intransigence and militancy of their unions, were to suffer in the long run: one weakness of the system was its very interdependence, and when Italian strikes held up production of machines, all Europe suffered. The solution, inevitably, was to switch production to Spain.) The bartering was helped by the fact that all the factories were running at full capacity. Had the economy been less robust, Faure now believes, the entire program could have been derailed by national rivalries.

True integration, though, still eluded the company. Faure's vision was of a European-model elevator that could be slotted as easily into the shaft in Valparaiso as in Avignon or Birmingham, but a single standard for Europe waited on the evolution of standard elevator codes, and those would not be achieved easily. For one thing, European economic integration played second fiddle to political expansion, as other European nations debated whether to join the fold—Britain and Denmark joined only in 1974—and the Community slowed down the process of standardization in order to proceed together. For another, standard codes were plainly in the interests of major players like Otis but fiercely resisted by smaller companies either unable to face the costs of conversion or content with market niches sustained by local codes; in the aggregate, the "artisans" represented a larger voting bloc.

What Faure did achieve, however, was to have major repercussions in the way Otis organized itself not only in Europe but around the world. Modelization and preassembly, accompanied by factory specialization, revolutionized Otis' prospects. In three years between 1964 and 1967, service contracts in the European Community had almost doubled, to 68,704. Sales of model elevators outstripped non-models in 1967. Profits inevitably lagged behind the enormous structural changes that had occurred, and rose only slightly over the period. The year 1968 was one of political unrest, particularly in France, but by the end of 1969 Otis' European revenues had doubled in five years. Otis was superbly well positioned to meet the challenges of the next decade.

The whole of International Operations had grown enormously since the war. Factories had been built or bought in Mexico, South Africa, Australia, New Zealand, England, Italy, France, Spain, Portugal, Austria, Argentina, Brazil, Venezuela, Uruguay, Peru, Lebanon and, of course, Japan. In 1970 some 34 Otis companies worked outside the United States, with offices in 294 cities—more than the 270 maintained in the United States. A further 118 cities were served by agencies. Six overseas companies had installed more than 15,000 elevators, and bookings abroad outstripped the U.S. total by $125 million.

The loading of Otis' International activity was vastly toward Europe; more than three quarters of its 1967 sales were in continental Europe and Britain—only Brazil and Canada matched their performance. At the same time, Otis' European share still amounted to only 16 percent of the potential market for elevators and escalators, 80 percent of which, it was reckoned, suited the model elevator target. Already International was using its European experience to instruct people in other parts of the world, and modelization was being introduced in South America, India, Japan and Australia. One sign that Otis was beginning to globalize its operations came in the reduction of International's staff activity: eight people went traveling in 1967, visiting 30 countries.

France's share of the total was in every way exemplary: Ascinter Otis employed more people, made more money (except for Japan), had higher sales and service bookings, negotiated more new-sales bookings, sold more service contracts, had more work on hand and performed more efficiently (except for Uruguay) than any other International company.* It also paid International's second-highest wages (after Australia) and sent the highest number of executives to New York. By 1970 the Gien factory had built a 12-story field operations test tower, the first of its kind in the world.

Certainly France was a good market in itself, but not intrinsically better than Germany, or Britain, or, indeed, Japan. France was ahead because Faure was French, and it is hardly surprising that the French government awarded him the Legion d'Honneur, making him the second Otis man to receive the honor, after Norton P. Otis himself.

---

* In the limited sense understood from the Construction Labor Efficiency Index.

One area of renovations that Faure had to address if specialization were to grow freely was the ownership structure of Otis' operations in Europe. Local partners had been vital to the establishment of flourishing business in national markets—Ascinter boosting Otis' share of French sales to 40 percent; DEMAG, Flohr's old owner, providing the company in Germany with the sort of assistance one would associate with Japan (technologies, finance and introductions in the construction world); and other partners around Europe lending the American giant a familiar face.

But the point about specialization was its flexibility: unless production could be moved about to take advantage of skills, labor rates, exchange rates and the like, then integration was meaningless. On the other hand, local investors would inevitably squeal if local production fell or if the system for allocating revenue and profit—the internal market—seemed to favor one side or another. Rather than face endless arguments and meetings, Faure decided in 1967 to bring all of Otis' operating companies under one umbrella and to persuade existing stockholders to swap their local holdings for shares in the new pan-European company. This would put flesh on the bones of the company Faure and J. Alexander Black, vice president of International Operations, had already created in 1965—Otis Europe.

On September 26, 1969, after two years of negotiation, it remained only to choose a chief operating officer and a headquarters. Faure, who had masterminded Otis' astonishing renaissance in France and now proposed to do the same for Europe, was a shoo-in, and headquarters would be exactly where he wanted it: Paris.

This was Faure's last creation before he was appointed head of International in 1970, but he stuck close to the action, persuading New York that Paris was the best possible location for an International vice president. This argument was irrefutable, particularly after Faure reorganized International itself in 1971, phasing out the centralized, monolithic structure of International Division in favor of three distinct regional groups, European Transcontinental Operations (ETO), Pacific Asia Operations (PAO) and Latin American Operations (LAO). He was anxious to escape the confining bureaucracy of New York, and, indeed, he worked with one secretary.

His choice of Paris proved enduring. In 1974 the company moved its offices into the 52-story Tour Montparnasse, then the tallest office structure in Europe, where it could have boasted, like the Otis Brothers themselves 100 years earlier, that "Our Passenger Elevator, illustrating its advantages over all other machines, can be seen at our office." The other regions found it harder to settle.

PAO was established first in Singapore, a city that had profited from America's involvement in Vietnam without, however, picking up the wilder atmosphere of old Saigon. A dour, efficient city-state, Lee Kwan Yew's Singapore offered foreigners a secure lifestyle, a Western legal system and a reasonable standard of education and living. What it did not do, however, was offer higher education to the children of employees or simplify PAO's central problem, that the region was so vast. In 1976, PAO headquarters was transferred to San Francisco, largely for tax reasons. As so often happens, the expected tax benefit was reaped only on a reduced volume of business, and PAO returned to Singapore in 1987.

LAO, too, moved around, though rather more in response to instability and rivalry in the region—the type of rivalry that made it impossible for either Argentina or Brazil to import components from each other. Indeed, the prospects for an ETO-style coordination of production in South America looked dim: this was one part of the world where the Otis family dealt with more feuds than reunions. A factory built in Argentina in the late 1960s to promote its products through the region proved a failure when the Brazilians refused to accept its products. South America, having sustained strong growth in the 1950s, had faltered in the 1960s and now entered a turbulent period of political extremism—leftist guerrillas in Argentina, Sendero Luminoso in Peru and gangsters, kidnappers and extortionists everywhere. Erik Warners went to Argentina in 1973 to preach the word on standard elevator codes and was met at the Buenos Aires airport by the Otis managing director and two men with long bulky suitcases. His host explained that he personally was spending every night in Montevideo, that Warners was already targeted by the "town guerrilla" as a kidnapping opportunity, and that their first stop would be a place in the woods where Warners could learn to fire a nine-millimeter revolver.

Warners waved this suggestion aside. "During the war I have been in the underground movement," he replied, "so I am used to handling a nine-millimeter revolver."

One evening Warners and a companion went to a bar and everyone put his revolver on the table to show that he was armed. That night Warners had a guard outside his door. The following morning, "the very moment that I left the room, the doors on the other side of the corridor opened up and there came two men with sub-machine guns point-blank at me. I could not do anything anymore and was disarmed in three seconds. So was the man next to me. Then out came a well-dressed, good-looking gentleman—the President of Panama, as it turned out. He was better armed and had better guards, and he walked around the corner." Warner and his companion got their guns back.

Others were less fortunate. A Frenchman named Daloubex was kidnapped, and Faure had to negotiate his release—one of the nastiest experiences in Faure's life. Daloubex, of course, had ignored the advice he had been given; he had gone out and chatted up some woman in a bar and was taken on the way out. Faure used professional kidnap negotiators, who eventually had him released, and gave Daloubex three weeks in Martinique to recover from the ordeal.

The Daloubex kidnapping came after Faure had ordered all of Otis' foreign nationals out of Argentina in response to terrorist threats, and in 1974 the decision was made to move LAO responsibility from Buenos Aires to Madrid. Subsequently LAO was located in Florida, and finally moved to Farmington, Connecticut. In view of the difficulties in traveling around South America, Farmington was almost as close to the market as anywhere on the continent.

J. Alexander Black, stepping down as vice president of International Operations in 1970, marveled at the growth of International's business over the decade. In 1963, he recalled, "the International Division comprised 32 companies and branches. Management was centered in New York, and Otis was excluded from many large markets. Today the number of operating companies and branches has risen to 47, and among the newcomers, due largely to the imaginative vision of the European Regional Headquarters Group, are such companies as Schneider-Otis in Spain, Freissler in Austria and smaller companies in Norway, Sweden and Portugal. The number of countries with agency representation increased from 64 to 86." He also pointed to the crushing workload borne by a small cadre of internationalists at Otis. "While volume increased by 159 percent," he wrote, "the total population of International Division Headquarters plus the population of the European, Latin American and Far Eastern Regional Headquarters only increased 47 percent from 98 to 144."

One country on the international scene that found Faure's preeminence hard to stomach was Britain, which had traditionally been the golden boy in Otis' international affairs. In a country that had lost an empire and not yet found a role, Waygood-Otis had seen many of its traditional markets develop their independence while the company remained in thrall to a mixture of managerial and union-based paternalism.

Waygood very nearly collapsed in those years. In the late 1950s the company made the fatal decision to relocate to Liverpool, prompted by apparently generous tax incentives provided by the government. As usual, the authorities had good reason to propose the bribe. Liverpool at the end of the century was one of Britain's great industrial centers, and it was not a particularly congenial place to live or work. It was rather as if Otis today were to move back to Yonkers from Farmington—into a bastion of working-class militancy. In 1964, after years of work and expense in fitting out a new factory, Waygood was meeting problems: "While there is a larger source of workers in Liverpool than in London, the skills of the workers are not as high as in London," the annual report admitted ruefully.

Britain's retreat from empire was both stately and abrupt: it arrived at the threshold of European integration still wafting the air of an imperial power and suffered rebuffs from de Gaulle in 1961 and 1967. Britain's evidently loose interpretation of the rules of the club did not jibe with the tighter integration sought by Germany and France, which were anxious not to bolt a foreign Commonwealth with all its complications onto a geographically distinct entity like the EEC, and left the British to consider their loyalties at leisure. Initial reactions in Britain were defensive, and so it proved at Otis, too, when at Waygood-Otis' request Barbour, coordinating manager of the European Region, was transferred from Faure's staff to the factory at Liverpool.

The problem of measurements had already arisen for Otis: drafts-men had been employed in most of Continental Europe shortly after the war to convert U.S. imperial measurements into metrics, and the complexity of the job had helped Otis' European companies establish engineering skills that soon blossomed into autonomous departments. As Jurgen Kuhn of Flohr-Otis explained, it was more than a question of reading conversions off a chart—the attitude Van Schoonhoven had so naively assumed when he sent Erik Warners in Holland a wooden ruler. "We were translating all the data from Otis into metric components. By this, obviously, we were not just translating. As engineers, we were also thinking there could be a more economical solution, and so on, and so we were deviating more and more from the common Otis design...."

Arriving in Liverpool, Barbour set the British company on a collision course with Continental operations, using his intimate knowledge of continental Otis' engineering and specialization to ensure that none of it could be made available to the Liverpool factory. The exclusion worked both ways, though, and Otis UK's isolationism no doubt set it back several years. It proved enormously costly: when Britain did join the EEC in 1974, legislative pressure forced the company back onto a track it had willfully abandoned only six years earlier. Partly, of course, the British shared International's early suspicion of small elevators and cleaved to their own tradition, which resembled America's, of forging complete large elevators and machines from scratch.

By then, however, the specialization program was in full swing on the Continent—cabs and doors produced in France, AT and BT machines in Italy, the VT machines later in Spain, escalators at the Stadthagen plant in Germany, where elevator control systems were produced, and car safeties and associated equipment in Austria. In the long term, the problem of compatibility made the Liverpool factory vulnerable to closure—something the British managers were nervously aware of. Nevertheless, they retained their faith in big machines, pressing their case in unlikely ways. Norman Cunningham belonged to the 1970 intake of bright young managers Faure was so anxious to recruit, and in 1973 he made an unorthodox bid to retain the production of gearless machines in Liverpool in the face of Otis' specialization plans. François Jaulin (who was to succeed Faure in 1985) had spoken at a meeting of European managers in Morocco. Others were due to speak, and everyone was looking forward to a relaxed dinner when Cunningham—who had been an actor in his youth—broke off his speech to say: "We have had a wonderful time here. Sometimes we do not agree with you." He took an old musket from behind a curtain, walked up to Jaulin, pointed the muzzle at him, and said: "If you close the factory in Liverpool, I will shoot you."

It can only be said that Cunningham misread his man. "We had to keep him by his pants from not firing this guy at this moment," recalled future Otis President J. P. van Rooy.

Otis' international expansion was reflected in a higher growth rate in the non-U.S. work force.
See Appendix.

Chapter 22

The Management Revolution

WHEN PERCY DOUGLAS DIED UNEXPECTEDLY in October 1964, playing a round of his beloved golf, Otis' board of directors had moved quickly to appoint Fayette Dunn as his successor. He was Douglas' own choice in the absence of a more suitable candidate, a lawyer who lacked hands-on elevator industry experience but who had developed his knowledge of the company as its general counsel since 1961.

Fayette Dunn had studied at the University of Michigan and at Northwestern, where he earned a J.D. degree, and his connections with Otis went back to 1935, when the Chicago law firm he worked for sent him to New York to manage its Otis account. By 1945 he was the company's assistant secretary, and as he moved up the legal ladder he became increasingly well known to members of the Otis board. In 1960, when Petersen decided to set up an in-house legal department, he invited Dunn onto the payroll. In 1964, when Dunn was catapulted into the job, the feeling was that Otis needed a safe pair of hands to guide it until a more appropriate candidate could be found—and Dunn himself shared the view that his appointment was temporary.

The idea of looking outside the company was still unthinkable. Dunn's arrival was certainly greeted with derision and even hostility by some Otis veterans because he was not a classic "elevator man," but he had at least served the company in the past. The problem of finding a suitable permanent successor occupied the board until 1968, when Dunn began to groom Ralph Weller, very much an elevator man, for the job. In the meantime, Dunn pressed on with the diversification programs launched by the man who had brought him on board in the first place, Leroy Petersen. During his own brief tenure, Percy Douglas had stalled the process, preferring to invest heavily in foreign and domestic elevator facilities, including the company's new state-of-the-art factory in Bloomington, Indiana, which would shortly become Otis' North American manufacturing hub.

Both Douglas and, after him, Fayette Dunn appreciated the need to loosen up Otis' very tight corporate structure, which concentrated all decision-making at the very top of the pyramid. The same Florentine system of line and staff had served the company since the 1930s, well before Otis had acquired its worldwide empire, and it increasingly caused congestion at the top. To bring some flexibility into the organization, Douglas and Dunn began dividing responsibilities among a greater number of vice presidents appointed to new divisions, both geographical and executive. So in 1964, Emmett Hines was made senior vice president for Regional Operations, comprising eight geographical areas under their own regional vice presidents, while an office for Diversified Operations was created to isolate executive responsibility for non-elevator work. On Hines' retirement in 1965, Dunn established Roy Olson as the new executive vice president for Domestic Elevator Operations, helping to foster cooperation between field and factory, while Robert Bry, who came to Otis from General Electric and had been managing Baker-Raulang, was appointed in 1966 to manage Diversified Operations, allowing some basic decision making to take place before it wound up on the CEO's desk.

Eugene Hull, who started his career as a specialist in industrial relations, effectively took over from Olson in 1968 as senior vice president for North American Operations, while Otis' worldwide business, as we have already seen, was divided into separate spheres of responsibility, including Europe, Asia and Latin America. Hull's job involved "profit improvement," which was taken to mean further diversification. Olson himself had left in 1968, having been passed over for the presidency of the company, which Ralph Weller assumed in November 1969.

For all the efforts of Otis' CEOs in the 1960s, North American traditions were hard to buck: rigidity was factored by history into the way all information, and all decisions, flowed in and out of New York. Overseas operations had already slipped out from under New York's direct tutelage, thriving on its ability to anticipate and respond to local market changes at almost every level. In the far more centralized structure of North American Operations, talented people were either sucked inwards or left champing with frustration at New York's myopia and the bureaucratic logjam—for the "bureaucracy" that Otis had so proudly created in the early years of the century had became a dirty word at last. It was not a climate that attracted smart thinkers to work for Otis; nor was it one that could teach such men as it employed how to roll with the punches and spot the main chance.

The profound centralization at Otis made it hard to foster general management capabilities below the highest level, but it isn't clear that it fostered them there, either. All change brings opportunity as well as risk, but in the turnover of CEOs that followed Petersen's retirement in 1961 after nearly two decades at the helm, Otis seemed saddled with the risks and missed out on the opportunities. Douglas died too soon; Dunn was a self-confessed stopgap; and Ralph Weller was a likable man who went in over his head when he accepted the top job. He acted the "regular guy's" dream of a CEO's life, preferring, as some recall, the bar at the Playboy Club to his desk on 260 Eleventh Avenue. He was to run Otis for the next six momentous years, and the direction in which he took the company, toward its fateful tryst with Harry Gray of United Technologies, serves eloquent judgment on his tenure.

When Hubert Faure became head of International Division in 1970, one of his first jobs, as we've seen, was to phase out the Division in favor of three regional groupings—Europe, South America and Pacific.

The timing was good, for important differences starting to emerge between each region were set to widen as the decade advanced. Driven by political and economic instability, South America was fast becoming a dangerous place to operate, where special knowledge and methods of business would be required to keep going. The European market was still a massive engine of growth, but already marks of maturity could be seen, and it seemed a long way from the undeveloped world of the Pacific.

In creating a Pacific Regional headquarters, Faure had his sights set on Japan. Japanese manufacturers had already managed to drive Otis' market share down to a measly 2 percent, and they were primed to use their powerful domestic base to make an assault on the Asian market, too, where as yet Otis' position was strong.

The company had been faced with a similar threat in another part of the world almost half a century earlier, when Stigler had used his unchallenged supremacy in the Italian market for elevators to lever his products into the European arena. Schindler had made the same progression out of Switzerland at the end of World War II. In each case, Percy Douglas had responded by taking Otis into the enemy camp, regardless of short-term costs, eroding the basis of his competitor's commercial security. To repeat the performance in Japan, though, required uncommon skills of diplomacy.

Japanese industry had effectively staged a lock-out of foreign competitors in the early 1950s. Otis, of course, was already inside when the drawbridge was raised, and was able to continue operations as a Japanese manufacturer in its own right. Mounting pressure, though, as much cultural as economic, had forced the company to look for a Japanese partner, and so began the ill-fated alliance with Toshiba. Toshiba's decision to break with Otis, while still holding a 25 percent stake in the company, not only drove Otis' market share down to 2 percent but made Toyo-Otis in Japan next to unworkable. Toshiba's medium-term goal, obviously, was to drive Otis out of Japan altogether. This was the intractable situation Faure inherited when he became vice president for International Operations in 1970.

Japan was to call for all Faure's accumulated skills in negotiation. His first encounter involved wresting back Toshiba's 25 percent share of Toyo-Otis, for though Toshiba had already gone into competition with Otis, it saw no reason to divest itself of part-ownership; on the contrary, it unquestionably planned to drive Otis out of the Japanese market and succeed to the remainder of Toyo-Otis' established business.

Faure prepared himself initially by reading 30 or so books on Japan and its methods of business. Far from simplifying the case, his wide reading only impressed on him the difficulties that lay ahead. He had the situation analyzed by James Abbeglen of the Boston Consulting Group, who prepared a very careful negotiating script and went so far as to analyze the seating arrangements when Faure, at the head of the Otis delegation, met with Toshiba's executives.

Faure's tactic was to exploit his ignorance of Japanese methods. He praised the country. He praised Toshiba. His confessed his inability to deal squarely with them, being at a cultural disadvantage—but he added that in all the research he had done, one thing stuck out: the Japanese, he understood, were a very fair people. The Toshiba team could hardly disagree.

It was in his power, he continued, to help them maintain that reputation for fairness. Rather than submit to Japanese negotiating rules, which put Otis at a disadvantage, he proposed to make the room extraterritorial. He and his team would begin negotiations just as though they were in the United States. It was only the start, but a week later Toshiba sold its stake back to Otis.

Faure had thus extricated the company from Toshiba's armlock, but Otis was not yet out of the woods. In the 1970s, as in the 1930s, absolute independence was not an option in the subtly regulated Japanese environment. Grandgerard's dictum that Otis needed a Japanese partner remained as valid as ever, but Faure was not keen to repeat the mistake of giving away too much controlling power.

The partnership that presented itself was a three-way cut between Otis, Sumitomo, a powerful bank, and its engineering ally, Matsushita. The partners would bring their financial muscle, their construction links and their elevator expertise together to form a company known as Nippon Otis. The success of the deal was to protect Otis, in particular, from suffering the fate of so many American manufacturers who woke up one day in the 1970s to discover even their domestic markets devastated by a Japanese onslaught. The success of the deal, however, was very much in the balance when Faure, head of International, opened negotiations.

The new partners proposed a 50-50 ownership deal, which Faure was reluctant to give; as the old alliance with Matsui in the 1930s proved, the cards were stacked from the start against a foreign partner working in Japan. "If you want equal terms," Faure told them, "then you're so powerful in Japan that to be on equal terms we need 60 and you'll only have 40 percent." At which they said, "Hmmmm. No question about that."

Faure proposed that the ownership issue be set aside in order to hammer out all the other points of the agreement–two years' work, as it turned out. During this period neither side made any reference to the ownership question, and up to the day Matsushita signaled their intention to sign an agreement, the split was still waiting for a decision.

Faure flew to Japan and had a business dinner with the Japanese team the night before the contract was to be signed–at a very, very grand geisha house, where everyone knelt around the table as ancient geishas prepared morsels of food beside their guests. Faure noticed one of his Japanese fellow guests making signs across the table before he suddenly turned and disappeared. Mystified, Faure's eyes searched the room. All of a sudden, the man was at Faure's elbow, having crawled silently around the table. "Forty-five for us, 55 for you," he said, and crawled away. The deal was signed the following day.

Percy Douglas, as Faure ironically remarked, had always believed in hiring dependable, unexciting men and avoided anyone too bright, but that was in the days of Otis' leisurely hegemony in the 1950s. As head of the International Division, Faure aggressively sought to attract intelligent and ambitious people to work for Otis. "The most valuable asset the Region has [is] its cadre of management personnel. The constant replenishment of this asset is vital to the survival of the organization," he wrote in 1970.[23]

His pursuit of François Jaulin five years earlier had been a case in point. When Faure moved up to head the European company in 1965, Otis was faced with the problem of choosing his successor in France, where the company was still feeling the reverberations of the Ascinter merger of 1963. Any promotion from within the company at this delicate time risked reopening wounds now healing between Ascinter and Otis factions, so Faure looked outside the company to settle on François Jaulin as an unimpeachable candidate. Jaulin was about to graduate from the top-flight French university, Ecole Polytechnique, from which he had been seconded to the elite Corps de Mines: this, in France, was fast-tracking with a vengeance, and both institutions were swathed in glamour that cut across all lines in the political spectrum. At Ascinter-Otis, the arrival of such a candidate was itself morale-boosting and resolved the potential antagonism between the two camps, in view of which Faure was even prepared to wait while Jaulin completed an obligatory term of government service. As soon as it was over he moved him into Faure's old job.

So began a dynamic relationship that was to last until Jaulin's untimely death in 1986. Having selected Jaulin to succeed him when he left Ascinter-Otis to head the European Region in 1965, Faure made him head of the European Region when he left Europe to become head of International Division in 1970. When in 1975 Faure became president of Otis, Jaulin took over at International. It was hardly surprising that when Faure moved into Otis' parent company United Technologies in 1981, Jaulin should become, in turn, Otis' president and COO, taking up probably the only job offer which would have induced him to leave France.

The relationship between Jaulin and Faure exemplified the twin goals of stability and creativity that Faure had tried to bring to the company, and that helped to sustain continuity through the 1970s, a decade of rapid change for Otis. Change and continuity were powerful factors in Faure's approach to management: change, because a company that fails to keep up with developments is doomed, and continuity, because a company that makes perpetual revolution inevitably loses the support of its people. People, Faure fervently believed, lay at the heart of every company's success.

Both men were French, but while Faure was a diplomat, a visionary and an enabler, who could get people to work with a word and continue working in his absence, Jaulin was an engineer by temperament and training; his greatest skill was to implement programs. They made a team, the one planning and explaining, the other ensuring that everything took effect. Faure had conceived of a pan-European model elevator line in the mid-1960s, but he left Jaulin to actually oversee the introduction of the first LM European elevators in 1973–75. Unlike Faure, who was never known to get angry, Jaulin's temper was legendary. As his colleague and successor J. P. van Rooy once put it, Jaulin was rational about things and emotional about people: "an intelligent bulldozer," he said, whose dedication was fierce and who suffered no fools.

As Jaulin began his rise through Otis' overseas hierarchy, more first-class managers were coming up through the European ranks or entering from outside—a cadre of seasoned professionals who would be firmly rooted in place when the pace of events heated up in 1975 and a new wind in the shape of Harry Gray's United Technologies came to winnow Otis. In 1970, Pierre Fougeron was finagled from the position of vice president of the Michelin Tire Company in America and brought to Ascinter-Otis in his native France, where he was responsible for marketing the LM product line between 1970 and 1973. J. P. van Rooy, too, had considerable experience in America before he was hired by Faure and Jaulin in the same year. He was dispatched to his native Belgium to sort out pricing problems and to help Jaulin, now head of International, implement the new system whereby the factories around Europe no longer took a profit (Jaulin likewise established the system of stock and contract factories). Van Rooy was expected to move on to Paris and run marketing, but an Italian crisis was brewing, and Jaulin sent him to Milan as managing director of Stigler-Otis. With typical dispatch, van Rooy learned Italian in a month, commuted on weekends to his home in Belgium and became the first managing director of Otis in Italy to visit all his branches. "To explain Italy," as he says, "you would need a book."

These men stepped up to situations in a straightforward, analytical frame of mind. Van Rooy, for example, recalls paying a visit to an Otis company in the early 1970s, when he ran marketing in Europe. "I remember very well entering a company at 10 in the morning when they claimed to have 25 percent market share. By the time I got out at 4 in the afternoon they were down to 12 1/2 percent."

An explanation must be sought for the contrast between management caliber in the United States and at International in the early 1970s. Faure may have bucked Percy Douglas' alleged recruitment standards and dismantled Douglas' centralized system, but he preserved Douglas' gentlemanly legacy of respect for others. Otis' ability to recruit in America may have been hampered by the more abrasive career traditions of the country, whereby American executives tended to judge emoluments more in terms of title and value, portable assets which could be carried right out of the industry altogether if the right offer was received. Yet an elderly elevator company operating in a mature market had little to offer the high flyers. By the 1960s, in Hubert Faure's delicate phase, Otis' U.S. management was "not distinguished." In Europe, after Douglas, it never looked back.

Otis in Europe had the exciting growth potential of a new business, with a massive presence in America that inspired confidence on top. People wanted to work for the company, whose future they traditionally viewed as being bound up with their own; it created an atmosphere in Europe in which good people directed their energies toward exciting challenges. By then, the atmosphere at Otis in North America could seem all wrong, drifting and traditional at once. The following story from Erik Warners is a reminder of the contrast, symbolized to some extent by the Americans' fetishizing of title over real content.

Warners recalls being appointed "acting manager" of Otis in the Netherlands in the 1950s. "I did not know what acting manager meant, and I said, 'Well, manager is manager, so I am fine. I am the manager.' Four years later Bill Reid came and said: 'Congratulations. You are now managing director.' I said: 'I had the idea I was it four years ago.' He said, 'No, acting manager is quite different.' I said: 'Good that I didn't know. I might have left the company.'"

When Pierre Fougeron joined the company in 1970 he was immediately struck by the honesty and dedication of the men he met both in Paris and New York. They were, he says, "very Otis. You had the feeling of a family, of a company it would be good to work in, and for, because of this kind of enthusiasm." One element was unquestionably Otis' historical reputation. "Otis is a great name. You are proud to work for that type of company," Fougeron explains, adding significantly, "It was a very old company, which, to Europeans at least, was very attractive."

Yet in the 1960s, Otis had grown tremendously, and the company's size was also an asset, for size offered variety: there were jobs at home and jobs abroad, jobs for high-flyers and for people who wanted to do nothing more than one thing well. Otis became, certainly outside America, a highly congenial place to be, largely because the company derived its value from its people. "It is people, people is Otis," as one employee remarked. Yet the American side of Otis, too, had its attractions for Europeans, who found Otis refreshingly unparochial. Working for the company brought down old barriers in Europe, where "You have the weight of the past—centuries of wars, and differences of opinion, and conflicts, and fights for the dominant position," as Fourgeron recalled, adding, "You still have that left. Today people still remember the past—some of them remember World War I. Most of us can remember World War II, and a lot of Europeans remember even further back, like the 1600s and 1700s, and so forth. This was not Otis in Europe, but Europe in the 1960s."

It *was* Otis, of course, to some extent. Despite Fougeron's disclaimer, it was too much to expect that national jealousies and rivalries could be ironed out of the organization overnight. As van Rooy put it, "The Germans and the French at the time, or the British—if one was of one opinion you might be sure that the others were of a different one." Van Rooy was able to put his finger on operational differences throughout Europe, too, which informed his understanding of how to successfully put decisions into practice. "The French...love to argue before [a decision can be made]. They argue before, and after that they strike. In Italy, you don't argue that much before, but they strike after and then they start arguing. The Germans, they don't argue before. They debate it before you take the decision for three months. Actually, then it's finished. Once they have it proved, it's finished." Being an Otis manager did not mean conforming to an international norm; it meant understanding regional differences. Years later, as president of NAO, van Rooy added Americans to his roster, saying he found them prone to debate a decision both before and after it had been taken.

Trying to grasp national differences so as to work efficiently with them was an instructive experience for the Europeans. When it came to diplomacy, handling awkward mergers or working alongside foreign colleagues, Otis' European managers had done it all. It is significant that North American technical, managerial and salespeople had their first gathering only after Faure became president of the company: Weller, like Dunn before him, had called them up to him "one by one." The unfamiliar breaching of the barriers was apparently an exhilarating experience.

Faure's European managers, in short, had adjusted to the task of managing in a decade of rapid change. Flexibility was their watchword, reinforced by a cultural bias toward negotiation, consensus and conciliation. America's more abrasive style could lead to entrenchment and to fights so vicious in prospect that no one wanted to start them. Union sensitivity to preassembly was a case in point. So was the functionalized

Charles Grandgerard,
Collins, P. J. Kessel,
ca. 1947

Otis paternoster installation
in Germany. An endless
chain of cars travel
continuously up at the left,
down at the right. No
doors are provided, and
passengers step on or off as
the cars go by, ca. 1947

Percy Douglas, 1949
President 1961–64

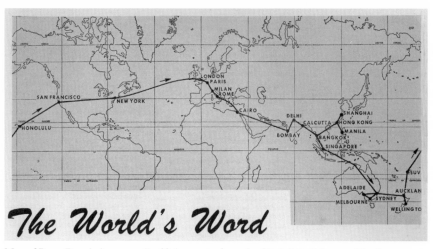

The World's Word

Map of Percy Douglas' 35,000 mile, 88-day route, from the *Otis Bulletin,* February–March 1949

Percy Douglas giving service award to Manuel Bandin, who exactly on that occasion completed 25 years with the company, October 8, 1953

Unveiling of the bronze plaque by Percy Douglas, assisted by Maria Yakominich, Montevideo, Uruguay, October 8, 1953

Bishop Z. Coleman of Dept. 22 at the Yonkers Works

Leroy A. Petersen
beside Autotronic
display, ca. 1948

Atlantic Refining Company building, Dallas, where Otis installed the first
Autotronic operatorless equipment. A passenger shows how to run your own
car—just press a button. From the *Otis Bulletin,* November–December 1952

Otis salesmen in Canada, ca. 1951

Escalator in the Washington
Park Race Track, Homewood,
Illinois, the most colossal of
the Otis 32-R series ever installed
(67 feet long), ca. 1955

Republic National Bank
Building, Dallas, ca. 1955

High-speed Otis escalators aboard the *USS Independence,* used to transport
pilots to their planes in shortest possible time, ca. 1959

The *Otis Bulletin,* January–February 1954, picturing President Dwight D. Eisenhower
on an Otis 32-R in the United Nations building, December 8, 1953

A car being lifted onto an elevator by extending metal fingers in the initial stage of Speed-Park operation, ca. 1961

Workmen in the Tokyo plant shown assembling the translucent dome inside the special car for the Tsutenkaku, ca. 1957

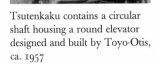

Tsutenkaku contains a circular shaft housing a round elevator designed and built by Toyo-Otis, ca. 1957

Burning joss sticks and paper are offered by a
Chinese worker in thanks for a successful and
accident-free installation of escalators, Hong
Kong Jockey Club, ca. 1957

A "panoramic escalator" installation at La
Samaritaine, a Paris department store, by
Ascenseurs Otis, ca. 1959

One of the 10 passenger elevators installed on the
S.S. Rotterdam is lowered into the partially finished
hull during construction, ca. 1959

Blackpool Tower, Ireland, ca. 1958

Diagram of Buoy Laboratory
in the Mediterranean, ca. 1963
1. Living quarters
2. Machinery space
3. Otis elevator
4. Laboratories
5. Ballast
6. Air tanks
7. Water tanks
8. Fuel tanks
9. 112-ton ballast

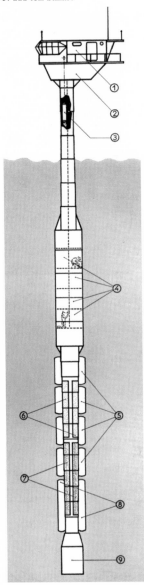

Fairmont Hotel's Otis observation elevator, ca. 1963

Priest blessing Stigler-Otis Cernusco plant, Italy, 1964

69UAL controllers being prepared for full function test at
Otis Liverpool Plant in United Kingdom, ca. 1965

Horace Taylor checking the wall-climber
elevator on the Umbilical Tower at the
NASA Kennedy Space Center's Launch
Complex #37, ca. 1966

127-foot Trav-O-Lator connecting the
El Cortez Hotel with the new Motel in
San Diego, California, ca. 1968

A tandem trailer carrying eight preassembled elevators in Buenos Aires
on its way to San Juan, Argentina, ca. 1966

Fayette S. Dunn
President, Chairman 1964–70

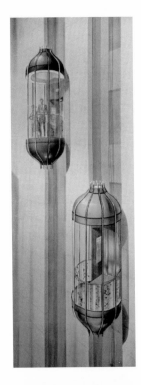

Mock-up of Atlanta
Regency's special
Autotronic elevator
which would travel
up the outside of
the Hotel's enclosed
Garden Court,
ca. 1966

Atlanta Regency's
special Autotronic
elevator in operation,
ca. 1971

An Otis elevator hoistway, surrounded
by a steel stairway and catwalks, rises
inside concrete shell of Johannesburg
FM Tower, ca. 1963

Photograph of Singapore, showcasing the Overseas-Chinese Banking Corporation Centre, under construction with its distinctive twin, half-circle service cores. This building would rise to a height of 660 feet. From Otis 1974 Annual Report

François Jaulin, 1977
President, Otis 1981–85

U.S. Secretary of Transportation
John A. Volpe enjoys a ride in an
Otis electric cart, ca. 1972

An elevator with low-height
operating panels for the
convenience of wheelchair users
at Vistula Manor in Toledo,
Ohio, the nation's first public
housing project planned to
meet the needs of the aged and
disabled, ca. 1969

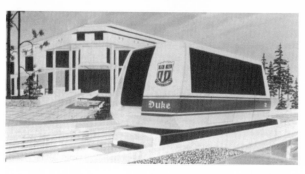

HOVAIR® system
proposed for Duke
University Medical
Center, ca. 1976

Ralph Weller and Hubert Faure
in front of elevator cabs, 1975

World Trade
Center
drawing,
ca. 1967

Harry Gray
Chairman, CEO, United Technologies
1974–86

Ralph Weller
President, CEO, Chairman, Otis
1969–75

World Trade
Center, from
Otis 1974
Annual Report

Hubert Faure, 1975
President, CEO, Chairman, Otis 1975–81

George David
President, CEO, Otis 1986–87
Chairman, CEO, United Technologies
1997–present

Shibayama Factory Product Application Tower (P.A.T.), 1977

command structure. "Business is about the survival of the fittest," wrote one American executive grimly: that was the *Otis Bulletin* of 1978, but it sounded remarkably like *The Indicator* of 1908.

European tradition was more consensual. In Germany, for instance, co-determination legislation gave unions representation on the board. "We tend to be closer to the Japanese than to English-American working culture," Jurgen Reuning explained. "Germans have a natural tendency to work in teams. We have a tendency to plan very much before we do something—to establish alternatives, to establish a good theory before we implement. It takes us a long time before we say, 'Yes, that's what we want to do.' Then you have a better consensus in your whole working team, so the implementation is much easier because everybody has participated in finding a solution." Anglo-American culture, on the other hand, "is very strong on making decisions quickly, and very weak on getting them implemented. Implementation in the U.S. is obstructed not so much by people arguing in meetings, but by sabotaging the actual implementation…. In Germany if I have a management meeting everybody stands up and says, more or less in a polite way: 'You are crazy!'"

Industry-wide gatherings at the new Otis were built upon positive experiences of cross-cultural fertilization, which first occurred in the dense cockpit of Europe. Reuning, for example, observed in 1991 that the Germans benefited from "a bit of Latin and South European spirit. Germans tend to be, in some cases, not so open, not so creative…. We can learn to have fun with business…." In the 1970s, likewise, the Spanish proved to be very good at eliminating unnecessary production costs. Abajo of Spain put the Otis rationale very well. If two people give each other 1,000 pesetas, they end up with 1,000 pesetas each. If they give each other an idea, though, each of them ends up with two ideas. The European mosaic, handled correctly, could be astonishingly fertile of ideas.

The give and take at Otis was something that attracted Fougeron. "I think it was the perfect blend of a worldwide company," he remarked in 1991. "Not too American, not too European, just a company that blends wherever it is." Otis increasingly possessed some of the benefits of the guerrilla strategy Faure had sketched out years before: a strong sense of overall unity and purpose, combined with an ability to blend in at every locality.

Europe was ready with its first common product in 1973, the LM apartment elevator, followed by the higher level Series 80 model line. What made the development possible was, of course, the European head-quarters organization in Paris, coordinating the work of designers, field installation and maintenance people, combined with the system of stock factories making specific components, contract factories assembling and delivering complete elevators locally, and buffer warehouses. François Jaulin, who directed the process as president of ETO, was to develop it as worldwide strategy when he became president of Otis itself in 1981.

Meanwhile, in the spring of 1975, the board of directors met to deliberate on a successor to Ralph Weller. Faure, who as president of International was also present, was asked to leave the room.

This was the moment for reservations to the clear choice to be aired. There was only one: whether Faure had the American experience to run an operation in the U.S. When Faure learned of this minutes later, he had a ready answer, though it came as a shock to some of the executives sitting in the room.

In the space of 30 years, he said, Otis had grown from a U.S. giant into a multinational company, working in more than 146 countries around the world. More than three quarters of its employees worked out-side the United States—only a handful of these were Americans. The company's revenues more than reflected the balance. Europe alone matched the United States in value and far outstripped it in volume. Faure then reminded his listeners in the boardroom that they had allowed him to run the whole of International already. North American Operations could be seen as a very large subsidiary of Otis worldwide.

Sales growth—then sales themselves—tailed off in the years
preceding Otis' acquisition by United Technologies.
See Appendix.

Chapter 23

Takeover

Hubert Faure had been in his new job as president of Otis exactly 16 days when Harry Gray, the CEO of United Technologies Corporation (UTC), launched a hostile takeover bid. The announcement was not a shock in itself—Faure had been predicting something of the sort for a year or more—although the source of the bid surprised Otis and Wall Street. UTC was essentially a defense company, which included Pratt & Whitney, Sikorsky Aircraft and Hamilton Standard; but Gray had been trying to wean the company from its reliance on government contracts. In 1974 he bought Essex Wire, a supplier to the car industry. In the spring of 1975 he renamed the company United Technologies from United Aircraft Corporation and instructed his investment banker, Felix Rohatyn of Lazard Freres, to cast about for an industrial company that might give UTC an entry into construction markets. Carrier Corporation was one of the companies he examined before settling on Otis Elevator Company.

Gray's appreciation of the elevator industry was remarkably close to Charles Otis' own in the 1880s: that it was unstoppable. In July 1975, UTC's chief financial officer, Ed Hennessey, showed Gray Otis' Annual Report, and the cover photo delivered a powerful message. Gleaming skyscrapers lunged heavenward from a rabble of sampans and houseboats in Singapore, the 10-year-old city-state on the South China Sea that was fast growing into the world's busiest port. Otis was there, of course. It was in Paris, in Hong Kong, in Brazil, in Australia—everywhere that tall buildings were rising. An international presence was just what Gray was looking for.

Otis' share price, meanwhile, had been steadily declining. From a 1974 high of $42 it had sunk to a low of $24.25. Gray saw this as more than a reflection on the current state of construction, still recovering from the oil crisis of 1973–74. At a meeting with Rohatyn in early September 1974, the banker sketched out a diagnosis of Otis' faults and difficulties— problems that the right corporate partner could convert into rich opportunities. The next step was to approach Weller.

Weller and Gray lunched alone. Gray warned Weller that Otis had gone irreversibly adrift in terms of new technology—the company's efforts to develop electronic control systems had come too late and were proceeding too slowly to match the competition. Weller's answer, that Otis' research would bring advanced microprocessors to elevator controls by the mid-1980s, was exactly what Gray wanted to hear. With UTC's engineering facilities and expertise in control systems, he replied, Otis could halve that timetable.

Weller spoke up for Otis as it stood: a billion-dollar enterprise, the biggest of its kind in the world, with half the U.S. market and a quarter of the world's. Gray's early tender of $37 a share was unrealistic, he said. Trading might be low now, but the true value was something on the order of $50. Perhaps it was an unduly laconic response, but Weller supposed that he had heard the last of the matter. Hostile takeovers, after all, were rare events then. The huge conglomerate mergers of the 1960s and early 1970s were over, and Wall Street, examining the long-term results of diversification, had fallen out of love with the idea. The bankers and lawyers who had helped put the conglomerates together were starting to earn their fees from pulling them apart again.

But Gray believed in synergy, and he was aware that the financial climate was actually favorable to takeovers. Around half of Otis' common stock was in institutional hands, and he was in a position to make a largely cash offer of $42 a share—a premium of $11 a share over current prices. He based his calculation not only on Otis' undervalued share price and the possibility that UTC could help Otis develop more advanced electronic control systems, but also on the fact that Otis could help UTC: it was a company whose massive service base generated a steady stream of cash, and which was already well positioned in markets around the world that UTC had yet to approach.

Despite Weller's rejection, Gray pressed on. At one October meeting, Gray recalled, Faure attended and briskly cut to the point: "What would it be like being an officer of Otis after an acquisition? What were some of the policies? How do we operate? How do we budget? How do we, in effect, control?"[24] Gray's presentation to the Otis board on October 17 concentrated on the technological advantage of a tie-in.

Wall Street was not impressed when the bid became public. Otis stock rose $6 a share on the first day, but UTC's fell: Gray was accused of living in the past, of egomania, insecurity, poor judgment. Could UTC develop an elevator with a rotor on the top? "It is difficult to picture the two companies being worth more together than they are separately," *The Wall Street Journal* opined. None of this helped Otis much. Gloomy reports only encouraged institutional investors to sell out, and Otis willy nilly moved into the marketplace.

Faure and Weller had little choice but to mount the best defense they could on behalf of Otis' remaining stockholders, while beginning the search for a "white knight." "Whether you liked it or not," Weller recalled, "someone was going to end up owning Otis or controlling it, so now you had to go through all the damn machinations of finding someone who would pay more money."[25]

"There were no suitors pounding at the doors," recalls George David, an executive who cut his teeth at Otis on the takeover battle and later went on to control the whole of UTC. David had been with the Boston Consulting Group before Faure lured him away from consultancy and into Otis in 1975.

David's appointment—with the new title of senior vice president for corporate planning and development—was a deliberate step toward beefing up the management capabilities of Otis in the United States. Born in Philadelphia, David was the son of a college professor who married one of his Bryn Mawr students. David's own academic career included four unproductive years at Harvard, he maintains, after which he put his head down at business school in Virginia before joining BCG in 1968. There he rapidly rose to become a vice president and partner.

He had already worked on Otis' account, investigating the rationale behind Otis' diversification program, when Faure brought him over in March 1975. David was instantly propelled to the forefront in the takeover battle: the best talker that Otis had, with the sharpest eye for the business facts, he was fielded to make financial representations to possible allies—first the Dana Corporation, an automotive parts manufacturer in Toledo, Ohio, then Lawrence Tisch at Loews and finally Lord Weinstock at England's GEC. None of them saw the opportunity.

UTC had already secured about 2.5 million of the 4.5 million shares it was after when the battle went legal, both sides arguing misrepresentation, fraud and other violations through the courts.

On November 12, after four weeks of battle, both sides dropped their lawsuits when Faure signaled to Gray that Otis was ready to deal. In return, UTC promptly sweetened its offer to $44 a share, $6 over book value. By the end of November it had bought 70 percent of Otis' stock for a grand total of $276 million—paid entirely in cash, with the help of a $50 million loan. Weller was assured of a job when Gray met him for "a long, friendly luncheon," and Gray's employees were told that Otis was a "profitable, strong, successful, well-managed" addition to UTC's business.

The endgame was for UTC to acquire the remaining Otis shares, and here it performed generously: most of the outstanding shares were held by individuals, among them a large number of Otis people, active and retired. The Justice Department finally dropped its antitrust investigation in March 1976, paving the way for UTC to present a plan swapping UTC for Otis stock that valued Otis shares at $45, more than $7 over par. Otis shareholders were disappointed that UTC was unable to finance the purchase of the outstanding minority shares on a tax-free basis, as Otis' lawyers had hoped, but what had begun as a hostile, predatory raid wound up as a rather benign exercise.

UTC could afford to be generous. From the vantage point of the 1990s, UTC clearly got a bargain. It bought Otis for about four times its own annual cash flow without diluting its own shares. In the bear market of the mid-1970s, the sale was not impeded by the kind of leverage and competitive bidding that would have come in the more robust economic climate of the 1980s. UTC recouped the cost of the deal from Otis' earnings in just over three and a half years; looking back, Gray admitted that the price was less than he had been prepared to pay, but he also reflected that he would not have gone much higher. The acquisition, he said, looked more brilliant 15 years later than it did at the time.

It was the best buy of his career.

Epilogue

IT IS STILL TOO SOON to write the definitive history of Otis' first quarter-century under the UTC umbrella. But the acquisition has been good for UTC as well as Otis. UTC acquired a company with $1 billion of sales and a global presence for $280 million. Revenues grew to $5.7 billion by 1999. At the same time, Otis benefited from an infusion of advanced electronic technology from the aerospace side of UTC.

Harry Gray did fulfill his promise to halve Otis' development time with the introduction in 1979 of Elevonic® 101, a completely microprocessor-based elevator control system. The first Elevonic® system was installed in 1979 at the New Jersey Public Service Electric and Gas headquarters in Newark, New Jersey. This was a triumph for a company that had pioneered gearless machines 70 years before. A fully integrated control system, Elevonic® 101 monitored every major function of the elevator and coordinated the motor generator and hoist motor with operational demands. An electromechanical gadget for tracking the car's position, which had been in use since 1924, was finally replaced with a digital device.

The Elevonic® system was made possible by aerospace controls technology that had been developed by Otis' sister business unit, Hamilton Standard, now Hamilton Sundstrand, a maker of aerospace systems from flight controls to space suits. Otis engineers worked together on the project with their colleagues from Hamilton Standard and the United Technologies Research Center. The new technology enabled Otis to leapfrog the U.S. competition and pre-empt Japanese companies from entering the North American market at that time.

Improvements kept coming: in 1981 Elevonic® 401 replaced the motor generator with a solid-state motor control system and computerized cab features. Everything on and around the 401 was smaller and neater than ever before. Less than 10 years later, Elevonic® 411M and 311M systems were introduced worldwide for the modernization market—both were derived from technologically advanced new-equipment systems. By then, Otis had already moved to recapture service contracts that were being lost to small competitors, temporarily at least, by introducing in 1983 a computerized, 24-hour dispatching service for mechanics called OTISLINE®. Five years later, the first remote elevator monitoring system was set up in North America, allowing elevator performance to be evaluated off-site.

After becoming president and CEO in 1986, George David began to counteract the decline of the company's engineering department in the United States. The state-of-the-art, 28-story test tower raised in Connecticut in 1987 became both symbol and substance of Otis' scientific renaissance. By 1988 the engineering staff of Otis had doubled, and its budget had more than tripled.

These investments paid off in terms of innovations that gave Otis a leg up in markets around the world. For example, Otis introduced in Japan in 1989 the innovative linear induction motor elevator, which eliminated the need for a machine room and used less energy and was quieter than hydraulic elevators. In 1992, Otis introduced fuzzy logic modules in gearless elevator systems in Japan, bringing new levels of efficiency to elevator dispatching in high-rise buildings. The same year the company unveiled in Japan a variable-speed, variable-frequency pump to eliminate the need for a main valve to control the speed of a hydraulic elevator.

In 1992, David became UTC's president and chief operating officer. Two years later he was CEO. In April 1997 he was elected chairman—the grand finale, maybe, to what looked like a reverse takeover of the parent company by Otis personnel.

If UTC had brought technical know-how to Otis, just as Gray had promised, then Otis—as Gray had hoped—had brought a new, international outlook to a company heavily locked into the U.S. market—a traditional company dependent on defense contracts and exports. With the end of the Cold War, defense spending was in decline. Perhaps most significantly, the end of the Cold War had ushered in a new, global economic order, one in which American ideas would be far more in demand than specifically American products.

As the 20th century drew to a close, something like a quarter of the world's population would be ready to jump into full economic partnership with the developed world. Like it or not, American companies had to be part of that or run the risk of marginalizing their presence—and their profits—on the world stage. They had to learn to invest, manufacture and sell abroad while maintaining their technological lead.

One company had been doing just that for decades. Five years after it acquired Otis, UTC had dramatically reduced its dependence on government purchasing, which dropped from 51 percent sales in 1972 to 22 percent in 1980 on a huge hike in actual sales volume. Besides air conditioning and electronics, the elevator market substantially broadened UTC's coverage and moderated the highs and lows of the business cycle. By 1980 some 40 percent of UTC's business was being done abroad.

In the meantime Otis itself had changed, extending its reach into previously untapped emerging markets. In Japan, probably the world's toughest and most sophisticated market for elevators, Otis had secured an alliance with Sumitomo Bank and Matsushita Electric, and gradually began to build up from the pitiful 2 percent market share it had inherited from the wreckage of its ill-fated alliance with Toshiba. After a slow start, Otis re-opened for business in China in 1984 with a manufacturing joint venture in Tianjin and subsequently formed joint ventures in Guangzhou, Beijing, Shanghai and Hangzhou (Otis originally began doing business in China in 1900). In Russia, Otis moved swiftly to establish a commanding position in domestic elevator production and service. In India, as the economy liberalized, Otis committed about $25 million between 1953 and 1999.

The experience that Otis executives had gained in global business smoothed their way to the top at UTC, as that very American company began to realign itself in the global marketplace. Otis executives were travelers; frequently now they were not American. Gray had retained Hubert Faure as Otis' president and chief executive, and Faure had become a UTC director in 1976. In 1981, Gray asked him to assume responsibility for a new business segment, Building Systems, which sought to exploit links among Otis, Carrier, which had been acquired in 1979, and a small telecom company Gray also had bought.

Faure was the first Otis executive to find his way to the senior management ranks of UTC. François Jaulin moved in Faure's wake from Otis' operation in France to European Transcontinental Operations (ETO) and in 1981 became Otis' president. He was Otis' CEO in 1985 and would doubtless have gone on within the parent company if his career and life had not been tragically cut short by cancer in 1986.

By that time the globalization and complexity of Otis' operations had changed the company's makeup: it no longer needed only "elevator men." Karl Krapek, who had come from General Motors to Otis in 1982 as vice president of operations, was running North American Operations in 1986. Three years later he was named Otis' president. He took over at Pratt & Whitney in 1992, joining UTC in 1997 as executive vice president and a member of the board of directors. He was named president and COO in 1999. J. P. van Rooy, who had been president of Carrier's international operations and executive vice president of the company between 1982 and 1986, succeeded David as Otis' president in 1991 and became chairman in 1997. When Gray retired, Robert Daniell succeeded him as CEO. George David succeeded Daniell in 1994.

David himself had two big policy ideas, and he didn't mind how often his people heard about them. One was Japan. He had always been fascinated by Japanese methods, and Otis' relationship with Sumitomo and Matsushita provided Otis—and eventually UTC at large—a direct link to the philosophies that made Japan such a powerful entrant into the developed world. David's longstanding interest in Japan helped him explore the Japanese approach to quality and innovation and to import his findings first to North American processes and products and subsequently worldwide, when he was appointed Otis' president.

Those years saw the world return to financial health after the oil shock and subsequent inflation of the 1970s. A spate of building followed world-wide, more than ever in the classical American model. In Paris there was La Defense; London had Canary Wharf; and Frankfurt grew as a European financial center. Europe, however, stuck, in essence, to the urban patterns it had established over the centuries. Even its skyscrapers were not so much organic developments of the urban fabric as bolt-on additions.

But as Europe's market matured, the company's focus began to shift again. Otis' involvement in Asia—the Pacific region—opened a third phase in the company's development. In the first, until around the time of World War II, Otis was a national company. The European revolution in the next 25 years made it international; Asia, in barely a decade, created a global enterprise.

Each phase was accompanied by cultural, organizational and technological shifts. The invigorating European experience taught the company how to listen to its markets, how to manage for consensus and how to apply the most rigorous processes to design and manufacture to keep ahead of the competition. Japan, as David liked to remind people, taught Otis about maintaining quality and exceeding expectations.

By 1999 there were more than 1.2 million Otis products in operation around the world, including elevators in 10 of the world's 20 tallest build-ings. Otis was servicing more than 1 million elevators and escalators worldwide. Otis employed nearly 63,000 people all over the world—about 8,000 based in the United States—and there were offices, operations or representatives in well over 200 countries. Sales of approximately 50,000 elevators and escalators gave Otis roughly 22 percent of the world's new-equipment market. The company generated revenues of $5.7 billion that year, of which 78 percent was generated outside the United States. While Otis produced 23 percent of UTC's revenues, it generated 27 percent of the parent company's profits. Otis was manufacturing in 15 countries, from Brazil to China and Australia to Spain.

Reflecting George David's rejuvenation of the engineering opera-tion, Otis was investing approximately $100 million in research and development. Engineering and testing centers were located in the United States, Japan, France, Germany and Spain. Engineering centers in sev-eral countries were linked electronically, making possible the instant and efficient exchange of technology worldwide. State-of-the-art engineering facilities included the world's tallest test tower (154 meters/505 feet) in Shibayama, Japan.

As the Internet began to transform commerce, Otis launched an e-business strategy in 1999. This new approach was based on a revised site on the World Wide Web (www.otis.com) and three new e-business products: e*Display (Internet-based information display in elevator cars), e*Direct (for on-line specifying and ordering of elevators) and e*Service (on-line service through a Web site for customers).

In terms of market leadership, global reach and engineering excellence, Otis had become not only a model for other UTC companies, but also a model for business in the 21st century.

When William Shannon, the editor of the post–World War II *Otis Bulletin*, read through young Charles Otis' journals of 1858, he was struck by how close the fledgling business had come to collapse. The journal is a dismal catalogue of bad debts and pressing demands that assailed the Otises, a near-despairing account of Charles' efforts to meet his creditors. Shannon wondered how the company had survived and came up with an interesting explanation.

"The employees didn't save it. Where would they get the $1,000 apiece [which the firm owed]? The Otis family couldn't save it. Their money was all gone. The real reason the business pulled through, and the reason we have our jobs today," Shannon wrote, "is because Mr. Bashford let Charley Otis have ten tons of coal when he knew the shop couldn't pay for it. Because Mr. Babbitt advanced $500 when he already was on the hook for a note due eight months before. Because people like Mr. Wooster were willing to risk their money on the ability and honesty of Elisha, Charley, Henry, Billy and the others in the shop." For Shannon, the message was clear: "Today we call that Capitalism, and no one has ever found a better way to do the job."

Otis' survival reflected the company's ability to meet change before change destroyed the business. Otis constantly and confidently evolved–remodeled its technology, reshaped its systems, overhauled its methods–in a process of adaptation that continues to the present day. Hubert Faure maintains that tradition and innovation are not as violently opposed to each other as one would think: within every enterprise they intertwine to create a productive tension which good management seeks to balance and exploit.

What is certain is that everything depends on the people who make up an organization—on their sense of security and loyalty, on the one hand, and on their willingness to innovate and take risks, on the other. That willingness is unlocked when people are recognized for their worth. Many of the controlling influences on Otis' development have been exerted by particular men like Charles Otis, William Delaney Baldwin, David Lindquist, Cecil Jackson, Percy Douglas, Hubert Faure and George David—all visionaries who took risks where they saw opportunities. If this book has focused on their work, it is because each of them contributed to the unfolding spirit of enterprise that sustained Otis and burst through the bonds of established tradition before tradition smothered them. That—as William Shannon might have said—is capitalism.

These leaders did not work alone. Catalysts for change, they still acted through the people around them—the people who implemented change and maintained order and continuity at every level of the organization. It is commonplace, no doubt, to talk of motivation, company ethos, esprit de corps. Otis has been fostering this spirit, consciously and unconsciously, since the 19th century—ever since Charles Otis suggested an extra payment to a man who had thought up a new method of punching holes. A company ethos to match the tenor of the age was evident in Baldwin's *Indicator* magazine (stern and upright), in Jackson's *Maintaineer* (swaggering and upbeat), in the *Otis Bulletin* (caring and democratic) and of course in the daily routine of managers and employees throughout Otis' history. Often it meant no more than sharing common concerns, as Faure discovered when in quiet moments he would perch on the edge of an employee's desk and simply chat—general conversation, family inquiries, business matters in the broadest sense. He found that everyone seemed to benefit from these informal discussions; they helped to generate an aura of confidence. They were small things that could mean much.

The value of Otis' "family" feeling is unquantifiable; yet it must have contributed to the ease with which changes to the company's organization were pushed through at crucial moments. Charles Otis and William Hale turned Otis Brothers into an efficient East Coast manufacturer, and Baldwin made the Otis Elevator Company number one in

North America. Percy Douglas launched the rational expansion of Otis enterprises around the world in a highly centralized operation focused on the United States. Hubert Faure remodeled the company on a regional framework, taking advantage of the meteoric growth of business in Europe, and then in the Pacific region, centralizing certain functions and decentralizing others. Most recently, George David has overseen the creation of a genuinely global Otis Elevator Company, with a similar mix of central and devolved functions, reflecting conditions and opportunities in a world no longer divided by curtains of iron or bamboo.

Endnotes (Part Two)

1   "Organization of the International Division" by W. J. W. Reid, vice president: transcript of a talk given to a group of Otis employees at New York headquarters, Otis Archive Subject File International

2   Interview with Arthur Mawson, January 7, 1991, conducted by George David Smith, Otis Archives

3   Organization of the International Division, pp. 4–5, March 1, 1960, by William Reid, Otis Archives

4   Interview with John McGee, October 4, 1990, conducted by George David Smith, Otis Archives

5   "War Production... By Otis" p. 39, Otis Elevator Company 1947

6   *Otis Bulletin,* April 1948

7   Interview with Michael DiZio, October 17, 1990, conducted by George David Smith, Otis Archives

8   Ibid.

9   International Division Annual Report, 1947, financial section, p. 7

10   Quoted in M. Lee, *History of Otis Elevator Company's Operation in France,* p. 11

11   This, and subsequent quotes, taken from interviews with Hubert Faure conducted by George David Smith on January 2, 1991, April 16, 1991 and May 15–16, 1991, unless otherwise stated, Otis Archives

12   Interview with Guy de Viaris of ETO, January 17, 1991, conducted by George David Smith, Otis Archives

13   see endnote 11

14   Ibid.

15   Ibid.

16   Ibid.

17   Lee, "History of Otis Elevator Company's Operations in Japan", pp. 18–19, Otis Archives

18   C. R. Scott, Jr., Works Manager, p. 68 of the 1964 International Division report, Otis Archives

19   Interview with Erik Warners, April 12, 1991, conducted by George David Smith, Otis Archives

20   see endnote 11

21   see endnote 12

22   see endnote 11

23   International Report, 1970

24   Interview with Harry Gray, October 31, 1990, conducted by George David Smith, Otis Archives

25   Interview with Ralph Weller, October 30, 1990, conducted by George David Smith, Otis Archives

Appendix

Even measured in today's dollars, Elisha Otis' company had modest beginnings. Datum calculated from price indices compiled by the United States Bureau of Labor Statistics. Chapter 1.

Elisha Graves Otis' account book on December 3, 1853, shows the following:

1 second hand lathe	$ 50.00
2 oil cans	1.50
1 desk & writing table complete	12.00
1 small work bench	10.00
Iron, steel, etc.	47.96
Account book and paper	1.25
Total Inventory	$ 122.71

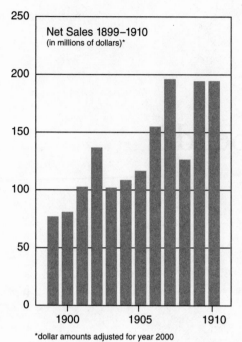

Otis' growth in the early
20th century paralleled that
of American cities.
Chapter 8.

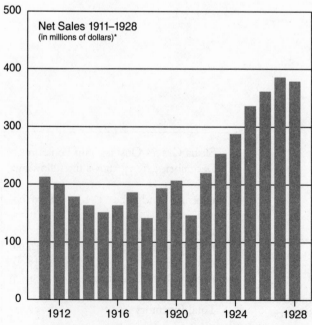

After slowing
during the World
War I years, Otis'
sales resumed their
rapid growth.
Chapter 11.

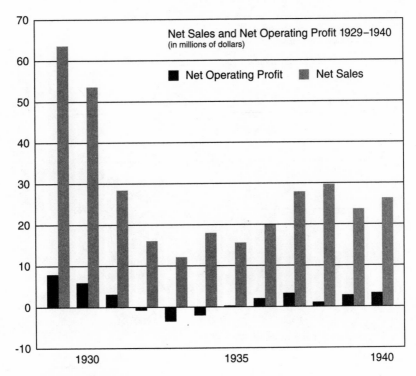

The Great Depression didn't spare Otis, as the company experienced its first prolonged profit shortfall. The rebound came slowly in the pre–World War II years. Chapter 12.

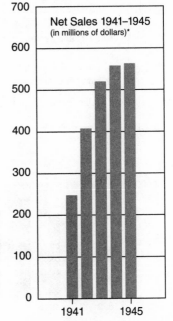

Annual sales more than doubled during World War II, as Otis lent some of its manufacturing capacity to the war effort. Chapter 15.

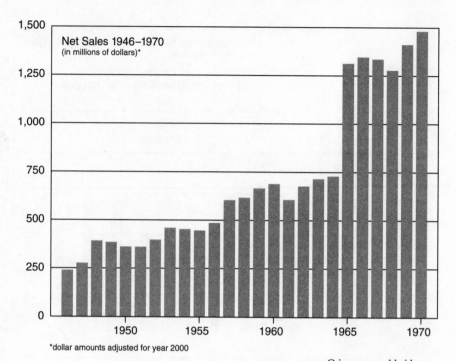

Net Sales 1946–1970
(in millions of dollars)*

*dollar amounts adjusted for year 2000

Otis grew worldwide
as postwar industrial
expansion created a more
robust global economy.
Chapter 19.

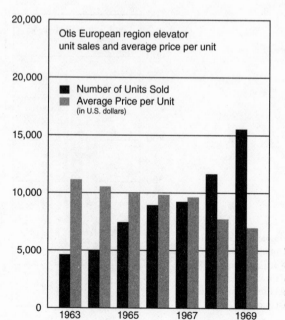

Otis European region elevator
unit sales and average price per unit

■ Number of Units Sold
■ Average Price per Unit
(in U.S. dollars)

The model strategy paid
off: as sales expanded,
economies of scale helped
reduce price per unit.
Chapter 20.

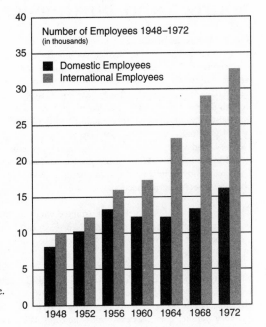

Otis' international expansion was reflected in a higher growth rate in the non-U.S. work force. Chapter 21.

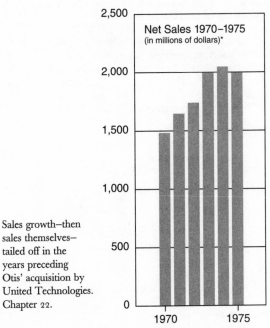

Sales growth–then sales themselves–tailed off in the years preceding Otis' acquisition by United Technologies. Chapter 22.

Sources and Further Reading

This book is based primarily on material in the Otis Historical Archives at the company headquarters in Farmington, Connecticut. For the 19th century, the secondary literature is good (see citations in later paragraphs), but gaps must be filled by using manuscript items at the archives. The core sources for the 20th century are the Otis Annual Reports to stockholders and the serial publications of the company, *The Indicator* (1908–1913), *Publicity Information Bulletin* (1927–1936) and the *Otis Bulletin* (1936–); these are also available at a few large business history libraries. The book also draws heavily on the Annual Reports of the International Division and the publicity compilations of the Communications Department. Oral histories of key Otis staff produced by George David Smith and transcribed by his colleagues in the Winthrop Group added important details to the narrative. Unpublished histories of elevators and of aspects of the company in the Otis archives by Dennis Barrow, Alan Bryant, Anne Millbrooke, Eino Latvala and Donald Shannon deserve special mention.

The Otis company published and distributed widely a short corporate history as a special stockholder report, *Otis Elevator Company: The First One Hundred Years,* New York, 1953. The November 1948 issue of the *Otis Bulletin* also contains useful historical articles.

On the history of elevators in general, see Jean Gavois, *Going Up,* New York: Otis Elevator Company, 1983, and Donald Jackson, "Elevating Thoughts from Elisha Otis and Fellow Uplifters," *Smithsonian,* November 1989, pages 210–234. The independent trade journal *Elevator World* has published many historical articles since its founding in 1953 and has recently established a history website (www.theelevatormuseum.com). While George Strakosch, *Vertical Transportation Handbook,* 3rd edition, New York, Wiley, 1998, deals mainly with modern machines, it does have brief reliable historical sections on such esoteric developments as the paternoster elevator. Of the many specialized monographs on the history of elevators, Robert Vogel's "Elevator Systems of the Eiffel Tower 1889," U.S. National Museum *Bulletin* 228, 1961, is a classic. A list of such works can be assembled by using standard sources such as the CD-ROM version of *America: History and Life* and the annual bibliography issue of *Technology and Culture.*

For the history of escalators, see William Worthington, "Early Risers," *American Heritage of Invention and Technology,* Winter 1989, pages 40–43, which covers the period up to 1920; David Cooper, "The History of the Escalator," *Lift-Report,* January/February 2000, pages 63–67; and Karl-Rainer Thiel, "Rolltreppen," *Kultur und Technik,* Winter 1989, pages 196–200. For that paradigm of escalator installations, the London Underground, see Ray Orton, et al., *Moving People from Street to Platform: 100 Years Underground,* Mobile, Alabama, Elevator World, 2000.

Photo Credits

Patent drawing: Elisha Otis' application for a patent on his safety elevator, from Record Group 241 (United States Patent and Trademark Office), National Archives and Records Administration, Washington D.C.

"King's Dream of New York" (1908–09) illustration: Moses King, © 1908, Bridgeport Public Library, Bridgeport, Connecticut.

Otis offices in Shanghai: From Liang Su Ning via Xin Wei Zhang of SOECHQ.

Otis Bulletin cover featuring President Dwight D. Eisenhower: From New York Herald Tribune (December 8, 1953); © 1953 New York Herald Tribune, Inc. All Rights Reserved. Reproduced by permission. Ira Rosenberg/NYHT Pictures.

Other images courtesy of Otis Archives.

Every effort has been made to research the copyright ownership of illustrations in this book and to obtain permission to reproduce images. If we have not discovered someone's rights to an image, we apologize and ask that he or she write to Intellectual Property Counsel, United Technologies Corporation, Hartford, Connecticut 06101, so that appropriate action may be taken.

Index

Abajo, Mario, 257
Air Cushion Company, 27–28
Air-cushion safety device, 27–28
Allied-Superb Bronze Company, 180
American Elevator Company, 66, 109
American Trading Company, 113, 158
Antitrust legislation and prosecution,
    96–102, 173–174. *See also* Trust,
    elevator.
Architecture, 126–127
Argentina, 109–110, 157, 190, 191,
    242–243
Ascenseur Otis Cie., 66
Ascenseurs Otis. *See* Otis-Pifre.
Ascinter, 225, 227–230
Ascinter-Otis, 229–230, 236, 238, 240,
    252–253, 254
ASEA, 194
Atelier Abel-Pifre, 114
Atlas, 194
Austral Otis Elevator and Engineering
    Company, 71, 109
Australia, 66, 70–71, 109–110, 155,
    157–158, 167, 190, 191, 203, 240
Austria, 110, 153, 237

Baker-Raulang Company of Cleveland,
    177, 179
Baldwin, William Delaney: Otis Brothers
    and Co., 75, 78; Otis Elevator
    Company, Inc., 85–89, 100, 104–108,
    111–112, 114, 116, 132–137, 189
BDR, 224–225
Belgium, 109, 156
Black, J. Alexander, 236, 243–244
Branches, 139, 153, 214–215, 240, 241,
    243–244; American Elevator Company,
    66, 109; American Trading Company,
    113, 158; Ascinter-Otis, 229–230,
    236, 238, 240, 252–253, 254; Austral
    Otis Elevator and Engineering
    Company, 71, 109; Flohr-Otis, 211–212,
    221, 228; Jacobo Schneider SA, 238;
    Nippon Otis, 251–252, 266; Otis
    Ascensorie Montecarichi, 156–157;
    Otis Electric Company, 77, 88;

Otis Elevator GmbH, 115; Otis-Fensom,
    111–112, 167, 216; Otis-Pifre, 154,
    155–156, 166, 198–199, 212, 213–219,
    224–225; Stigler-Otis, 156–157, 200,
    227, 254; Toyo-Otis, 158–160, 163,
    219–224, 235–236, 250–252; Waygood-
    Otis, 71, 115–116, 154, 155, 157–158,
    160, 163, 198, 224, 237, 244–246. *See also*
    Competitors; Foreign markets; Otis
    International Division.
Brazil, 109, 190, 191, 193–194, 240, 242
Brown, Thomas E., 68–69, 74
Bruns, William, 183
Bry, Robert, 179–180, 186
Burger, Samuel, 81

Canada, 66, 111–112, 118, 167, 240
Car design, 43–44
Chile, 66, 109
China, xii, xiv, 67, 110, 191, 202, 266
Columbian Exposition (1893), 72–73
Commercial passenger elevators, 17, 21,
    25, 27–30
Competitors, 28, 79–85, 86, 98–99,
    157–158, 174–175, 183, 184, 185–186,
    187–188, 194; Air Cushion Company,
    27–28; Ascinter, 225, 227–230; ASEA,
    194; Atlas, 194; BDR, 224–225; C. R.
    Crane, 55–57, 78, 84; Dover, 175–176;
    Electron Company, 75; Ellithorpe, 27;
    Fensom Elevator Company, 111–112;
    Flohr, 212, 221; Fraser Electric Elevator
    Company, 89–90; Graves Elevator, 57;
    Haughton & Armor, 174; Hitachi, 224,
    236; Jacob Schneider, 237–238; Johns,
    71, 157; Kone, 194; Matsushita,
    251–252, 266, 267–268; Mitsubishi,
    224, 236; Montgomery, 174, 176;
    Reno, 106; Sabiem, 156–157, 200;
    Schindler, 194, 250; Alonzo B. See,
    82–85, 99; Sprague Electric Elevator
    Company, 84, 90, 111; Standard
    Waygood, 157; Stigler, 156–157, 200,
    250; Stokes & Parrish, 55–56, 78;
    Tufts Manufacturing Company, 25–26,
    27, 30, 34–35; U.S. Elevator, 187–188;

Waygood, 71, 111, 115–116;
Westinghouse, 173–174, 176, 184,
187–188, 201, 224, 227; Whittier
Machine, 56, 57; Zardoya, 238. *See also*
Branches; Otis International Division.
Controlling interests. *See* Mergers and
controlling interests.
Counterweights, 9, 37, 95
C. R. Crane, 55–57, 78, 84
Cunningham, Norman, 245–246

Daloubex kidnapping, 243
Daniell, Robert, 267
David, George, xiii, 261–262, 265,
267–268
Depression, Great, 134–139, 144–146, 155,
162, 275
Development of elevators. *See* Elevator
development.
Douglas, Henry P., 111–112, 183, 189
Douglas, Percy, 163, 182, 183, 189–212,
213, 214, 216, 220–221, 227, 229, 236,
247, 248, 250
Dover, 174–176
Dunn, Fayette, 181–183, 231, 236–237,
247–249

Edison, Thomas (Edison Machine
Works), 76
Eickemeyer, Rudolf, 75–79
Eiffel Tower, 64–70
Electrical Engineering Company, 81
Electricity, 26, 29, 41, 73–79, 83, 88–90,
92–93, 128, 130–131
Electrobus Division of Tork-Link
Corporation, 185
Electron Company, 75
Elevator development: and American
labor shortage, 13, 16, 23; architecture,
126–127; car design, 43–44; commercial
passenger elevators, 17, 21, 25, 27–30;
counterweights, 9, 37, 95; electricity,
26, 29, 41, 73–79, 83, 88–90, 92–93,
128, 130–131; Elevonic 101, 264–265;
Elevonic 401, 265; Elevonic 411M
and 311M, 265; engineering,
40, 126–132, 173, 183–184, 187–188;

in Europe, xii, 63–64, 65–66, 68, 74,
214–215, 224–225, 227–228, 231–234,
237–240, 253, 258; fuzzy logic modules
in gearless systems, 265; gearless
traction elevator, 94–96, 98, 127, 128;
Group Multi-Voltage control (GMV),
130–131; hydraulics, 13, 25, 28, 29, 30,
35–40, 44, 48, 55, 71, 78, 89, 94, 98, 126,
174–176, 187; linear induction motor
elevator, 265; operatorless elevators,
169–172, 223; passengers, 128–130;
postwar suburban boom, 177–179;
Pratt-Sprague "screw and nut" machine,
90; remote monitoring system, 265;
residential elevators, 77; safety, 26–28,
40, 68–69, 95–96, 132; skyscrapers,
xi–xiii, xv, 45–47, 58, 71, 91–95,
123–124, 127, 128, 177–178, 184–185,
214; solid-state motor controls, 187;
speed governor, 40; steam engine, 17,
21, 25, 27–29; variable-speed, variable-
frequency pump, 265; Vertical Screw
Railway, 25, 26, 35
Elevator operators, 169–172, 223
Elevator (word), 42–43
Elevonic 101, 264–265
Elevonic 401, 265
Elevonic 411M and 311M, 265
Ellithorpe, 27
Engineering, 40, 126–132, 173, 183–184,
187–188
Escalator (word), 106
Escalators, xiv, 75, 105–107, 158, 176,
228–229, 235–236
Euclid Crane and Hoist Company, 180
European elevator development, xii,
63–64, 65–66, 68, 74, 214–215,
224–225, 227–228, 231–234, 237–240,
253, 258. *See also* Foreign markets.

Faure, Hubert, 117, 207–210, 213–219,
224–234, 236–246, 249–262, 267,
269–270
Fensom Elevator Company, 111–112
Field, S. D., 76
Field and factory operations, 125, 146,
181–182, 186–187, 248
Flohr, Karl, 212, 221

Foreign markets, xv, 66–67, 70–71, 109–116, 133, 139, 153. *See also* Branches; European elevator development; Otis International Division; *names of specific countries.*
Fortis, 237
Fougeron, Pierre, 254, 255–256
France, 66, 109, 114, 153–156, 190, 191, 193, 198–199, 211–219, 224–225, 227, 229–231, 236, 240–241
Fraser, E. M. (Fraser Electric Elevator Company), 89–90
Freissler, 237
Fuzzy logic modules in gearless systems, 265

Gearless traction elevator, 94–96, 98, 127, 128
Gendre, 237
Germany, 109, 114–115, 153–154, 156, 167, 190, 191, 193, 211–212, 241
Grandgerard, Charles, 159–160, 162, 190, 201–202, 203, 219–220, 251
Graves Elevator, 57
Gray, Harry, 176, 249, 259–264, 267. *See also* United Technologies.
Great Britain, 66–67, 109–110, 111, 114, 115–116, 153–155, 163, 167, 190, 191, 193, 198, 244–246
Great Electrical Scandal, 173–174
Group Multi-Voltage control (GMV), 130–131

Hale, William: American Elevator Company, 66, 109; Hale and Crane–Crane Elevator, 86; Hydraulic Elevator Company of Chicago, 36, 38–40, 54; Otis and Hale, 49–51, 66, 78; Otis Brothers and Company, 49–50, 54–55, 57, 74
Hale and Crane–Crane Elevator, 86
Hall, W. F., 67, 70
Haughton & Armor, 174
Hitachi, 224, 236
Hoists: automatic safety device, 14–15, 16, 25, 26–28, 50; history of, 8–10, 13
Hong Kong, 202

Hungary, 110, 153
HVP Hydraulic, 187
Hydraulic Elevator Company of Chicago, 36, 38–40, 54
Hydraulics, 13, 25, 28, 29, 30, 35–40, 44, 48, 55, 71, 78, 89, 94, 98, 126, 175–176, 187

Ihlder, John, 77
India, xiv, 110, 190, 201–202, 240, 266
Indicator, The, 117–125
International Union of Elevator Constructors (IUEC), 138–139, 186
Internet commerce, 269
Italy, 109, 156–157, 190–191, 194, 200, 212, 250

Jackson, Cecil, 142–147, 183
Jacob Schneider, 237–238
Jacobo Schneider SA, 238
Japan, xi–xv, 110, 112–113, 158–160, 190, 191, 219–224, 235–236, 240, 250–252, 265, 266, 267
Jaulin, François, 245–246, 252–253, 258, 267
Johns, 71, 157

Knapp, J. C., 146–147
Kone, 194
Krapek, Karl, 267
Kraus, Kermit, 219

Labor shortage and U.S. elevator development, 13, 16, 23
Lindquist, David, 127–132, 183
Linear induction motor elevator, 265
Lockwood, William, 32, 50

Maintaineer, The, 140–147
Maintenance and upgrading, elevator, 127, 140–147, 183, 222, 223, 265
Malaysia, xiv
Management issues, 102–104, 162, 186–187, 205, 210, 214–215, 217–219,

231–234, 236–237, 238–239, 249, 254–258. *See also Indicator, The.*
Matsushita, 251–252, 266, 267–268
Mergers and controlling interests, 98–99, 180, 185, 229; Allied-Superb Bronze Company, 180; Ascinter, 227–230; Atelier Abel-Pifre, 114; Baker-Raulang Company of Cleveland, 177, 179; C. R. Crane, 55–57; Electrical Engineering Company, 81; Electrobus Division of Tork-Link Corporation, 185; elevator trust, 79–85, 86, 98–99; Ellithorpe, 27; Euclid Crane and Hoist Company, 180; Fortis, 237; Fraser Electric Elevator Company, 90; Freissler, 237; Gendre, 237; Graves Elevator, 57; Hale and Crane–Crane Elevator, 86; Hydraulic Elevator Company of Chicago, 36, 38–40, 54; Mitsui Trading Company, 158–160, 219–221; Moto-Truc, 180; Nielson, 237; Reflectone, 180; Reno, 106; Schneider, 237–238; Stokes & Parrish, 55–56, 78; Toshiba, 222–223, 235–236, 250–251; Transportation Technologies Inc., 180–181, 185; Tufts Manufacturing Company, 34–35; Voorwartts, 237; West Coast Manufacturing Company, 180; Whittier Machine, 56, 57; York Company, 180; Zardoya, 238. *See also* Otis International Division.
Mexico, 109
Mitsubishi, 224, 236
Mitsui Trading Company, 158–160, 219–221
Montgomery, 174, 176
Moto-Truc, 180

National Association of Elevator Contractors, 174
Netherlands, 109, 206, 228–229, 237
New York World's Fair (1854), 7–8, 14, 16
New Zealand, 190, 203
Nielson, 237
Nippon Otis, 251–252, 266
No. 2 Hoist Machine, 7–8, 14–15, 16
N. P. Otis & Brother, 76; Charles Otis, 22, 23–24, 30–31; Norton Otis, 22, 23–24, 76

Otis, Charles: character, 19, 75, 130; death, 62; N. P. Otis & Brother, 22, 23–24, 30–31; Otis and Hale, 51; Otis Brothers and Co., 31–33, 35, 49, 52–62, 79; Otis Elevator Company, 16, 17–20, 21–22, 130, 147, 217; patents, 21, 28; relationship with Elisha Otis, 18, 20, 21–22; speed governor, 40; and Alfred Wilde, 5–7, 17
Otis, Elisha: automatic safety device, 14–15, 16, 25, 26–28, 50; character, 18, 19, 20; death, 22; early life and career, 10–12, 15–16; and hoists, 13–14; New York World's Fair (1854), 7–8, 14, 16; patents, 14, 21; relationship with Charles Otis, 18, 20, 21–22; steam engine, 17, 21
Otis, Norton: character, 19, 24, 75; N. P. Otis & Brother, 22, 23–24, 76; Otis and Hale, 50–51; Otis Brothers and Co., 31–32, 49, 75–76, 81; Otis Elevator Company, 17–18, 22, 130; Otis Elevator Company, Inc., 85, 103; patents, 28, 76; political career, 75; promotion of elevators, 130
Otis and Hale: William Hale, 49–51, 66, 78; Charles Otis, 51; Norton Otis, 50–51.
Otis Ascenseurs. *See* Otis-Pifre.
Otis Ascensorie Montecarichi, 156–157
Otis (brand recognition), 101–102
Otis Brothers and Co.: William Delaney Baldwin, 75, 78; Thomas E. Brown, 68–69, 74; Samuel Burger, 81; Thomas Edison (Edison Machine Works), 76; Rudolf Eickemeyer, 75–79; Eiffel Tower, 64–70; elevator trust, 79–85, 98–99; foreign markets, 66–67, 70–71, 109–116; William Hale, 49–50, 54–55, 57, 74; W. F. Hall, 67, 70; John Ihlder, 77; William Lockwood, 32, 50; Charles Otis, 31–33, 35, 49, 52–62, 79; Norton Otis, 31–32, 49, 75–76, 81; Otis Electric Company, 77, 88; William Roebling, 82; R. C. Smith, 76

Otis Bulletin, The, 178, 205
Otis Diversified Operations, 186–187
Otis Domestic Elevator Operations, 186
Otis Electric Company, 77, 88
Otis Electronic Division, 169
Otis Elevator Company: Charles Otis, 16,
  17–20, 21–22, 130, 147, 217; Norton
  Otis, 17–18, 22, 130
Otis Elevator Company (Europe), 109
Otis Elevator Company, Inc.: antitrust
  legislation and prosecution, 96–102,
  173–174; William Delaney Baldwin,
  85–89, 100, 104–108, 111–112, 114, 116,
  132–137, 189; William Bruns, 183;
  Robert Bry, 179–180, 186; Robert
  Daniell, 267; George David, xiii,
  261–262, 265, 267–268; Henry P.
  Douglas, 111–112, 183, 189; Percy
  Douglas, 163, 182, 183, 189–212, 213,
  214, 216, 220–221, 227, 229, 236, 247,
  248, 250; Fayette Dunn, 181–183, 231,
  236–237, 247–249; Electronic Division,
  169; elevator trust, 79–85, 86, 98–99;
  Hubert Faure, 117, 207–210, 213–219,
  224–234, 236–246, 249–262, 267,
  269–270; field and factory operations,
  125, 146, 181–182, 186–187, 248;
  gearless traction elevator, 94–96, 98,
  127, 128; Harry Gray, 176, 249,
  259–264, 267; Great Depression,
  134–139, 144–146, 155, 162, 275; Group
  Multi-Voltage control (GMV), 130–131;
  HVP Hydraulic, 187; *The Indicator,*
  117–125; International Union of
  Elevator Constructors (IUEC), 138–139,
  186; Internet commerce, 269; Cecil
  Jackson, 142–147, 183; François Jaulin,
  245–246, 252–253, 258, 267; J. C.
  Knapp, 146–147; Karl Krapek, 267;
  David Lindquist, 127–132, 183; *The
  Maintaineer,* 140–147; maintenance and
  upgrading, 127, 140–147, 183, 222, 223,
  265; management issues, 102–104, 162,
  205, 210, 214–215, 217–219, 231–234,
  236–237, 238–239, 249, 254–258;
  National Association of Elevator
  Contractors, 174; Norton Otis, 85,
  103; *The Otis Bulletin,* 178, 205; Otis
  Diversified Operations, 186–187; Otis

Domestic Elevator Operations, 186;
  Otis Electronic Division, 169; "The Otis
  Way," 176, 187; Leroy Petersen,
  168–169, 177, 181–182, 215, 247, 248;
  postwar suburban boom, 177–179;
  William Reid, 161; George H. Reynolds,
  90; Sprague patents, 90; stockholders
  and share prices, 85–86, 134–136, 138,
  191–192, 260–261; Sultan sedan,
  107–108; test towers, xi–xiii; timing
  systems, 131; Unit Multi-Voltage
  control (UMV), 131, 132; Jesse
  Van Alstyne, 137–139, 153, 162, 169;
  J. P. van Rooy, 246, 253, 254, 256,
  267; Ralph Weller, 187, 248, 249, 258,
  260–262; World Trade Center,
  184–185, 187; World War I, 126,
  153–155, 274; World War II, 155,
  165–167, 275. *See also* Otis International
  Division; United Technologies.
Otis Elevator GmbH, 115
Otis Europe, 241
Otis International Division, 153–164,
  214–215, 216, 241–244, 249; Mario
  Abajo, 257; J. Alexander Black, 236,
  243–244; Norman Cunningham,
  245–246; Daloubex kidnapping, 243;
  Percy Douglas, 163, 182, 183, 189–212,
  213, 214, 216, 220–221, 227, 229, 236,
  247, 248, 250; Hubert Faure, 117,
  207–210, 213–219, 224–234, 236–246,
  249–262, 267, 269–270; Pierre Fougeron,
  254, 255–256; Charles Grandgerard,
  159–160, 162, 190, 201–202, 203,
  219–220, 251; François Jaulin, 245–246,
  252–253, 258, 267; Kermit Kraus, 219;
  maintenance and upgrading, elevator,
  127, 140–147, 183, 222, 223, 265; Otis
  Elevator Company (Europe), 109; Otis
  Europe, 241; Otis Maine, 159; Bill Reid,
  216, 255; Jurgen Reuning, 257; Pierre
  Roussel, 224–225, 229–230; Fred Town,
  162–163, 190; J. P. van Rooy, 253, 254,
  256, 267; Leversee Lansing Van
  Schoonhoven, 162–163, 196, 228–229;
  Otto Erik von Klosterlein, 228; Erik
  Warners, 228–229, 242–243, 255. *See also*
  Branches; Competitors; Foreign markets;
  Mergers and controlling interests.

Otis Maine, 159
Otis Patent Safety Hoisting Machine,
24–25, 27–29
"Otis Way, The," 176, 187
Otis-Fensom, 111–112, 167, 216
OTISLINE, 265
Otis-Pifre (Ascenseurs Otis; Otis
Ascenseurs), 154, 155–156, 166,
198–199, 212, 213–219, 224–225

Paris Exposition (1888), 64–70, 106
Passengers, 128–130
Patents, Otis, 14, 21, 28, 76, 83,
90, 106
Petersen, Leroy, 168–169, 176–177,
181–182, 215, 247, 248, 249
Philippines, 202
Portugal, 237
Postwar suburban boom, 177–179
Pratt-Sprague "screw and nut"
machine, 90
Pump, variable-speed, variable-
frequency, 265

Reflectone, 180
Reid, Bill, 216, 255
Reid, William, 161
Remote monitoring system, 265
Reno, Jesse, 106
Residential elevators, 77
Reuning, Jurgen, 257
Reynolds, George H., 90
Roebling, William, 82
Roussel, Pierre, 224–225, 229–230
Russia, xiv, 110, 154–155, 266

Sabiem, 156–157, 200
Safety, elevator, 26–28, 40, 68–69,
95–96, 132
Saxer, Al, 147
Schindler, 194, 250
Schneider, 237–238
See, Alonzo B., 82–85, 99
Seeburger, Charles, 106
Service, elevator. *See* Maintenance and
upgrading, elevator.

Shibayama test tower, xi–xiii
Singapore, 203, 242
Skyscrapers, xi–xiii, xv, 45–47, 58,
71, 91–95, 123–124, 127, 128, 177–178,
184–185, 214
Solid-state motor controls, 187
South Africa, 157, 190, 191, 201
Spain, 109, 110, 153, 190, 237–238
Speed governor, 40
Sprague, Frank (Sprague Electric
Elevator Company), 84, 90, 111
Standard Waygood, 157
Steam engine, 17, 21, 25, 27–29
Stigler, 156–157, 200, 250
Stigler-Otis, 156–157, 200, 227, 254
Stockholders and share prices, 85–86,
134–136, 138, 191–192, 260–261
Stokes & Parrish, 55–56, 78
Subsidiaries. *See* Branches.
Sultan sedan, 107–108
Sweden, 109, 237
Switzerland, 237, 250

Test towers, xi–xiii
Thailand, 202–203
Timing systems, 131
Toshiba, 222–223, 235–236, 250–251
Town, Fred, 162–163, 190
Toyo-Otis, 158–160, 163, 219–224,
235–236, 250–252
Transportation Technologies Inc.,
180–181, 185
Trust, elevator, 79–85, 86, 98–99.
See also Antitrust legislation and
prosecution.
Tufts Manufacturing Company, 25–26,
27, 30, 34–35

Union Elevator and General Machine
Works Company, 7–8, 14–15, 16
Union relations, 138–139, 186
Unit Multi-Voltage control (UMV),
131, 132
United Technologies, 253, 259–269.
See also Gray, Harry.
Uruguay, 240
U.S. Elevator, 187–188

Van Alstyne, Jesse, 137–139, 153,
    162, 169
Van Rooy, J. P., 246, 253, 254, 256, 267
Van Schoonhoven, Leversee Lansing,
    162–163, 196, 228–229
Vertical Screw Railway, 25, 26, 35
Von Klosterlein, Otto Erik, 228
Voorwartts, 237

Warners, Erik, 228–229, 242–243, 255
Waygood, 71, 111, 115–116
Waygood-Otis, 71, 115–116, 154, 155,
    157–158, 160, 163, 198, 224, 237,
    244–246
Weller, Ralph, 187, 248, 249, 258,
    260–262

West Coast Manufacturing
    Company, 180
Westinghouse, 173–174, 176, 184,
    187–188, 201, 224, 227
Wheeler, George H., 106
Whittier Machine, 56, 57
Wilde, Alfred: and Charles Otis, 5–7,
    17; New York World's Fair (1854),
    7–8
World War I, 126, 153–155, 274
World War II, 155, 165–167, 275

York Company, 180

Zardoya, 238